Escape, Evasion and Revenge

The True Story of a German–Jewish RAF Pilot who Bombed Berlin and became a PoW

Marc H. Stevens

Pen & Sword
AVIATION

First published in Great Britain in 2009 by
Pen & Sword Aviation
An imprint of
Pen & Sword Books Ltd
47 Church Street
Barnsley
South Yorkshire
S70 2AS

ISBN 978 1 84884 106 2

A CIP catalogue record for this book is
available from the British Library

Typeset in 10pt Palatino by Mac Style, Beverley, East Yorkshire
Printed and bound in the UK by CPI

Pen & Sword Books Ltd incorporates the Imprints of Pen & Sword
Aviation, Pen & Sword Maritime, Pen & Sword Military,
Wharncliffe Local History, Pen & Sword Select, Pen & Sword Military
Classics, Leo Cooper, Remember When, Seaforth Publishing and
Frontline Publishing

For a complete list of Pen & Sword titles please contact
PEN & SWORD BOOKS LIMITED
47 Church Street, Barnsley, South Yorkshire, S70 2AS, England
E-mail: enquiries@pen-and-sword.co.uk
Website: www.pen-and-sword.co.uk

Dedication

To my father's wartime comrades. Many of them made the supreme sacrifice. Dad's rear gunner, RAF Sgt Ivor Roderick Fraser, died over Berlin on 7/8 September 1941, when his parachute failed to open, and has no known grave but is immortalised on the Runnymede Memorial.

To my heroes. I met in person 'Tex' Ash, 'Wings' Day, 'Mike' Lewis, John Matthews, and Douglas Wark, and by telephone 'Jimmy' James; I just missed meeting George Girardet and Alan Payne. We younger people will never forget what they did, even though our gratitude seems an inadequate response to their magnificent service. My father had only two heroes of whom I am aware: Winston Churchill and 'Wings' Day. The men whose names I list here are *my* heroes – truly members of 'the Greatest Generation'.

To my relatives who died in the Holocaust. This work pays homage also to those members of my family, none of whom I ever met, whose lives the Holocaust so brutally shattered and then stole.

To those people closest to me. My grandmother Henni (Seckel) Hein gave everything she had in order to save her children, while perishing herself. My father fought the bastards tooth and nail, confounding them at every turn. My Aunt Trude went without so much for her entire lonely life. Marianne taught me to persist – 'like a dog with a bone.' And my mother, Claire Stevens, was so unselfish in her devotion to my brother and me and gave me the happiest and most loving childhood one could imagine.

Toronto, 2009

All that is necessary for the triumph of evil is that good men do nothing.
Edmund Burke (1729–97)

We few, we happy few, we band of brothers;
For he to-day that sheds his blood with me
Shall be my brother; be he ne'er so vile,
This day shall gentle his condition;
And gentlemen in England now-a-bed
Shall think themselves accurs'd they were not here,
And hold their manhoods cheap whiles any speaks
That fought with us upon Saint Crispin's day.

William Shakespeare
Henry V, Act IV

Contents

Acknowledgements

My research began and ended at the National Archives (formerly the Public Record Office) in Kew, London. Its collection of historic documents going back hundreds of years was a revelation for me, and in 1988 it opened my eyes as to what might be possible for my research. It took me many visits over an eighteen-year span, but I finally found everything necessary to write this book. All the documents at the National Archives are crown copyright, as are all their sources that I cite below.

The brilliant research of books by Charles Rollings and Oliver Clutton-Brock inspired me. These two men are some of the most knowledgeable (and helpful) sources concerning the Second World War's Commonwealth and Allied prisoners of war.

Other books, mainly the memoirs of heroes such as Bill 'Tex' Ash, 'Wings' Day, 'Jimmy' James, 'Mike' Lewis, and Oliver Philpot, became my constant companions. It is indeed an honour for me to have met, or at least spoken briefly with, most of these men. Their stories make for incredible reading and illustrate the clarity of their thought and their knowledge that what they did was for the greater good. Their sacrifices and courage are humbling to those of us who have never served.

Many people have helped me during this arduous journey over the last fifteen or so years. Wing Commander 'Mike' Lewis met Dad as a fresh prisoner of war in Holland and escaped with him from a heavily guarded German train. Decades later he had to put up with my incessant questioning about wartime flying and aircraft (although I am a licensed glider pilot) and about squadron life and being a prisoner of war. He became in essence my technical expert and fact-checker. My late aunt Trude Hein inspired me with the story of her sad and lonely life. Marianne Fedunkiw made me believe that I could indeed write this story. Mark Herron supported me in ways that only a best friend can. Steve Martin, who likely has the world's largest collection of Great Escape-related artefacts, met with me at Sagan in 2005, and explained to me the 'lay of the land' of *Stalag Luft* III, while inspiring me to continue my writing efforts.

Several members of my extended family assisted me. John Selby, a distant cousin in England, at our first meeting at my aunt's funeral told me to 'WRITE

IT!' and helped with hours of additional last-minute research in London. Alison Wertheimer, another distant cousin and an author, whom I also met at Aunt Trude's funeral, also urged me: 'WRITE IT!' Brigitte and Nick Beer, also distant cousins, shared an interest in our family's German genealogy.

Dr Peter Schulze, a historian in Hanover, Germany, spent many years producing a catalogue of all the Jewish inhabitants of my father's hometown. It is an incredibly helpful document for people seeking to trace their Hanoverian family roots. I am extremely grateful as well for the day he spent with me in September 2005, leading me on a tour of the graves of my Jewish ancestors. It was a very moving experience, to meet a side of the family that had been previously unknown to me.

Douglas Radcliffe of the Bomber Command Association at the RAF Museum assisted me early on with advice and motivation on how to search for all the information on Dad's wartime service and then to compile it.

John Parry edited a complex manuscript through extremely trying personal times.

My mother did everything possible to dissuade me from writing this book. As with most parents' exhortations to their children, her attempts at persuasion had exactly the opposite effect.

To them all: thank you!

Foreword

Wing Commander WJ ('Mike') Lewis (RCAF), DFC, CD

Life as a member of aircrew in Bomber Command during World War II was uncertain and often very short. They worked hard and played hard. But the odds were that they would end in disaster and death. But some of us were fortunate that we evaded that disastrous ending and became prisoners of war.

Life as a prisoner of war was a rudimentary existence and brought its own onerous demands. Near-starvation diet was the most pre-eminent of that existence, but mental strain made its own demands. Freedom was our goal and that could only be achieved by escape or the ending of the war by victory by the Allies. Our safety net was the Geneva Convention, under which our lives were protected.

But in this book you are going to read about a man who was not protected by the Geneva Convention. He lived for more than three years and eight months under the threat that, if the Germans discovered his true identity, they would march him out of the prison camp and shoot him. That man was Peter Stevens.

I first met Peter at *Dulag Luft* (the German interrogation camp for new prisoners of war). He had been shot down the same night that I was (7/8 September 1941) and after some tentative give and take we knew that we were each valid comrades. Soon we were shipped (along with others) to a POW camp at Lübeck (*Oflag* X C). While we were there, we determined to escape whenever the opportunity arose. That opportunity came when the whole camp was moved to a new compound at Warburg (*Oflag* VI B); some thirty-five kilometres north-west of Kassel.

We were loaded onto railway freight cars; fortunately only about twenty-five to a car plus two German guards; each armed with a rifle. Peter and I found that there was a small door up on the side of the car and it was large enough for a man to squeeze through. We warned our fellow POWs of our intent and asked them to co-operate when the time came. Just before dusk the train slowed at a signal well out in the country between Hamburg and Hanover. We had removed the wire that had tied the little door shut. We asked our fellow POWs to stand up and hold out their blankets so as to block the view of the guards; presumably before settling down for the night. When they did so, Peter and I went out through the little door; Peter first. Just as he was dropping to the ground and I was through the door, the train suddenly shuddered to a halt! When this sudden halt occurred, every guard looked out to see what had caused the halt and there was Peter just reaching the ground and myself dropping. There was no stopping! We knew that, even if we stopped, we would surely be shot, so we just kept going. There was a small woodlot nearby, so we ran for it. Bullets came whizzing by our ears like little bees buzzing around our heads. Every guard on the train was having target practice! But we made it into the woods and after a short search, the train pulled away. Unfortunately the short search had discovered our small cache of food that we had tossed out ahead of us. So there we were, having escaped but in our captors' land with no food!

We had not determined our ultimate goal – across the Baltic or Switzerland. We now had to make that decision and Peter said that he wanted to go south. So we set out walking south on the railway tracks. At dawn the next morning we came upon a small wooden shack, a shelter probably erected for railway workers caught out in inclement weather. We decided to stay the day there and start off again at dusk. As we sat there during those dark hours, Peter told me his personal history, the story that you are going to read in this book.

To tell that story would pre-empt this book. But, to say the least, we travelled south by foot and hitch-hiking on freight trains to Hanover. We visited houses in the dark of night, we visited the Hanover Jewish ghetto in daylight and, given money, we travelled by train (in a passenger train in a compartment together with two German soldiers going on vacation) to Frankfurt. But we were recaptured in Frankfurt.

I alone shared Peter's story for about a year. But I felt that someone further up in the hierarchy should be aware of his danger, so I persuaded Peter to tell his story to the Senior British Officer (SBO), the famed Wing Commander Harry 'Wings' Day. We shared that secret until the end of the war in Europe.

What a brave man Peter was, putting his life 'on the line' in more ways than one! But his son Marc is going to tell you his whole life history and you can judge for yourself. I still look back on our companionship with great pleasure and revel in our joint escapades!

Toronto, 2004

Preface

This story is, to all intents and purposes, true.

My father and I lived together for twenty-two-and-a-half years, from my birth in 1957 until his death in 1979. But while we dwelled in the same house along with my mother and older brother, we did not interact much. Although Dad was not shy, he did not know how to behave around children. On the rare occasions when he played with us, took us out for a Sunday drive, or showed us around construction sites and took us for an ice cream, he seemed quite reserved. He took pleasure in our successes, laughed at our jokes, and loved making us laugh. And so perhaps he did come to know *us*, but we never really had a chance to know *him*.

This book is the culmination of my many years of work, beginning in the late 1980s, to try to know my father. I'd always known that he was a highly decorated war hero, but growing up with such a fact is enough to make it irrelevant in one's own mind. Over the course of my research, I have finally come to *know* my father. If only he were still here, so that I could tell him how proud I am of what he did and to be his son. And to thank him.

Since I was not alive to witness at first hand most of the events about which I write, I have used many sources to seek to recreate my father's life before my birth. It is with the help of these people and this research that I have pieced together events that I believe to have happened as I describe them. It is certainly possible, however, that some may have transpired differently than I have written. It is not my intention to deceive; I attempt to tell my father's story as best I am able to surmise. I have not added any untrue or fictional material. Everything in this book actually took place; it is only in the minute details that I may have inadvertently misrepresented the truth ever so slightly.

I do not intend this volume to be a day-to-day description of life as a prisoner of war under the Nazis. Many fine books do an excellent job of that, and some have served as source material for this work. Peter Stevens lived a full and eventful life both before and after the war, but I concentrate on incidents that occurred during his time as a prisoner of war.

Other sources included my father's own (few) words and those of his sister and his wife (my mother); records of the Royal Air Force at the National Archives (formerly the Public Record Office) in Kew, England; visits to three Second World War airfields in England (Hemswell, North Luffenham, and Coningsby); interviews with many people who knew my father; the ten or so books that mention his escape activities; and genealogical research by me and others.

I interviewed my mother, Claire Stevens, my aunt Gertrude ('Trude') Hein, George Bowen (during his visits to my boyhood home), Harry 'Wings' Day, 'Jimmy' James, Frida Leider, 'Mike' Lewis, John Matthews, Rodger Morro, Charles Rollings, and Douglas Wark.

Thousands of Jews enlisted and fought in the war, especially in Britain and the United States. This book in no way attempts to belittle their courageous efforts but rather tells the story of one man who took the Nazi dragon by the tail and gave it a good shake.

I grew up understanding that my father had been born in Germany to Christian parents and that his widowed mother had sent him to England in the 1930s, ostensibly because she did not like political developments in Germany. I learned my father's real name and that an English couple (whom I met as a ten-year-old in 1967) had adopted him and changed his name to Peter Stevens. I came also to understand that this information was a serious family secret and that I was to divulge it to no one. It was only in the late 1980s and the 1990s that I discovered the whole truth...

Part One: Fire Over Berlin!
(7 September 1941)

Chapter One

Long Day's Journey

Sunday 7 September 1941 dawned bright and sunny in the English Midlands, but there were no pilots awake to witness it. RAF North Luffenham, a base belonging to 5 Group of Bomber Command, had welcomed 144 Squadron and 61 Squadron just forty days earlier. The airfield, about twenty miles directly east of Leicester and eighty miles north of London, awoke like many bomber bases – very slowly.

Bomber pilots of the Royal Air Force (RAF) were famous for their late-night activities during the war, both in their aircraft and out of them. The previous night, with bad weather over the Continent preventing flights and knowing that they hadn't flown on operations (ops) for a few days, the boys of 144 Squadron had taken it relatively easy. Certainly, they had made the short trek over to their 'local', the Wheatsheaf Inn, opposite the base's main gate in the village of Edith Weston. But a few of the smarter, more experienced ones had not drunk with the reckless abandon that they reserved for the night after an op. Despite it being a Saturday, they had known that the squadron's number was just about up and there was a good chance that they'd be flying over Germany the following night.

Pilot Officer (P/O) Peter Stevens lay asleep in his billet in the officers' quarters. He was twenty-two, bright and well spoken, with a deep voice and Oxford accent, and sported a full head of dark, curly hair. Having joined the squadron at the beginning of April, he was now one of the base's more experienced bomber pilots, but difficult to know well. He socialised and drank with fellow officers, but most of them felt that he was just a little bit too reserved, that they couldn't really become close to him. The other pilots thought him extremely intelligent and unusually worldly for someone so young. Stevens had flown over twenty combat missions, and this made him a veteran, who knew what to expect the day of an op. He was not prone to fits of temper or emotion; rather he appeared to be someone who would bear up well under pressure.

And so, while the pilots had precious few hangovers among them on 7 September, not many were out of bed in time for breakfast. Sleep was as valuable a commodity as food to them, especially when they flew only at night, often for up to seven or eight hours at a time. While 144 Squadron's aircraft had no co-pilots as such, their automatic pilots were so rudimentary that the human being in the cockpit had to hand-fly virtually the entire time. That meant that the pilot had to stay in his seat for the entire flight. In fact, the Hampden was so small that he had nowhere else to go, even if he wanted to. The fuselage was narrow in the extreme, perhaps no more than thirty-six inches wide. This made it very uncomfortable for the crew, and the RAF was well aware of that fact.[1] Its odd appearance made the plane the object of much derision, becoming known as the 'Flying Suitcase' and the 'Ferocious Frying Pan'.

By 1941, the twin-engine Handley Page Hampden was almost out of date, but the pilots still loved their 'Flying Tadpole', as they had come to know it affectionately. Many pilots found it a sheer delight to fly. For a bomber, it was relatively small, very fast, and highly manoeuvrable. With a top speed of 265 mph, it was 30 mph faster than the underpowered but very stable Vickers Wellington Mk I and 35 mph faster than the ungainly Armstrong Whitworth Whitley, its two main RAF contemporaries.[2]

The pilots considered the Hampden the veritable 'sports car' of Bomber Command. Its 1936 design was considered state-of-the-art when conceived, but advances since then made it by summer 1941 almost ready for retirement. An all-metal monoplane with such a slow top speed and a maximum bomb load of only 4,000 pounds was now almost obsolete. Now over 100 mph slower than German fighters, it was facing disastrously high losses. Unfortunately the airmen of 144 Squadron were to complete the most Hampden operations and suffer the most losses of any wartime Hampden squadron.[3]

Because the unusually narrow Hampden would not permit two pilots in the cockpit, the RAF used fully trained pilots as navigators, at least for their first several ops with a frontline combat squadron. If anything incapacitated the first pilot, the second (whose duty station was in the nose below and ahead of the pilot) could crawl up through the tunnel under the pilot's seat, pull him out from behind, and step in to replace him. In theory.

RAF officers were considered gentlemen and thus had the unusual privilege of an enlisted man (a batman) serving as their private valet. By 10 a.m., the officers' batmen at RAF North Luffenham had knocked on their doors, and the pilots were beginning to stir. When they made their way individually down to the Officers' Mess for some grub, the pilots could already tell that their earlier suspicions had been correct. As usual, the mechanics and other members of ground crew were rushing around looking very busy, and the Hampdens spread across the airfield were already taking on fuel. All the signs were there: something was up for tonight! As the pilots accumulated a critical mass around the dining tables, their hushed tones were all whispering about possible targets for that night.

Soon matters became official when the squadron's commanding officer arrived and posted orders on the bulletin board: full squadron briefing at 6 p.m. The rumour mill now went into overdrive: the old hands speculated on the target, and the new boys gathered to ask each other what flying combat would be like. The veterans, each with more than ten operations under his belt, knew how difficult and dangerous any op would be and cared only about the target. A mine-laying trip would be relatively short and not as dangerous, but a flight into the heart of Germany, whether to the heavily industrialised Ruhr valley or to a major centre like Cologne, would be both long and potentially perilous.

The absolute worst, however, would be Berlin. 'Jerry' was very determined about protecting his capital city. Thankfully, 144 Squadron had avoided that target since mid-April, and most of the pilots thought that Hampdens weren't up to the task. After all, Berlin was at the extreme limit of their operational range, which would allow for only half the maximum bomb load of 4,000 pounds. At full load, the Hampden would fly 870 miles. Berlin was much further: some 1,200 miles there and back. Not only that, but they would have to fly slowly and conserve fuel in order to achieve that kind of range. All of that meant more time over occupied territory – more time as a target for some ugly night fighter pilot or for those bastards on the ground with their potentially lethal anti-aircraft flak guns, or 'ack-ack.'

It was standard operating procedure (SOP) that all pilots took up their 'kite' for a brief test flight on the day of an op. They used this 'night flying test' (NFT) to look for any mechanical snags that might interfere with a combat operation. A squadron's 'operational readiness' – the percentage of time its aircraft were in condition to fly whenever they were called on – determined its ranking at RAF Headquarters. A good squadron test-flew its planes regularly, even when there was no operation for that night. This practice minimised unwanted surprises when fully loaded aircraft turned out to be unserviceable just before or after take-off.

Bomber Command keenly measured the success of its operations, and one of its primary methods was to 'guesstimate' the number of aircraft that in fact bombed the target. Unless all the planes returned (an extremely rare occurrence), Bomber Command could only estimate the number that had successfully bombed the target, since it could not know the fate of every missing aircraft.

Immediately after their brunch, at about one o'clock, Stevens and Navigator/Second Pilot (Nav) Sgt Alan Payne had met up with P/O Roake, another old-boy pilot with whom Stevens (as navigator) had done his first six combat ops. Together they headed for the squadron's Operations Room and confirmed their assigned aircraft and duty instructions. Signing the flight authorisation book, each pilot confirmed and accepted his written orders. Stevens was pleased to see that his plane was one he'd flown before, serial number AD 936. In fact, Stevens and his crew had flown that Hampden just four days earlier, when bad weather had forced the recall of the entire group. The plan had been to bomb the German U-boat pens in the port of Brest (occasionally they went to Brest to drop mines in the sea). Like most pilots, Stevens allowed himself a certain amount of superstition and disliked having to fly a combat op using an aircraft he'd never flown before.

Both Stevens and Roake and their navigators caught a truck out to their respective Hampdens, across the airfield on paved dispersals. They waved good luck to one another and consulted the ground crew as to aircraft condition and fuel load. Ambling over to his waiting bomber, Stevens performed the required brief walk-around pre-flight inspection.

Payne and Stevens then climbed aboard, and the pilot went through the pre-start checklist. This included adjusting his altimeter to the current local barometric pressure, which gave him the correct reading for the already known field elevation at North Luffenham. This step was crucial before every flight, as local air pressure could change daily. When it did, it resulted in inaccurate altitude readings, which could cause a pilot to believe (especially at night or while flying in clouds) that he was higher than in reality. Again, the RAF had more than a few accidents resulting from this oversight and had to write letters to grieving parents because of them.

On completion of the checklist, Stevens looked out over the inner port wing to the mechanic standing about ten feet in front of the port engine. The fuel pumps had no independent power, and so the massive radial engines needed manual priming with fuel in order to start. The mechanic confirmed with a hand signal to the pilot that this had been done. Stevens, with his left index finger pointing upwards, made a circular motion. The mechanic mirrored the motion, telling the pilot that he was clear to start engine number one. Stevens flipped the magneto switch to 'Both' and engaged the starter for the number one engine.

As the port prop slowly began turning, he counted the rotations until the prop was turning too fast to see and he was sure that the engine had fired. He eased the throttle back to 'Idle', and inspected the port engine gauges. Stevens saw the tachometer was registering the correct number of rotations per minute (RPMs) and the cylinder-head temperature and oil pressure rising to normal levels. He then repeated the process with the starboard number two engine. After about two minutes, when everything seemed to be operating correctly, he gave the thumbs-up signal to the mechanic, who turned to face the control tower and aimed a bright white directional lamp in that direction. The response was a green light, which gave the pilot clearance to taxi.

The RAF had long ago learned to maintain radio silence during NFTs, as the Germans tended to listen in from the coast of occupied territory. In the war's early days, RAF pilots on NFTs would radio their control towers freely, letting the enemy know that operations were scheduled for that evening and to prepare a surprise for the bombers. Sometimes German fighters dashed over from France and shot down a few bombers on their mid-afternoon NFT ritual.

While chocks blocking each main gear wheel still held back the plane, Stevens pushed both feet hard on the brake pedals and gingerly moved the twin throttles forward to about 50 per cent power. Both engines responded crisply, and, as the RPMs increased, the Hampden began to rock its large, bald tyres against their chocks. When he was sure that the engines were running well, he returned the throttle levers to 'Idle.'

Stevens looked back towards the ground crew and gave the opposing-thumbs-outward sign, meaning 'chocks away'. The rigger (one of the mechanics) knew not to duck between the deadly props and instead went the long way around via the wingtip. He pulled at the ropes joining each pair of wooden blocks jammed up against the main undercarriage wheels, and the chocks came away. The crewman again walked outward along the wing, then forward to where the pilot could see him. He held the chocks up to show the pilot that his aircraft was free to move. When he had moved clear, he stood to attention, looked the pilot square in the eye, and gave him a formal salute. Stevens smiled and returned the salute somewhat more leisurely, then looked in both directions and advanced the throttles of the two big Bristol Pegasus XVIII radial engines, each capable of making almost 1,000 horsepower. It didn't take much throttle to get the very lightly loaded Hampden moving, and he backed off the throttles quickly, so as not to reach 60 miles per hour (mph) before he knew it.

Since the Hampden was a tail-dragger, the pilot steered on the ground via differential braking and throttle. When he wanted to turn left, he would put his left foot on the brake and advance the starboard throttle. The combination would cause the plane to arc gracefully in the intended direction. However, tail-draggers could be devils on the ground, especially at higher speeds, when only two wheels were in contact with the ground. Accident reports covered all manner of incidents and accidents resulting from this awkward arrangement.

RAF North Luffenham was a true airfield, virtually nothing more than a vast field. It was almost brand new, having opened only in December 1940,[4] and had no real runways. While take-offs and landings were somewhat bumpy at best, all take-offs and landings could at least head directly into the wind. This is critical for aircraft carrying maximum gross allowable take-off weight, or even a bit more. In practice, a pilot would ascertain the wind's direction from the windsock and then taxi to the point furthest away from that direction before commencing his take-off run directly into the wind. This method also helped to maximise the length of ground (or 'runway') available for use, giving pilots the best possible opportunity to become airborne, and to gain enough altitude to clear any objects such as trees, houses, or church steeples lying directly ahead.

Stevens had well over 400 hours of total flight time (though only 120 as pilot-in-command) and was one of the more experienced pilots on 144 Squadron. He had to smile to himself as he taxied to the downwind side of the airfield, however, because he was only twenty-two years old. He had almost *2,000* horsepower at his fingertips, and he had never even learned to drive a car! Needless to say, this was pretty heady stuff for someone not so long out of high school.

As Stevens used his left hand to advance the throttles to take-off power, the nearly empty Hampden fairly jumped forward. 'It is a genuine pleasure to fly these NFTs,' he must have thought. He found that when the aircraft was this light, it handled just the way he imagined a Spitfire would. As the Hampden gathered speed down the airfield, Stevens had to feed in left-rudder pedal to counteract the increasing torque of the big propellers, and push the control yoke slightly away from him, allowing the tail wheel to lift off the ground. The aircraft was now moving quickly, and he could steer using the rudder pedals alone. Before he knew it, the aircraft began to feel light. The airspeed indicator told him that the wings would now generate enough lift to sustain flight, and he pulled back lightly on the control yoke.

Sure enough, the Hampden lifted off and continued climbing. As soon as he knew it was flying and safely off the ground, he reached for the undercarriage handle and moved it to 'Retract'. Ever so slowly, the engine-mounted hydraulic pumps moved the fluid in the struts, and the two main landing gears in turn moved aft into their bay under each motor. After about twenty seconds, when the job was complete, the plane climbed even better, thanks to the decrease in aerodynamic drag from the big wheels.

The typical NFT lasted only about thirty to forty minutes, just long enough to push the engines up to operating temperature and to test the main systems and ensure there were no snags that might scrub an op that night. Stevens climbed to 2,000 feet above ground level (AGL), then flew west towards the designated test area and went through the prescribed checklist. Finding no problems, he consulted over the intercom with Sgt Payne, who agreed that all his systems were functioning correctly. Heading back towards North Luffenham, and again maintaining crucial radio silence, he joined the downwind leg of the circuit pattern to the busy runway.

Reducing power to speed descent, Stevens lowered the undercarriage and then the semi-automatic flaps. The increased drag from the landing gear accelerated the descent. Turning onto the base leg of the circuit, and then onto final approach, he adjusted his altitude to the prescribed glide slope and airspeed by holding the nose level and using just the throttles. Too high and he would reduce power, too low and he would add some. At about ten feet above the ground, he reduced power just a notch, then pulled back gently on the yoke until it was almost touching his belly. At that moment, the main wheels touched. A perfect landing – very rare in his experience! Taxiing back to the dispersal area where his aircraft was usually parked, he was again careful not to over-control the beast. Once there, he made a 180-degree turn and, when the plane was facing forward, cut off the ignition and fuel to both engines.

Seeing that one of the riggers had lodged the chocks under the wheels, Stevens climbed down out of the open cockpit. He walked back towards the wing's trailing edge to the ladder that the armourer had already placed there and climbed down the three short steps to the ground. He hadn't bothered to change uniforms for the brief flight and was still wearing his everyday battle dress. After conferring briefly with Sgt Payne, he gave his authorisation to the grouped mechanics for the aircraft to fly on the upcoming operation. Back at the squadron Operations Room, he entered the flight in his logbook – he was always meticulous about such details. Even if today's NFT had lasted only twenty-five minutes, it still meant something and counted in his total hours. Over a full tour of duty, NFT time would add up to an additional ten hours or more. Counting hours was and remains a very 'pilot thing'; ask most pilots today their number of hours and, unless they are General Chuck Yeager (the first man to break the sound barrier), they will probably give you a fairly close approximation without thinking too hard. For combat pilots, number of hours was almost an unseen medal for the left breast of their uniform. Earning these hours was hard (most especially in combat, which they marked in red ink in the logbook) and constituted a private badge of courage.

After returning to his room and checking his flying kit, Stevens looked at his watch and realised that he had just enough time to make it to the Protestant church service at 2.30 p.m. Like most of the pilots, he had been in bed and had missed regular Sunday-morning worship. While he was not remotely Protestant, he felt that divine intervention could not do any harm and that attending looked good, adding to his cover and masking his true identity. He was sure to run into one or more of his own crewmen there, and they would respect him all the more. Sure enough, when he entered the chapel, he again ran into P/O Roake. They exchanged smiles, but the service was about to begin. There was a bit of small talk afterwards, and then they walked back to the officers' quarters together.

Stevens returned to his room and laid out his combat flying kit on the bed, making sure that he had all his emergency survival gear in the appropriate pockets and linings. He had taken the advice of a pilot he'd met when he'd first arrived at the squadron on 1 April and had written out his own checklist. As a pilot, he found checklists both standard procedure and incredibly useful. He ran through his and popped down to the Mess to pick up some fruit to take along. On a very long flight – probably eight hours – he would need energy boosters along the way. The squadron medical officer would supply the chemical variety, but munching on an apple or a banana would feel good and give him a bit of a sugar high when he felt drowsy.

By three o'clock, the pilots had all eaten a good hearty meal and those required to do so had flown their NFT. As they usually did on the day of an op, they returned to their rooms for a nap before their final briefing. Leaving strict instructions that their batmen should awaken them at 5.45 p.m., they retired to their bunks. While everyone lay on their freshly made beds with eyes closed, only a few of the more experienced actually had some shuteye.

Before they knew it, there were knocks on all of the doors and then the sounds of feet stomping into just-shined shoes. The Operations Room was just a seven-minute walk from their digs, and immediately outside its double door the officer pilots, navigators, and wireless operator/air gunners (WOP/AGs) joined up with their non-commissioned-officer (NCO) crewmen to go in as a unit. Off-duty fraternisation between ranks in the various ranks' Messes was unusual, but there was no differentiation in flying combat. Men of all ranks came to know each well under the strain of combat conditions, and there was typically little formality on board a bomber. Everyone used nicknames, regardless of rank. Peter Stevens was simply 'Stevie' to his crew, and that was quite all right with him.

It was now 6 p.m.; as per standard operating procedure on the day of an op, authorities had locked down the base. From this point on, nobody could leave except in a fully loaded bomber.

Half of the men at the briefing were still expecting to see Group Captain (the RAF equivalent of a full colonel in the USAAF) JF Barrett take the stage. But they soon remembered that the Germans had shot down the popular officer just five days earlier as he flew over Berlin in an Avro Manchester bomber (an earlier, woefully underpowered and dangerous twin-engine version of the fabled four-engine Lancaster), killing all seven souls on board. That memory strengthened the resolve of everyone in the room.

Butterflies were churning in many stomachs when the base's new commanding officer (CO), a group captain unfamiliar to the assembled crew, made his way onto the small platform. Standing just behind him was 144 Squadron's CO, Wing Commander WS Gardner.[5] As usual, the map behind the base CO was under a cover for the moment.

He began his remarks in a very serious manner, saying that the target that night was very important and would require maximum effort. He could not give details of the size (i.e. total number of aircraft from all squadrons detailed to take part) or the nature of the op (in case, as was very likely, the Germans captured and interrogated some of the men in the room) but he made it very clear that this was something out of the ordinary.

When the curtain over the map was drawn back, the entire squadron gasped as one. The target for tonight, despite all logic to the contrary, was 'The Big City': Berlin – the belly of the beast. The new men were, each in their own way, quite nervous and uncertain. The old boys, able to anticipate exactly what they would face, were just as anxious, but they didn't let it show. They had the presence of mind to be both alert and positive. Aggression was the order of the day, and that they exhibited in spades.

They all received the usual information at the briefing, and many duly recorded it on the backs of their hands. Take-off times, compass headings, initial (aiming) points, specific targets, and special instructions (such as 'Be sure to get photographs of any damage and fires if you can, and have a good look at the railway junctions') were all important to both pilots and navigators. The senior officers gave detailed instructions for the squadron for its time over the target. Each pilot had to do everything possible to be there at a precise time, for several hundred Allied bombers would pass through 'the eye of a needle' in space less than an hour. At least the WOP/AGs and the AGs didn't have to concern themselves with such details.

Next, the squadron's intelligence officer explained the various types of opposition the men could expect both en route and over the target area.

Because the Germans defended Berlin more than any other city, opposition would be massive, and for very good reason. It was not only the country's capital, but also the largest industrial centre. Factories there belonging to AEG, BMW, and Siemens pumped out a quarter of the *Wehrmacht*'s *Panzer* tanks and half of its big artillery guns. There would be night fighters to worry about en route there and back, and the intelligence officer mentioned the main enemy-fighter bases and warned the men to stay well away. As their flight path would include a fair distance over land, flak too would be a worry for a good two-and-a-half hours before they reached Berlin. But those five hours over occupied territory would be the longest of his life, each man must have thought. They all imagined the hellfire of flak over the target and the squadrons of deadly fighters to be evaded on the way home. Made aware of the British intruders on their way into the target, German fighter pilots would be ready and waiting to hit them hard as they headed back to England.

The assembled group then received a very sober and complete briefing on the expected meteorology ('the Met') to be encountered during the eight-hour mission – the weather. Pilots and navigators took special notice of the forecasts for their flight out, their time over Berlin, and their return flight. They took notes about cloud cover, always welcome during the trip, to block searchlights. But they would need occasional breaks in the overcast to confirm their location, especially over Berlin. They couldn't easily bomb what they couldn't see, and they weren't keen on bombing innocent civilians.

Lastly, the Group Captain gave the final order: 'Synchronise watches!' and, with a motivational word for good luck, dismissed the men. Finally the briefing was over, which gave them all the more time to fuss and worry about the op.

Earlier in the day, those airmen who were flying ops that night had given their personal letters (addressed to wives, girlfriends, or parents) to men who would remain behind in England. The comrade was to mail the note only if the writer did not return. Each man prepared himself mentally for combat. Most had a procedure: some thought of a good friend who'd gone missing in action or a family member lost in the Blitz, and steeled themselves to deliver retribution. Others simply avoided thinking about the mission at all.

Though only twenty-two, Stevens was an 'old boy', having survived twenty-one combat ops. He seemed an upper crust, very 'la-de-da' fellow. His deep voice and calculated Oxford-sounding accent were quite at home in the Officers' Mess, and, while he never really opened up, the group accepted him as a 'good old chap'. Here was one place at least where his private school education held him in good stead, even if his colleagues would have been shocked at the names of his schools. Regardless of one's innate intelligence, the RAF initially commissioned newly trained recruits as officers because of their education or class background, which appealed to Stevens's snobbish nature. He liked the hard-earned respect he received as a combat veteran and enjoyed the attention of being an officer. And, like most of the squadron veterans, he knew not to become too close to the new boys: they might not last long, and it was not worth the effort to establish friendships that might end soon. It was general practice in most units not to befriend a man until he had returned from ten ops.

The next stop on Stevens's schedule would be the Officers' Mess, for a good, albeit brief, wholesome dinner. A pilot flying ops never knew when he would have another decent meal, so, apart from missing the occasional early-morning one, he was sure to load up whenever possible. Besides, the food was damned good. While the rest of the nation coped with severe rationing of meat, sugar, eggs, fresh fruit, and the like, men on active duty faced no such constraints. The RAF's High Command knew that it was asking a great deal of aircrew, who in return deserved the very best the country had to offer.

Entering the Mess, Stevens spotted Roake again; when he had loaded up his tray with rare roast beef and mashed potatoes oozing gravy, he went and sat down beside him. 'Hello old boy, getting all the necessary blessings, I see?' laughed Stevens. Roake smiled and calmly replied, 'Well, I see that I'm not the only one looking for eternal salvation – or is it damnation, I can never recall!' At this bit of typical pilots' black humour, they both had a good laugh.

The rest of the meal was relatively quiet, with the officers going over the upcoming op in their minds and trying to think up new ways to ensure their safety and eventual return. They could look forward to the food, as returning bomber crews received a three-egg and bacon breakfast, even if it was at 5 a.m. Despite their now-full bellies, the prospect of eggs and bacon in just eleven short hours sounded wonderful!

As they finished their dinners, one by one, each silently rose and, with a simple thumbs-up or a wink of the eye, wished the others a speedy and safe return. They all knew the thoughts running through each other's minds – one of those rare times and places when men did indeed all think alike.

Notes

1. Sir Arthur Harris, *Bomber Offensive* (Toronto: Stoddart Publishing Co. Limited, 1990), 33.
2. Chaz Bowyer, *The Encyclopedia of British Military Aircraft* (London: Arms and Armour Press Limited, 1982), 92–143.
3. Martin Middlebrook and Chris Everitt, *The Bomber Command War Diaries: An Operational Reference Book 1939–1945* (Leicester, England: Midland Publishing Limited, 1996), 746.
4. Bruce Barrymore Halpenny, *Action Stations 2: Military Airfields of Lincolnshire and the East Midlands* (Wellingborough, Northants: Patrick Stephens Limited, 1981), 148.
5. Jonathan Falconer, *Bomber Command Handbook 1939–1945* (Gloucestershire: Sutton Publishing Limited, 2003), 248.

CHAPTER TWO

Night Flight

After dinner on 7 September, the bomber pilots at RAF North Luffenham individually went to dress for the op. Each put on a good but worn-in set of comfortable battle dress fatigues (there was nothing worse than sitting in an aircraft for up to eight hours in a brand new, itchy woollen uniform). Then, it was the brief walk from their quarters to the stores room, where they picked up their parachutes and personal sidearms. They could not check the parachutes (they wouldn't know how or what to check in any case), but each flirted with the young women who took loving care of the lifesaving silk, and then those who chose to carry the optional firearms spun their revolver barrels to ensure a full load. Next, it was off to the squadron Operations Room, where they laboriously climbed into their flying gear. The cumbersome overalls were very welcome at 15,000 feet in an unpressurised, barely heated aircraft on a cool night.

Each Hampden bomber crew of four men – pilot, navigator/bombardier/second pilot, wireless operator/air gunner (WOP/AG), and air gunner (AG) – then assembled outside, waiting for the truck to take them to their aircraft, somewhere in a wide area around the airfield. In case of German attack, this method of scattering parked aircraft prevented major damage to very valuable resources. In September 1941, not much besides the RAF stood between the Germans and complete European domination.

There had not been much good news since the British sank the *Bismarck* in late May and Hitler's launch of a sneak attack on his ally the Soviet Union on 22 June opened a second front. The United States, while aiding with materiel, was still not in the fight, leaving the Commonwealth – Britain, Canada, Australia, New Zealand, and South Africa – to fight the Nazi juggernaut on their own. German U-boats roamed the North Atlantic at will, preying on supply convoys from North America. Britain desperately needed those supplies, which included food, fuel, equipment, and Canadian soldiers, aircraft and aircrew.

The war in North Africa was not going well for Britain, as *Feldmarschall* Erwin Rommel, the famed 'Desert Fox,' had recently assumed command of the German forces there. The British garrison at Tobruk (Libya) had been under siege since April, and Germany had routed the Allies from Greece and the Balkans. The only – and minor – victory in the ground war had come in Ethiopia, where the British had vanquished the Italians and reinstalled Haile Selassie as emperor.

Smokers enjoyed a final cigarette outside the Operations Room, and then the dispersal truck came along. Three crews, a total of twelve very bulky men, climbed in the back. It was now 7.30 p.m., and the first take-off was to take place at 8.15. Bouncing along in the back of the ugly green army truck, the men soon arrived at the paved stands where the aircraft were parked. Each crew disembarked in turn, and Stevens's was the last to exit.

While Sgts Fraser and Thompson climbed in through the single small hatchway leading into 'the tin' (the lower rear gunner's position), Stevens had a quick word with his navigator/second pilot, Sgt Payne. They compared notes on take-off time, initial heading, and squadron rendezvous position, and then Payne climbed aboard through the second hatch in the top of the fuselage, immediately over the top of the main wing spar. While Payne made his way forward through the narrow and cramped tunnel under the pilot's seat, Stevens began the pre-flight inspection of his bird. For take-off and landing, and whenever the plane was taxiing, the navigator would climb back up into the centre of the fuselage and sit on the wing spar, just behind the pilot. In this way, he could take over from an incapacitated pilot at a moment's notice. After Payne had ensured that everything in the nose was squared away for take-off, he returned to his position and sat immediately behind the pilot.

The 'erks' – the ground crew members who maintained each aircraft – were there waiting for the pilot of 'their bird'. They discussed the minor snags Stevens had reported from his brief NFT – a formality before Stevens accepted the aircraft in writing. 'Funny,' he thought, 'you can't even go to war without signing forms!' Next the armourer certified that the specified bomb load was indeed loaded within the confines of the bomb bay. Berlin being beyond the Hampden's maximum range with a full 4,000-pound load, they would carry only 2,000 pounds of high explosives tonight. The rest of that weight would be traded off for the necessary extra fuel to reach the extreme distance of the target and make it home again safely. Stevens made a point of checking the fuel load with his crew of mechanics and riggers, then verified it on paper. He damned well would not run out of gas on *this* flight, his longest ever. Many bombers had crashed for want of fuel either over the North Sea or even back over British soil. It just wouldn't do to survive the trip to hell and back and then run out of petrol while searching desperately for home.

Four 500-pound high-explosive devices in the bay looked small next to the unused space for more bombs, while the rack under each wing just outboard of the engine remained empty. Under-wing bombs would add too much drag for so long a flight, and the extreme range rendered them unusable. Stevens inspected the internal bomb mountings very carefully, as he couldn't afford to have one fall off at an unexpected moment. He actually gave each one in turn a good push and pull, carefully avoiding the arming device in the nose of each.

The fuses were in the tip of each bomb, and the navigator, who would aim and release the bombs, would arm these electrically. As a final fail-safe measure, each fuse also had a tiny propeller. When the navigator released the bombs, the safety wire leading from the propeller to the aircraft would break, allowing the propeller to spin freely and arm the detonator. Stevens didn't touch the wee propellers. *That* would be asking for serious trouble!

Sure that everything was correct with the bomb load, he moved on to the airframe. He took a quick look at the port main undercarriage and tyre, then walked to the starboard engine nacelle, which he inspected for debris and oil leaks. Finding nothing amiss, he proceeded outward along the wing and ran his hand along the leading edge, feeling for any damage. At the wingtip, he looked at the navigation light, and then he continued around to the trailing edge of the wing. Grasping the starboard aileron, he gently moved it up and down to ensure that it had the full range of movement necessary to control the wings' attitude in flight. Moving inboard, he examined the extended flaps, and then, heading aft, he ran his hand along the rear fuselage. Reaching the large twin tail, he inspected the leading edge of both the horizontal and vertical stabilisers, as well as the twin rudders.

The unusual-looking Hampden was a pure delight to fly, but one of its flight characteristics required full use of both rudders to correct. In 'stabilised yaw', the left rudder blanketed the right one, usually in an uncoordinated left turn. The effects could be devastating and culminate in a flat spin. If *that* happened, the aircraft had ceased flying and was in great danger. The pilot could only try to induce a dive, from which a safe recovery was possible. The best way was to pull the starboard throttle back to 'Idle' and advance the port one to take-off power, while trying to move as much weight as possible into the nose. With luck, one might end up in a regular (i.e., diving) spin, from which one could recover with enough altitude (300–500 feet or more). Stevens always made sure that both rudders were in perfect condition.

Looking at the elevator at the very aft end of the aircraft, he decided that it too was fine. Next he got down on his belly and looked very strange indeed as he inspected the partially retractable tail wheel, which helped steer the plane on the ground. If it had problems, the Hampden might be uncontrollable while taxiing and might crash fully laden into a building or another aircraft. 'Wouldn't be a pretty sight,' he perhaps thought. Upright again, he walked forward to the small hatch of the 'tin' and gave its handle a mighty pull. A month earlier, he'd had to abort an op a half-hour after take-off, when the hatch had fallen off in mid-flight! Stevens had been the laughing stock of the Mess for two weeks after that episode, and he didn't want to repeat it.

Walking forward, he repeated all the checks on the portside wing, then moved to the front of the fuselage, under the cockpit. He ran his hand along the side of the fuselage, almost as a caress, and paused momentarily, as he did before every op. 'Bring us back safely, old girl. You've got a long ride tonight, and lots of very angry "Jerries" to get through,' he willed to the aircraft. Stevens then felt each of the little hollow aluminium pitot tubes leading out and forward from the side and bottom of the airframe to satisfy himself that they were well secured. Each of them was indispensable, as they allowed the flight instruments on the dashboard to inform the pilot about airspeed and altitude. As he moved to the Perspex-covered nose of the aircraft, he saw Payne squaring himself away in the navigator/bombardier's position. He gave a tap on the clear acrylic and, as Payne looked up, flashed a quick smile and the universal 'thumbs-up' sign. Payne grinned back and responded in kind.

With the pre-flight inspection complete, the pilot walked back around the port wing to where it joined the fuselage. He bent over and looked in through the Plexiglas window on the lower gunner's position and waved to Sgt Fraser. Looking up again, he saw Sgt Thompson at work at the upper rear-gun emplacement. Stevens whistled and, when Thompson looked over, smiled and gave the 'thumbs-up'.

A rickety-looking four-rung steel ladder rested against the port-wing root, allowing the pilot to climb up onto the wing itself, whence he would gain access to the cockpit. Before he used it, however, he relieved himself. It would be a very long flight, and, like all airmen, he carried a thermos of hot coffee. The caffeine would be welcome, but not the feeling of bursting his bladder. While the Hampden carried an 'Elsan' port-a-potty just forward of the rear gunners' positions, the pilot would not be able to use it in flight. Everyone else could if necessary, but the pilot was stuck in his seat – this time for eight hours. So Stevens took a pleasant, leisurely pee beside his aircraft.

He then climbed the ladder onto the wing, with one of the mechanics following him, and walked forward to the cockpit. The pilot's entrance to the Hampden was unusual, for a bomber. All he had to do was slide the pilot's canopy rearwards and climb into his seat from the side, almost as if climbing into a Spitfire fighter. Like all young men entering the RAF early in the war, he had dreamt of becoming a 'gladiator of the air' – a fighter pilot. While the Hampden wouldn't do 350 mph (like a Spitfire or Hurricane), it was certainly the fastest and best-handling RAF bomber in the air. The controls were light and responsive, and it was easy to stand it up on one wingtip, something Stevens did occasionally on an NFT, just for fun. He would have loved to try a barrel roll, but, even though the aircraft could cope, his superiors would not approve.

Placing his parachute pack on the seat, where it became his cushion, Stevens faced forward and hoisted his right leg up and over the port fuselage into the cockpit. He then swung his left leg over, and this left him standing so that the top half of his body was outside the aircraft, above the windscreen. This was not easy to do, as his heavy flight suit made him feel a bit like the Michelin Man. He sat down on the parachute pack, and the mechanic helped him adjust and connect the various shoulder harness and lap belts. Giving the fellow a quick wave, the pilot cleared him to depart. 'Now,' he thought, 'down to business.'

For if Stevens was anything as a pilot, he was business-like. The cockpit was his office, and he did everything there by the book. He commenced going down the pre-start checklist and was ready within a minute.

Following the same procedure as earlier that day, he started first the port engine, then the starboard. While they were coming up to temperature, Stevens held his breath for a moment and listened very hard to each engine. Not only did he use his hearing, but he also put both hands on the control yoke and *felt* the engines – or at least their vibrations. If something were slightly out of balance, if one of the crankshafts were about to spin a bearing, he might just feel the early warning signs. They were his lifelines, and if there was the slightest doubt about their health this was his last chance to check. As it was, he could sense nothing amiss and liked what he had heard and felt. The engines seemed to be running perfectly. Next, he used the engine-powered hydraulic system to raise the flaps from fully extended to fully retracted. While most aircraft required a small amount of flap for take-off, the Hampden's patented automatic leading-edge slats gave that extra bit of low-speed lift necessary to get off the ground.

Having connected his oxygen mask/microphone to the radio/intercom system, he tested it by asking the crew to check in, one by one. By habit, they each clipped on their oxygen masks with the integrated microphones and replied.

'Wireless operator to pilot, everything ready.'

'Air gunner to pilot, clear.'

'Navigator to pilot, ready here.'

With the engines warmed up, the pilot used the hydraulic controls and started one last task: 'Pilot to navigator, closing bomb bay doors.'

'Pilot to crew, okay chaps, here we go. Let's keep everything safe on this one, and everyone comes home.'

Following guidance from the control tower, once again with different-coloured Aldis lamps, Stevens waited for clearance and then joined the convoy taxiing slowly towards the furthest downwind section of the airfield. He handled the aircraft particularly gingerly on the ground, as it was now a very dangerous weapon, loaded with 2,000 pounds of high explosives and several thousand pounds of high-octane – extremely flammable – aviation fuel. Everything about this Hampden was now high, and Stevens knew he was sitting on top of a large bomb, just itching to explode. He would do his damnedest to ensure that it didn't. It was more than just his life, after all. The rest of the boys were relying on him now.

It was approaching dusk as Stevens turned his plane into the wind and, receiving the appropriate lamp signal, slowly advanced the throttles to take-off power. This time, the Hampden was much slower to react. At a taxi weight of a few hundred pounds over its maximum allowable gross weight (21,000 pounds[1]), she would require a very long take-off run. Stevens was ready for that and entered the airfield as far back as possible. As the kites ahead in line became airborne, Hampden AD

936 responded well to his demand. He deliberately kept her on the ground longer than normal, as he would need more speed to make her fly at so heavy a weight. Finally, when the end of the field appeared to be just a few seconds away, he gently pulled back on the yoke, feeling the wings take the machine's weight off the main undercarriage. He had now committed himself and raised the landing gear to decrease drag. She was flying, but would she climb?

Soon he had to find out. Coming close to some trees up ahead, Stevens asked her to climb, and ever so gradually she did. While he monitored the engine temperatures and pressures, he guided the machine ever higher, striving for the transit altitude of 15,000 feet above sea level. He could just barely make out the shapes of the five aircraft ahead of him, and there were six to follow. All of a sudden, as he climbed through 3,000 feet, out of the corner of his left eye he saw a huge explosion on the ground behind him. The fireball rose, and the night slowly enveloped it. Everyone in the crew saw it; they gasped into their microphones but instantly clicked them off, realising that dwelling on what had just happened would help no one.

In fact, the aircraft of P/O Reginald John Roake, Stevens's best friend on the squadron, had suffered an engine failure almost immediately after take-off. Unable to maintain altitude, let alone climb, the stricken Hampden had resisted all his admonitions and could not keep sufficient airspeed for the wings to generate enough lift to remain aloft. In airman's terms, she had stalled and spun in. At the altitude from which it had happened, only 300 feet, the end had been mercifully quick. There were no survivors. With enforced radio silence, no one in the air could know which crew had just 'bought the farm'. Roake's Hampden had augured in at 8.55 p.m., just three minutes after take-off, crashing on the Empingham–Ketton road, north-east of the base.[2] Roake was twenty-three years old.[3] His father, a captain in the Royal Army, had earlier distinguished himself in service to his country, being awarded the Military Cross (presumably in the First World War). Clearly it was a family of extreme dedication.

Of course, Roake's crash was a painful reminder to all aboard of what could happen to any of them at any moment. That was the worst: not knowing. Would it be a mechanical malfunction, or an enemy fighter, or an anti-aircraft cannon shell rising from the ground, or a mid-air collision with one of their own aircraft in the dark of night, or would one of their own planes drop a bomb on them from a thousand feet over their heads? Any one of these was a distinct possibility, and each of them occurred with unpleasant regularity. While almost paralysed with fear, each man bearing it in his own, private way, they all had one common wish: that if it happened, it should be quick and painless. Roake's crew had been lucky, they all agreed wordlessly. But the absolute worst would be horrible injuries or disfigurement and survival. Fire terrified every member of the aircrew. Imagine spending the rest of your life with no recognisable face. Each of them did imagine it, regularly. They were afraid not of dying, but of *living* under such conditions.

Eventually, after about fifteen minutes aloft, the aircraft had reached the minimum altitude for crossing the cold and dark North Sea and turned eastwards. Several among the forty-four remaining men of 144 Squadron in their flying coffins were sure that this was their night – tonight they would die. Stevens, at least, had never entertained such thoughts. For he was once again a man on a mission. He would show those Nazi bastards. He would do to them what they had tried to do to his family. He would become a weapon, and the safety catch was about to be released.

Though sweating under the heavy cotton overall and the woollen battle dress, he wondered whether he wouldn't freeze on the long journey. He could have worn battle dress and a full layer of heavier winter sheepskin. But as the aircraft continued to climb towards 15,000 feet, the air continued to cool, until at 10,000 feet, with the cockpit canopy partially open for ventilation, Stevens began to feel more comfortable. He usually flew with his oxygen mask dangling from one side of his leather flying helmet, but at that altitude he grabbed his mask and locked it into both sides of the helmet. Clicking the intercom, he advised, 'Pilot to crew, 10,000 feet, go on oxygen and confirm. No getting drunk tonight.' The early symptoms of hypoxia (lack of oxygen) resembled those of an overabundance of beer, and they would all need their wits about them. All three men reached for their flow control and turned the lever to 'On'. They then reported back to the pilot, knowing that they would not stay fully conscious in the unpressurised Hampden without it. Above 20,000 feet, they would eventually die from oxygen starvation.

Reaching the east coast of England, Stevens engaged the simple autopilot. Crossing the North Sea would take about forty-five minutes, and then he would have to fly 'hands on' until they passed the European coast on the way home. Stevens still had to monitor all the instruments, but for a while he could relax ever so slightly. The routeing for tonight would take the Hampden almost 150 miles across the North Sea, making landfall on the Dutch coast near the southernmost tip of the Frisian Islands.

Once they reached the Dutch coast, they would need all senses on alert, and the pilot would have one hand tightly around the control yoke at all times. Only good sense would stop him from using the autopilot over enemy territory. An emergency could happen at any time, and Stevens knew well that he would have to hand fly the plane during the period of heightened danger.

Unknown to Stevens and his crew, there was quite a parade in the sky that night. The RAF had dispatched a total of 294 aircraft from various bases in England: 197 to Berlin, fifty-one to the submarine works at Kiel, thirty-eight to the dockyards at Boulogne in France, and eight Hampdens to lay mines off the Frisian Islands.[4] And so, for most of the way, Stevens and crew had a host of unseen company, another 246 aircraft. This armada crowded the routes and drastically increased the potential for mid-air collision.

Well out over the North Sea, the Stevens gave permission over the intercom, 'Okay lads, test your guns. Just make sure that you don't hit any of ours!' With that, each of the rear gunners, as well as the navigator (who had his own gun in the nose for use when he wasn't navigating or dropping bombs), cocked their machine-guns and let go a very short burst, aiming upwards (except for the rear air gunner in the lower position, who had to aim straight downwards) so as to minimise the risk of hitting a friendly plane. While they were busy with that, Stevens test-fired his own gun, which was in a fixed mount just below him and to his left. He always enjoyed firing it, as it made him feel once again like the Spitfire pilot he had always longed to be.

Occasionally one of the crew would see flashes or searchlights coming from the continent ahead, but the only thing that could reach him here over water was a night fighter or, if he was unlucky, a flak ship off the coast looking for intruders such as the Hampden and its crew. Unfortunately, the *Luftwaffe* was very skilled at hunting, as Stevens knew very well at first hand. Two Junkers Ju 88s had jumped him over Belgium just a month earlier. Amazingly, he and his injured crew had all survived, but one of the German pilots had paid the supreme price in the encounter, and this had given Stevens a great deal of satisfaction. He was not at all shy about killing Germans, for the Nazis had ruined his country and then his family. He was quite prepared to fight evil with evil.

Despite the confidence that he gained from the knowledge that German fighter pilots were not invincible, Stevens reminded his men every fifteen minutes to keep a close eye out for any intruders, any reflection of moonlight off metal, or, worse still, the flash of tracer shells. They were flying relatively slowly, about 170 mph, in order to save fuel. This would help ensure a flight home but made their Hampden a sitting duck for the night fighters.

The trip so far had been cold and very lonely. There was too little going on, at least for the two air gunners in the rear, and, despite scanning the sky for any sign of visitors, they could not help allowing their minds to wander. Fear was the enemy, and time was the enemy's friend. The longer that they were not actively doing something, the more time there was to think. The more time for that, the more time for fear. At least the pilot and the navigator had things to do.

Being busy, however, did not negate the fear that the two pilots felt. They both found themselves listening to the engines, checking for anything amiss. Occasionally they would feel a slight vibration and worry about a developing misfire or perhaps an engine about to self-destruct. Nobody knew what caused the engine failure that doomed Roake's plane a few hours earlier; probably nobody ever would. Such catastrophes just happened, but a pilot could still trouble himself about it.

After one-and-a-half hours out from North Luffenham, the Hampden approached the coastline where northern Holland begins to melt into the North Sea, becoming a small chain of islands. Stevens wished that he could have continued further north and stayed well offshore all the way to Denmark in order to avoid the flak guns on the Dutch coast searching for him and his comrades. But that would have added perhaps 200 miles to their round trip, and there just wasn't enough fuel on board. Just 150 miles ahead and slightly to the north lay the peninsula where Germany reaches north towards Denmark, splitting the North Sea from the Baltic. Jutland!

Each of the crewmembers had heard about Jutland in school and its famous naval battle of 1916. An incredible 250 British and German ships, including forty-four of the largest dreadnoughts ever,[5] took part in perhaps one of the most significant naval battles of all time. But whereas the others in the crew thought it was a great victory, Stevens as a boy had learned of it as an ignominious defeat.

'Navigator to pilot. Enemy coast ahead.'

The crew always appreciated a word from the skipper at a nervous moment, and Stevens accepted the mantle of command the way he thought a British gentleman should.

Pilot to crew. Okay chaps, here we go. From here on in, it's American rules: shoot first and ask questions later. They're counting on us back home. We all know how heavy the defences will be, but if we do a good job tonight, we shouldn't have to come back anytime soon. Let's go and say hello to *Herr* Hitler. Let's give the little corporal a greeting card from hell.

Of those poor, lonely souls on board, only Stevens knew at first hand just how much Hitler and his cronies deserved what he was about to deliver. And he wished with all his might that one of his bombs would find its target and rid the world of this unspeakable evil. A desire for revenge welled up within him, powerful and unstoppable.

As they crossed the Dutch coastline, everyone on board knew that they would be flying a tightrope from then on. Had the *Luftwaffe* fighter pilots or the *Wehrmacht* soldiers manning the anti-aircraft guns on the ground known that Peter Stevens, born in Hanover to a wealthy Jewish family, was still legally a German citizen, they would have taken extra delight in killing him. For to the Nazis he would be not only an enemy; he and his people were responsible for all the evil that had befallen that nation throughout the last several generations. Nobody on board the Hampden except Stevens knew that he was a German Jew – a member of a group that Nazis considered the filth of Europe.

Hampden AD 936 had already been in the air for some ninety minutes, and as it had so far flown only over water, little had prepared the men for what they were about to face. Within minutes of crossing the coastline, they could see large groupings of searchlight beams criss-crossing the sky near Amsterdam, forty miles to the south. Before they knew it, the searchlight band grew much closer to their own track, looking for targets. Obviously some were emerging: the entire crew would see tracer shells arcing up to try and hit an RAF bomber. This was a very difficult task for a single gun, but as the number of artillery pieces increased so did their coverage and their chances of success.

German anti-aircraft defences would be slightly lighter over northern Holland than over Germany itself, at least away from any large cities. Once over the narrow Ijsselmeer, the Brits would fly slightly south-east to avoid the large city of Groningen. Stevens wanted ideally to be about thirty miles south of that town but no further than that, in order to give 'Happy Valley' a very wide berth. The heavily industrialised Ruhr Valley had such good defences, with anti-aircraft artillery and night fighters, that flying anywhere near it was sheer lunacy. The course just south of Groningen would give the Hampden a safety margin of some 100 miles north of the Ruhr – enough to miss the brunt of the flak batteries, but the night fighters would have ample range to come after it. Entering northern German airspace, Stevens would be sure to split the well-defended cities of Bremen to the north and Hanover to the south. Then all he had to do was fly 250 miles through the heart of the Third *Reich* to Berlin. 'Ahh, Hanover,' Stevens may have thought wistfully to himself, 'what bittersweet memories.'

There wouldn't be too much opposition for the first 100 miles over enemy territory (occupied Holland), but the last 400 to Berlin would be sheer hell. Not knowing the Brits' target, the Germans would first assume Hamburg, a manufacturing and logistics centre and important ocean port. When it was clear that the British raiders were bypassing that city, the next assumption would be the naval base at Kiel. When they stayed well south of Kiel, there would be no doubt remaining that they were aiming for the capital. The Germans would spare no effort to ensure that the *Terrorfliegers* all died before they reached their target.

Trying to thread the flak needle between Bremen and Hanover would not be simple. Defensive searchlight and anti-aircraft gun emplacements ringed both cities to a radius of at least ten miles beyond their boundaries. Without navigational radio beacons and in the dark, it would be difficult for the Brits to avoid large targets and still head directly for Berlin. While Bremen and Hanover were about sixty miles apart, their route would also take them over mainly agricultural territory with no obvious military targets. The Germans knew that any bomber flying this route had only one likely target: Berlin.

The Germans had placed anti-aircraft guns in thick bands spreading from north to south across their intended path. And so, for the next 200 miles or so, the noose would seem to be tightening. In peacetime, they would have been able to identify each of the larger centres by the dense ring of lights downtown. A strict blackout, however, made it difficult to distinguish them or to pinpoint their own position.

At least the aircraft was flying better. By now, it had burned off several hundred pounds of fuel and was a bit easier to handle. With the outside air at about –12°C (10°F) and about 4°C (40°F) inside, Stevens was again thankful that he'd not chosen the sheepskin. It would have been too warm, and whenever he felt too hot he became nauseous. The other three men had taken their cue from him and were also chilly but not freezing cold.

Suddenly, just thirty miles past Hanover, the sky around them became pure white. They had flown right into the cone of a searchlight, which blinded them all for a moment. Stevens took emergency evasive action, maintaining their course but diving to gather speed. The faster they travelled, the sooner they would be out of the light's range. Now there was another concern: did radar or a human on the ground control the beam? They would know shortly. If radar, the beam would shut off very quickly so as not to blind a nearby German fighter pilot whom the radar operators were guiding, and they could expect hot metal arriving in moments. If human, the beam would try to stay with them while ground gunners adjusted their aim.

The crew wanted to scream to Stevens over the intercom, 'GET US OUT OF HERE!' but doing so would not help. Stevens would do anything to break free of the beam immediately. Puffs of smoke were approaching the aircraft, which nearby explosions of flak shells were rocking. The Germans' aim was still off by several hundred feet, however, as the additional airspeed gained in the dive fooled their calculations. Nonetheless, the two air gunners could hear small collisions of shrapnel fragments with the outside of the fuselage. Fortunately the shells had exploded far enough away that their decelerating metal bits could no longer penetrate the Hampden's aluminium carapace.

The continuing beam meant that there were probably no fighters close by. The additional 60 mph from diving soon paid off, as the Hampden emerged from apparent daylight into the cool safety of the darkness. There was a silent sigh of relief from everyone on board.

The Germans now knew where they were and, by extrapolating their course, could be sure that they were targeting Berlin. The element of surprise was now gone, and Stevens and his crew would face tough flying and determined opposition. This daunting realisation made the silence on board even gloomier.

All at once there was a terrific racket, as air gunner Sgt Fraser opened up with his pair of .303 machine-guns. 'What is it?' yelled Stevens over the intercom.

'Not sure, Skipper,' came the reply. 'I was pretty sure I saw a reflection off metal.'

'Well,' Stevens replied for all to hear, 'let's be careful and make sure we don't shoot down one of our own.'

Notes

1. Harry Moyle, *The Hampden File* (Tonbridge, Kent: Air-Britain [Historians] Ltd, 1989), 23.
2. W. R. Chorley, *Royal Air Force Bomber Command Losses of the Second World War, Volume 2, Aircraft and Crew Losses 1941* (Leicester: Midland Counties Publications, 1993), 141.
3. Website of the Commonwealth War Graves Commission: http://www.cwgc.org/search/casualty_details.aspx?casualty=2709593
4. Middlebrook and Everitt, *The Bomber Command War Diaries*, 200–1.
5. R. Ernest Dupuy and Trevor N. Dupuy, *The Harper Encyclopedia of Military History*, 4th ed. (New York: HarperCollins Publishers, 1993), 1,056–7.

CHAPTER THREE

The Heart of Darkness

A fter another thirty minutes heading eastward, Sgt Payne called to Stevens, 'D'you see it, Stevie?' 'Yes, I do now,' was the response. They had both seen the protective ring of searchlights surrounding Berlin. Once they entered that ring, there would be no need to worry about German fighters, which would never enter the 'Zone of Death'. The flak gunners on the ground would not be able to distinguish between friend and foe and would shoot at any aircraft they could see. It was the same around London, in fact. Every RAF bomber pilot knew to stay well clear of the capital when returning from an op, even in broad daylight. Gunners on the ground would shoot first and ask questions later.

Droning on towards the target, the Hampden's crew was quiet yet purposeful. Stevens checked with the navigator regularly for wind drift and time remaining to the target. By the time Sgt Payne told him the final course to steer to reach the 'initial point' (IP), they had already begun flying through the searchlight beams. At the IP, they would make their last course correction, putting them on final approach to the aiming point, whence they would identify the target and release their bombs.

Nearing the centre of the Third *Reich*, Stevens felt an unusual sensation. After all, it was only five years since he had last visited the city. He asked himself whether any of the other crewmen had ever been in peacetime Berlin, such a beautiful and cultured place. Unlikely, he thought. He wondered how it had changed, sure that it now looked very different, courtesy of the RAF. He remembered with fondness watching Jesse Owens win so many gold medals at the 1936 Summer Olympics and his satisfaction at this great embarrassment to the *Führer*. Hitler had refused to bestow these laurels on a black man, who belonged to *another* people that the Nazis considered sub-human. He also recalled his last meeting with his mother, how awkward it had been, but how gently she had bidden him farewell. Where was she now? How was she coping? Despite his childhood animosity, Stevens hoped against hope that she was well and had avoided both British bombs and Nazi persecution, but he had his doubts. His mind strayed just slightly to the rest of his relatives still in Germany. For all of his aunts, uncles, and cousins he felt concern, yet he suspected that they were probably dead. Even stronger in his mind than such concern, however, was the anger that demanded revenge. He vowed silently, 'Many Nazis will die tonight.'

A call from the navigator returned Stevens to the present. As the sky erupted with metallic fury, Payne advised: 'Three minutes to target, steady on course.' This was the pilot's cue, and he reached over and flicked the switch that commanded the bomb bay doors to open. Payne backed away from the bombsight just long enough to look at the electrical panel on the side of the fuselage and flipped the switches that would arm the bomb fuses. Over the intercom, Stevens confirmed with him that he had tripped the appropriate bomb-selector switches and that the master bomb switch was now 'On'.

'Pilot to navigator, you have the aircraft.'

From this point on, Payne controlled the Hampden. He would be command and control, all in one. For the crew had a single mission, to deliver the bomb load to the target. And that job was now squarely in Payne's hands. He would coax the plane to the unique spot whence the bombs must fall perfectly. He would take into account prevailing wind, airspeed, altitude, and several other factors. He had become like a surgeon ready to excise a tumour, but knowing that one slip could kill hundreds of innocent civilians. His conscience was not ready for such a burden, and he would therefore do everything possible to hit the target. He made final adjustments to the bombsight lens and double-checked that he had entered the correct altitude and wind information. Then, looking downward through the reticle of the precision instrument, he issued minute left- or right-course corrections to Stevens, who was doing everything he could to keep the aircraft straight and level – never easy even at the best of times. Now, at the very worst of times, it was all but impossible. Flak shells were bursting around them, rocking their fragile little craft back and forth, up and down. If the show had not been so awesomely beautiful, it would have terrified them. Finally, it was time.

Focusing his right eye through the eyepiece of the complex bombsight, Payne regained his bearings and began searching for the railway junction that was his signal to press the 'tit' and release fire. Thanks to incendiary bombs that the first wave had dropped, there were a few fires in the surrounding area, which adequately illuminated objects on the ground.

There was the spot! As it reached the crosshairs in his reticle, Payne hit the release and muttered under his breath 'There you go, you Nazi bastards, see how you like it!' He screamed over the intercom, 'Bombs gone!!!' but the pilot had already felt the great lift the plane had experienced as 2,000 pounds had fallen free. Stevens's first chore was to close the bomb doors and make the aircraft as slippery, smooth, and fast as possible.

The Hampden had jumped up almost a hundred feet as the deadly cargo disappeared. This was the pilot's signal to break off the attack and get out of there as quickly as possible. But Stevens could not fly just willy-nilly in any direction, for fear of colliding with a friendly aircraft. He had to follow precise routeing instructions to reach a safe area away from the immediate target before he could resume his planned course for England.

Despite their relief that the bombs had gone and they were leaving the central target area, crewmembers were painfully aware that they remained a target. Quite ironic, Stevens thought, a target over a target. The air gunners had very little to do but sightsee. Each reminded himself that they would see no fighters until they passed fifteen miles of anti-aircraft artillery. The *Luftwaffe*'s two primary twin-engine night fighters – Junkers Ju 88s and Messerschmitt Bf 110s – would not dare enter the killing zone.

Because the Hampden had now burnt off over 1,200 pounds of fuel and disposed of 2,000 pounds of high explosives, the plane would fly higher and faster. Stevens now harnessed that advantage. As soon as he had felt the bombs go, he had advanced the throttles to full power and dropped the nose to obtain a burst of speed and help clear the killing zone of deadly shrapnel bursting around him. At the higher airspeed, it would take them only four minutes to clear the target area. Then they would have to contend with the fighters again. But if they could only fly west-north-west as far as the coast, they would have a decent chance of reaching ...

Suddenly there was a blinding flash, a mighty thunderclap, and the aircraft slewed to the right, the port wing lifting and rolling the Hampden onto its side. Stevens fought to retain control of the bucking plane and worried that he had lost it. He commanded a left turn, but there was almost no control. He tried using full left rudder, and it helped, but there was something drastically wrong. He yelled into the intercom, 'Is everyone all right?'

There was no reply from the navigator in the nose, but the two air gunners in the rear replied in the affirmative, and Sgt Fraser asked if the plane was all right. Stevens wasn't sure and asked each of them for a damage report. The gunners, after a quick survey inside and out, now saw the cause of much of their problem. Fraser called back, 'We're missing a large chunk of tail and rudder on the port side, Skipper.' Again, nothing from Sgt Payne.

'Keep me posted, and someone check on Doc [Payne],' replied Stevens. In the meantime, he tried to evaluate the situation as best he could. The port engine was now running very roughly, and airspeed had bled off from over 220 mph down to only 150. 'At least we're still flying,' he thought. But then Fraser hailed again on the intercom, 'Skipper, we're leaking fluid from the port wing. It might be fuel.'

It *had* to be fuel. Stevens felt the death knell as the message sunk in. His eyes went straight to the twin fuel gauges, and he felt his stomach twist in knots as he saw the level of fuel in the port wing tank drop visibly in less than a minute. But his primary concern for now was to fly the aircraft. Too many accidents had occurred and people died because the pilot was so busy dealing with an emergency that he forgot to fly the plane. Stevens would not make *that* mistake. Now he began to realise that they might not return to England. His mind became a mechanical calculator, working overtime. Figures of airspeed, distance to England, and rates of fuel consumption raced through his brain and kept coming up short. Flying so slowly and certain to lose half of its fuel, the plane could not reach home. It had become a question of life or death. The Hampden would be easy pickings for the fighters at this speed. Would they survive?

Sgt Thompson grabbed his torch and advanced through the darkened fuselage and crawled under the pilot's seat and down into the nose section, to check on the navigator. Immediately he found 'Doc' dazed but uninjured. He checked him from top to bottom and could find no blood or holes in his flying overalls. Thompson gave him a good shake and asked him if he was all right. Payne replied in the affirmative and seemed to come back into the reality of the moment.

'I guess we took a bit of a hit there,' was his only comment, 'is everyone else okay?'

Thompson reassured him that everyone was alive and kicking but told him of the damage to the aircraft. Before he went back to his own position, 'Doc' warned him to be on the lookout for any additional damage and to be ready to bale out at a moment's notice, if necessary. On the way rearward, 'Tommy' stopped just behind Stevens and shouted to him: 'Doc's okay!' Stevens gave a silent thumbs up in response.

The aircraft was still handling very sluggishly, and Stevens wasn't at all happy. He already knew that he'd been hit in the port wing and that the port aileron was no longer whole. He gingerly began to test each of the other flight controls, measuring their reactions against what he innately felt as 'normal'. He immediately noticed the rudder's loss of effectiveness, but he could live with that. What concerned him much more was the lack of elevator authority, necessary to raise or lower the nose. He wondered whether he hadn't lost part or all of that critical control surface. By far the most dire thought, however, was that of the leaking fuel's catching fire and the remaining high octane in the tanks exploding. As a precaution, Stevens decided that it would be safer to drop below 10,000 feet, the safe bale-out altitude without oxygen bottles. He immediately reduced engine power while dropping the nose ever so slightly. This combination would decrease altitude while not increasing airspeed enough to endanger the damaged aircraft.

'Tommy to Steve, we seem to be losing small bits and pieces of things. I'm seeing debris go by the Tin on the Port side.'

While all of this had been happening, Stevens had also been thinking ahead. He had made the required turn to the north and was on the verge of clearing the target area. Then another flash of blinding light hit them, this time a constant beam. Moving this slowly and clearing the flak zone, they would soon fall victim to the fighters. Weighing up the possibilities and knowing England to be unattainable, he turned his thoughts to the safety of his men. They were now clear of the worst of the flak. Facing the fighters would be suicide, whereas life as a prisoner of war was still life. Calmly but resolutely, he made the fateful call, 'Pilot to crew, abandon aircraft! Bale out, bale out!' To himself, he gave them his blessing, 'Thanks chaps, you've done everything you could. Now, go while you still can. Good luck to you all, and be safe.'

Part Two: Georg Franz Hein
(1919–39)

CHAPTER FOUR

Childhood at 19 Rumannstrasse, Hanover (1919–26)

The 1914–18 war was finally over. Life was beginning its return to some semblance of normalcy, business was picking up. Victor Hein's family had never been in direct danger, living well away from the front, in Hanover. Germany had lost the Great War, but that wasn't the Heins' problem. As Jews, they were always very careful to avoid politics, especially when war was its natural consequence. Because of this seeming insouciance, wars usually did little damage to his people. Yet they often received blame for causing, or at least financing, the conflicts. In any case, centuries of European warfare offered a valuable lesson: do not take sides. The Heins' distant relatives the Rothschilds had it right: bankroll wars, but don't fight in them. Nonetheless over 80,000 German Jews had fought for their homeland in the war, and 12,000 had died.[1] Luckily, at age forty-three in August 1914, Victor had been too old to fight. A good thing, too: he had never held a gun and appeared to people who knew him as one of the meekest men alive.

But then, Victor Hein was not in the same league as the Rothschilds. Born to an upper-middle-class family in Baden in 1873, he had been quite successful. The family had done well for a couple of generations, and Victor's father, Selly Hein, had had the great misfortune of having his primary business nationalised at the turn of the century. Selly had started one of the many private courier services that existed prior to the federal government creating a centralised German Post Office, in 1886. Since Selly's efforts had been quite successful, and Communism did not yet exist (other than on paper), the nationalisation of his company (Stadbrief Expedition Mercur) on 31 March 1900 was accompanied by compensation from the German government of 262,044.33 Marks. A very rough calculation of the conversion makes that amount the equivalent of several million dollars in today's money.

When Selly died in July of 1900, Victor inherited the family publishing business. By February 1919, at age forty-seven, he'd accumulated a modest fortune of his own through ownership of a national trade magazine, *Die Manufakturist*, which published articles on subjects of interest to factory owners and managers.

Of course, as with most such publications, the bulk of revenue came from advertising, not from circulation. The magazine included the nation's most highly regarded personnel exchange, with classified ads for people looking for jobs and jobs in need of people. The horrific carnage of war had left more jobs than people, and that was good for advertising revenues.

That was a strange thing about wars, at least for the last hundred years; who won and who lost mattered little to the middle class. As long as its members kept their collective heads down (and didn't enlist in the armed forces), they were relatively safe – at least until the invention of the aircraft. Since air power had not yet come into its own, the Great War had not devastated German cities. Afterwards, industry went wild, commerce boomed, and people who thought earnestly about the consequences and planned ahead did well. Victor was particularly bright and thoughtful.

There was still, however, the maddening issue of runaway inflation. Money just wasn't worth what it used to be, but little did Victor know what hyperinflation meant. Within five years, Germans would need literally a wheelbarrow full of money to buy a loaf of bread. Prices rose every day, and so did interest rates. That was a very bad thing, if one happened to owe a lot of money. Being a prudent and conservative businessman, Victor didn't. High interest rates suited him just fine, thank you very much.

Life for the Hein family was pretty good. In 1912, thirty-nine-year-old Victor had married Henni Seckel, twenty-six, a bright and fiery woman, with considerable talent at the piano and flaming red hair that matched her temperament. She had given him a son, Erich, in 1915, when the war looked remotely winnable. Now the conflict was over, and Henni's belly was huge with their second child, due any day.

Both the Hein and Seckel families were Liberal (or Reform) Jews. Over several centuries they had, like most upper-middle-class German Jews, assimilated. They considered themselves far too logical to let their religion run their lives. While they attended religious services regularly, they also mixed with people of other faiths. After all, that was good for business. But more than that, the two families had education and were active in community life, which they felt their duty as good Germans.

Victor Hein was small and slight; some observers might even have called him 'mousy'. He was balding and wore a moustache, which added to this characterisation. He had four brothers and two sisters (although one of the girls had died in infancy). He was the middle child, and his brothers became quite successful in their own right. Paul, seven years his junior, had received his PhD in chemistry. Adolf, eleven years younger, was a lawyer who had earned his doctorate in that discipline.

Henni Seckel was even smaller than Victor at four feet, ten inches, yet she ran the home. Her parents had spoilt her, the youngest of four children, and she usually got her own way. She too came from a family that expected excellence.

Her older brother, Martin, was the director of a bank. Siegmund, Henni's father, had been a merchant in Peine (about thirty miles east of Hanover) but had also been very civic-minded. He had started off his political career as an alderman and had finished with the 'Key to the City' and as a 'Free Man of Peine,' a major honour.

Even though the Heins and the Seckels were not particularly religious, they had observed all of the correct rituals at Erich's birth. But they were more pragmatic than many other Jews and did not want their religion to dominate life. Besides, why call attention to themselves? History revealed far too many Jews who had become too prominent, too successful, and it had cost them dearly in the end. Too many countries had evicted their Jews. Victor was much more cautious. He felt very strongly that religion was a matter for an individual and his or her God, whichever God one chose to worship. He also thought very highly of the separation of church and state. It gave anti-Semites less power, if not less opportunity, to wield against Victor's people.

Heins and Seckels had lived in or near Hanover for hundreds of years. The young couple's parents hailed from Hildesheim (for the Heins) and Peine (for the Seckels). Virtually all the family's recorded history had taken place within 100 miles of Hanover. The Jewish cemetery there dated back to the seventeenth century.

The three Heins occupied a ten-room flat at number 19 Rumannstrasse, so there would be plenty of room for the new baby. Even with the maid and butler/chauffeur living in the servants' rooms behind the large kitchen and servery, a new mouth to feed would not crowd their home. Perhaps they'd have to move into a slightly larger place if Victor agreed to Henni's request for a governess when she had more than one child to look after. Perhaps, too, she would then want her parents to move in with them, so they could help with the new baby. They lived only 300 metres down the street and even being so close didn't get in the way. A nice old couple, they were good with young Erich and were very much looking forward to becoming grandparents again.

The luxurious flat, which occupied the entire second floor of number 19, was in one of the nicest parts of Hanover. It was only three blocks away from the Hohenzollernstrasse, an imposing boulevard, and the Eilenriede, a large and beautiful park in the centre of town. Another block or two away, and facing the park, was the music conservatory where Henni was something of a celebrity. Ten or so blocks to the west, just past the central Hauptbahnhof railway station, stood the Opera House, the Heins' 'home away from home'. Henni and Victor were patrons of the opera and had a reserved box for every performance.

At home, both husband and wife liked and surrounded themselves with fine things – French crystal, German Meissen and Rosenthal china, English sterling flatware, Dutch and Flemish art. The walls were dark walnut, and Henni ensured that the servants oiled and polished them often enough that the grain fairly leapt off them. The Bösendorfer grand piano dominated the music room, and Henni played often, filling the building with tapestries of sound. None of the neighbours complained; Henni had performed on stage in Berlin, Prague, and Vienna. As it happened, she was sitting at the piano on the evening of 14 February, playing a Beethoven sonata – something soothing and not too challenging – when her waters broke. Victor was a gentle man with a true reverence for his wife, and he hoped that she would deliver the child with as little pain and suffering as possible. He rang for Henni's physician, asking him to 'come round as quickly as possible'. In the meantime, the maid helped Henni to her bed to prepare for the birth. Everyone present expected a long process, with little opportunity for rest.

It turned out to be a rather short, albeit painful, event. Before noon on 15 February 1919, Henni Hein gave birth to a healthy infant, a boy, which she presented to her proud husband. The child, named Georg Franz, had an abnormally large head, whose passage through the birth canal had caused his mother sheer agony, which she would have great difficulty in forgetting. Some people might even say that she would hold it against the child for the rest of her life. The family summoned Henni's devout father, Siegmund, to view and pronounce his blessing on his second grandson, and in this he took very great pleasure.

After such difficulties, Henni recovered slowly. Siegmund and Victor therefore had to postpone their plans for the traditional Jewish celebration for the birth of a boy. Georg's public circumcision (the Briss) took place three weeks after the birth, to allow Henni to recover. All of the Heins' friends attended the daylong party, which culminated in a black-tie event that evening in the ballroom of the city's best hotel. Henni received an extravagant new gown for the occasion. Another son was exactly what Victor wanted, and he was very proud of the baby, although Henni had secretly longed for a daughter. She vowed to herself to keep trying until she had one, as painful as it might be.

The earliest problem in the household after Georg's arrival was his parents coping with lack of sleep. Victor was relatively fortunate, however. Because of the family's wealth and way of life, it could have easily hired a wet nurse for the baby and located the nursery far enough from the master bedroom to prevent the baby's cries from disturbing his parents' sleep, or at least his father's. Henni still slept fitfully and awoke easily but did not bother her husband with situations (such as a hungry baby) with which he could not possibly help. She believed that that was her duty, not his. Of course, the governess took care of the infant most of the time.

The elder boy, Erich, was quiet, introverted, and not jealous of the new focus of attention. This was convenient, since Georg was fussy, demanding as much as he could possibly obtain. Erich tolerated his young brother quite well despite his crying, still wanting to help his mother with the baby.

Sadly, and unexpectedly, Henni's mother, Rieke, died at sixty-seven, only three weeks after Georg's arrival. This certainly put a damper on the festivities for the birth and hit Henni particularly hard. In fact, Henni just couldn't seem to recover from this terrible blow. 'Just when things seemed to be going so well,' she agonised. The war had ended, a new baby had arrived, things should have been so perfect. As much sympathy as Victor could offer just wasn't enough, and it seemed to him as though Henni might be unable to cope with this loss. Did she blame the baby? She certainly wasn't reacting to him as one would expect – she seemed almost to ignore him. Victor worried about Henni's mental state and urged Siegmund to do whatever he could for her. They grieved together, and in time, and with the help of the doctor and his little black bag of miracle drugs, Henni slowly came around.

On 28 June of that year, exactly five years after the assassination of Archduke Franz Ferdinand and his wife in Sarajevo that led to war, the diplomats and so-called peacemakers signed the Treaty of Versailles, officially ending the Great War. The conflict had been essentially a stalemate until the Americans entered it in April 1917, and by the late summer of 1918 German losses were unsustainable. So would have been Allied losses, but for the monthly infusion of 300,000 fresh American troops.[2] By September 1918, the Germans had privately asked for peace talks, and civil rule quickly broke down. The German navy had mutinied, and Communist insurrection resulted in chaos. Kaiser Wilhelm II had abdicated and fled to Holland on 10 November, and the armistice had taken effect the next morning, at the eleventh hour of the eleventh day of the eleventh month of 1918.The human cost had been horrendous – hence 'The Great War' and 'The War to End All Wars'. Germany and its allies had lost approximately 3,132,000 dead plus 8,420,000 wounded, out of some 22,850,000 troops (a casualty rate of almost 51 per cent).[3] Germany itself had suffered a casualty rate of 55 per cent, with 1,809,000 dead and 4,247,000 wounded out of armed forces of 11 million. In the Allied powers (including France, Britain and the Empire/Commonwealth, Russia, Italy, and the United States), 4,889,000 people serving had died and 12,809,000 received wounds out of 42,189,000 service people (a casualty rate of 42 per cent).

The innately proud Germans took defeat hard. It is probably accurate to say that they felt themselves superior to every other nation in Europe, except for Britain, which they viewed as their equal. Not only had Germany lost the cream of its youth, but now the international community expected it to acknowledge complete responsibility for the war and to make cash reparations. The signing of the peace treaty at the Palais de Versailles just outside Paris attracted world leaders. US President Woodrow Wilson took a major role, along with Prime Minister Georges Clemenceau of France and Prime Minister David Lloyd George of Britain.

The peace settlement that the Allies finally dictated was very difficult for the Germans to accept. By the nature and scope of the conflict (humanity had never before seen its like), the agreement was extremely complex. Of course, Germany would disarm. But it also had to foot the blame and grovel somewhat, which was completely out of character for its people. Far worse was the (to them) incomprehensible level of reparations, which the Allies set at 132 billion gold Marks (roughly US $33 billion),[4] plus interest. This amount was about 7 per cent of Germany's gross national product, and it was to pay the levy over thirty-seven years. John Maynard Keynes, the eminent English economist, commented that it was probably three times more than Germany could afford.[5] While complex clauses and loopholes might lower the amount, there was no guarantee that Germany could avail itself of all of them.[6]

This number was simply unbelievable for the German man on the street. That spring and summer in Hanover, the Heins were trying to return their household to some semblance of order. Young Erich was to begin school in the autumn, and he had led a very sheltered life to that point. His mother taught him everything he would need to know to relate to his new teacher and friends. The new baby grew like a sprout, and while he was hard to please, home was relatively peaceful. Business continued to go well for Victor, as rebuilding the country generated lots of activity. Industry boomed, and despite Germany's having to pay reparations, there were signals that the number of available jobs would continue to outstrip the supply of workers for some time. Despite an uncertain political situation, Victor knew that his cash reserves were strong and that he could withstand almost any siege.

Life was good in Hanover for people of wealth and privilege. Social engagements resumed soon after war's end. The opera and the theatre returned to their pre-war activities. Music always filled the Heins' flat, whether from the massive Bösendorfer concert grand piano or from the new Victrola, an early player of gramophone records.

Before she knew it, Henni was pregnant again. Although they had not planned this addition, they would accept it as a gift from God. Victor was a little more pragmatic than that, but he was certainly not unhappy with the news. After all, it would help to distract his wife from her mother's death. Since they already had two boys, he knew that a little girl would thrill Henni. If she was happy, then so was Victor. Besides, he had come from a family of seven, and he was not averse to a large group of children, especially if there was sufficient help. This they could afford.

On 24 August 1920, Henni's secret wish came true, when she gave birth to a tiny, perfect baby girl, whom she named Gertrude Freda. The infant really was small, suggesting premature birth. Gertrude, or Trude, was beautiful, with a character as sweet as her looks. She gave her parents no trouble whatsoever and was soon sleeping through the night. She delighted her parents and Erich, but the new arrival seemed to shock and dismay Georg, now a year and a half. The newcomer replaced him as the centre of everyone's attention.

While Germany was going downhill in the early 1920s, Victor's prudence and hard work in business ensured his family's survival, no matter what. He was always working on a new project, diversifying the firm, and every venture seemed successful. He was often burning the 'midnight oil' at the office, which frustrated Henni no end, yet she could not bring herself to chastise him too vigorously. After all, his efforts sustained their handsome lifestyle.

The Heins had a very comfortable existence indeed, thanks to Victor. They had a spacious flat and live-in help, and they would 'dress' for dinner each evening (at least when Victor was home for that meal). They took vacations by the seashore and travelled to Switzerland and the Italian Alps when they could. In short, while they were not ostentatious in the least, they did not 'go without'.

At home, Henni (along with the governess) enjoyed the children's company. The two women spent the daytime reading to the youngsters or walking with them in the park. The maid and the cook performed most of the housework. After supper, the flat filled with music. Whether it was live, with Henni at her beloved Bösendorfer, or came from recordings of Mozart and Wagner's operas, there was rarely a moment without music in the household.

The newly bereft Siegmund Seckel became a fixture in the family's life. He didn't want to impose, so he maintained his own home just as it had always been, but he loved being with his daughter and grandchildren. The joy of the young ones eased the pain of losing his beloved wife, and Henni worshipped him; he was truly welcome in their home.

For whatever reason, there were no more babies, but that didn't concern Henni. Her family was complete. She was exceedingly happy, and so her husband too was contented. Despite political and economic turmoil around it, the Hein household thrived.

All through 1925, however, Victor Hein did not feel well. He couldn't put his finger on anything in particular, but even the minimal physical challenges of everyday life were difficult for him. Regular visits to the doctor produced no definitive answers, yet he knew that something was wrong. In December, his physician found his heart a bit weak, along with his lungs, but this could not explain shortness of breath and constant fatigue. Victor was only fifty-four – not old at all for a merchant. The doctor prescribed a tonic along with two weeks at a health spa, but nothing stronger – no accurate diagnosis was possible.

For New Year's Eve 1925/6, the family had planned the usual celebrations. Some close friends were hosting a ball at a nearby hotel, and the family finery was out: a new evening gown for Henni, and white tie and tails for Victor. The children saw their parents off to the party, and the governess had arranged a small party for them and their cousins and close friends.

The ball was a huge success, with a top-notch thirty-piece orchestra and wonderful food. The Heins had shared a table with two of Victor's brothers and their wives. The dancing was fine, mostly waltzes. The midnight toast with champagne wished everyone happiness, prosperity, good health, and long life. The party broke up at about 2 a.m. On their return home, Henni checked on the children, who were all tucked up warmly in their beds. She and Victor were in their own bed and asleep by three o'clock.

Imagine the shock and horror then, when Henni woke up at 10 a.m., to find a cold and motionless Victor beside her. She screamed. Some time during the morning, Victor had simply expired. Aged only fifty-four, Victor Hein was dead.

Notes

1. Austin Stevens, *The Dispossessed: German Refugees in Britain* (London: Barrie & Jenkins Limited, 1975), 22.
2. Dupuy and Dupuy, *The Harper Encyclopedia of Military History from 3500 B.C. to the Present*, 1,075–8.
3. Ibid., 1,083.
4. Margaret MacMillan, *Paris 1919: Six Months That Changed the World* (New York: Random House, 2001), 480.
5. David Aretha, ed., *The Holocaust Chronicle* (Lincolnwood, Ill.: Publications International, Ltd, 2001), 20.
6. MacMillan, *Paris 1919*, 480.

CHAPTER FIVE

On His Own: At the Castle Boarding School (1926–33)

In 1920s' Germany, mourning was typically long and drawn out. The family displayed the body at home, but only fairly briefly. For observant Jews, the burial had to take place within twenty-four hours. And so, on 2 January 1926, the family buried Victor Hein not too far from the grave of Henni's mother, in the Jewish Cemetery in the Strangriede in Hanover.

All of a sudden, the world had come crashing down on Henni's shoulders, and she was by no means ready. Victor's brothers and her own brother, Martin, were there to help. What would become of the family's publishing concern? Henni certainly knew nothing about running a business, and while she was willing to take over and run it, she was aware that she lacked the necessary experience. In the short term, family members helped out. Siegmund Seckel was there at every turn, ready to assist and offer good, sound advice. Without his calm, almost serene presence, Henni would not have managed.

Even worse was the situation at home. Erich was ten – old enough to understand death and even to volunteer to help his sad and pained mother. His offer deeply touched her. Georg and Trude had much more trouble understanding. It took months of soothing and gentle explanation to help them grasp that their father was never coming home. Trude accepted it without complaint, but Georg resisted the news fiercely. He began to behave very badly, throwing temper tantrums at the slightest upset. It did not help that his health had become a concern. He began complaining of serious, painful headaches and also had trouble breathing. Henni's father moved in with the family, and things calmed down for a while.

But young Georg would not accept Siegmund as a father figure, and Henni was soon beside herself. She consulted the best doctors in Hanover. They prescribed medicines for the migraines and asthma, but the psychiatrists were unable to soothe the overwrought boy. It was as though he blamed his mother for his father's death. Not only had she earlier abandoned him for his little sister, now she had taken away the only other person who paid attention to him, the father he had worshipped. And since Henni associated him with her mother's death, she was not well disposed to deal with Georg's bad behaviour.

Meanwhile, with Siegmund's help and guidance, *Der Manufakturist* continued operations and even turned a small profit. This lifted a great load from Henni's mind, as she worried also about her twenty-odd employees and their families. If the business failed, who would look out for them?

Henni became increasingly desperate about her younger son. She begged her father, brother, and brothers-in-law for help, but nothing they tried would calm him. There was no substitute for his father, and Georg would not listen to reason. He was, after all, only seven years old, and logic hadn't yet found a place in his brain. Being at her wits' end, Henni took extreme measures. She searched for the best institution in which to place the boy. She could no longer handle his outbursts and feared that Georg might harm his sister.

In the summer of 1926, she discovered news of a boys' school that came with high recommendations – the Schloss Marquartstein, in a small town roughly halfway between Munich and Salzburg, just ten miles north of the Austrian border. Henni and Siegmund made the arrangements and in August delivered Georg into the care of strangers.

The school was actually in a small castle, almost nine hundred years old, on the side of a small foothill of the Alps in the lush forests of Bavaria, overlooking the village of Marquartstein. It couldn't have been more picturesque, yet Georg was not the least bit happy about this most recent upset in his life. Here he was, still only seven, and now, to his mind, his family had completely abandoned him. He cried his eyes out for weeks. The staff knew that he was a special case and made every attempt to treat him with extra kindness and love. It was nonetheless a boarding school, with certain ways of doing things. The older boys were not accepting of a little boy who did nothing but whimper and complain of headaches. They treated him badly, bullying him at every opportunity.

His mother felt horrible at taking this extreme step, but her male relatives felt it would be good for Georg, and most especially for poor Henni. Yet she experienced terrible guilt and made the then-special effort of calling her son by telephone at least once a week. For the first month, when she called him on the telephone in the headmaster's office, he refused to speak.

After a while, things became more bearable for him. Georg slowly made a few friends in his class. Still he was sullen, and the headaches and asthma continued to sap his energy and make him a poor playmate. His teachers considered him very bright, yet his maladies (both physical and psychological) continued to plague his results. The instructors praised him whenever they could, and this helped. Georg, it seemed, craved attention, and the staff soon learned how to provide it in a positive sense. What the lad did enjoy at school was sports and being outdoors. He ran and played outside as if there were no other purpose in life. While he didn't mind reading, especially adventure stories, running took his mind off his problems. He was especially competitive for a boy his age, and that surprised the teachers.

Soon it was time for the Christmas holidays, and even though he was Jewish he went home to Hanover. As a seven-year-old, he could not travel alone, and his grandfather journeyed south to collect the boy. On the way home, Georg would not discuss his mother or even refer to her in the third person. For her abandonment of him, Georg reasoned that this behaviour was fair play. He did, however, look forward to seeing Erich and their cousins and to the wonderful food. He was not fond of the meals at the school – perhaps nutritious and well prepared, but not that to which he had become accustomed in Hanover. Candy and pastries – at home, Georg would eat nothing else!

Henni greeted them at the *Bahnhof*, and Georg refused to talk. She gathered him up in her arms to give him a big kiss, but he wanted none of it. It became clear that he would talk only to boys or men, and so his grandfather took him in hand. His cousins and uncles spent a lot of time with him, and he revelled in the attention. Soon, however, the New Year came and, with it, time to return to school. Georg was extremely reluctant to leave, throwing more tantrums and even begging his mother not to send him away. But his behaviour reminded Henni of how she had been unable to cope just six months earlier, and she shipped the lad south, back into exile.

In early 1927 in Marquartstein, Georg Hein began to feel somewhat independent (insofar as a seven-year-old can). He no longer cried at night, and his schoolmates stopped treating him like a baby. The schoolmasters threw Georg a small party for his eighth birthday on 15 February, a luxury they accorded no other student. In the foothills of the Bavarian Alps, winter sports were serious business. This did not upset the boy whatsoever, although he had trouble learning how to ski. There were winter field trips to neighbouring ski hills and to concert halls and festivals in Munich and Salzburg. Other local explorations included a trip of forty miles to the famous mountaintop retreat of Berchtesgaden – later Adolf Hitler's vacation retreat, which he called the 'Eagle's Nest'.

Georg had inherited his parents' fondness for music, but he was in effect tone deaf. Still, he loved listening, most especially to Mozart and Beethoven. He also developed a fascination with choral music, even though he couldn't sing a note in key.

While never overtly happy in Marquartstein, he found enjoyable activities. The scenery was glorious, especially in winter. The snow-capped Tyrolean peaks (the village was almost 5,000 feet above sea level) were awe-inspiring, especially for a young boy from a big city nowhere near the mountains. Snow covered the ground around the school-castle from late October through late April and the nearby high mountain peaks for an extra month in each of spring and autumn.

More fun still was the *Schloss* itself. Count Marquart II built it in 1075 AD, and it had its own drawbridge and dungeon! For a boy of seven, it was a fairy tale come true. The castle had changed hands many times over the centuries, and that had meant alterations to the building: additions, demolitions, secret passageways, and, of course, legends! The staff, while on the whole very strict and proper, used this history to gain students' attention. They tested the boys on the history of the castle and the surrounding region and rewarded good results with 'exploration time'. The youngsters looked forward to Sunday evenings, when one of the masters would gather them and tell them one of the legends.

The schoolwork itself was difficult, and the atmosphere (apart from the earlier kindnesses to Georg) rigid. The teachers were quite strict, and the education was top-notch. The school expected a great deal of hard work from the boys, and woe betide he who did not meet its rigorous standards. Georg's work was above average – he was very intelligent – but he continued to suffer from behavioural lapses, and the staff's patience was beginning to wear thin. The teachers had made exceptions because of the loss of his father, but they would not countenance wanton disobedience. They reprimanded Georg on occasion and familiarised him with the occasional crack of the cane.

While the boy's headaches gradually became less frequent, he still had trouble breathing, though not enough to require his leaving the school. Several times the school summoned the local doctor to provide treatment for his lungs. More than once the physician suggested that – even though the clean, fresh mountain air was good for the boy's lungs – the school's incessant cold and high humidity were very harmful for him. The dampness resulted in a constant battle against mould, which grew in the underground rooms and passageways and occasionally in the lavatories. The cleaning staff did very good work, but against an enemy that was virtually unbeatable.

Eventually spring arrived and, with it, the end of the school year. This time, his grandfather Siegmund was unable to travel, as his health was deteriorating. He was, after all, eighty-two! One of the teachers volunteered to accompany the boy on the train to Hanover on his own way to Hamburg. Henni and Siegmund were waiting at the station, along with Erich and Trude. Georg was once again sullen and non-communicative with his mother, which hurt her deeply. She felt tremendous pain and guilt about sending him away, and her inability to mother him constantly troubled her. While her brother and brothers-in-law regularly reminded her that her action was the best for everyone and that Georg was not suffering, none of this made her feel better. She believed strongly that she had done the right thing, but it was hardly compatible with true motherhood.

The summer passed quickly for Georg at home and on family outings to the countryside and the seashore. The children seemed to enjoy each other's company, and Georg's tantrums were rare and manageable. But the family learned that Siegmund was dying. Henni loved him and relied on him very much, and took this news particularly badly. Siegmund took his last breath on 25 August 1927, just a few days before Georg was to depart again for Bavaria.

The family laid him to rest beside his beloved wife Rieke in the Strangriede Cemetery.

Siegmund had lived a full and fruitful life, but Henni collapsed into anguish and depression. Her brother, Martin, and Victor's brothers, Paul and Adolf, did everything they could to help. They decided that Henni needed as much rest and quiet as possible, so Georg would have to return to Bavaria. Someone contacted the school and arranged for the teacher from Hamburg to stop for Georg on his way south.

The situation in the Rumannstrasse flat was not good. Henni just wasn't herself and began losing touch with reality – a classic case of depression. With a great deal of sedation and time she slowly returned to near normal. The brothers ran the firm in their spare time, but this was a poor solution, and the business quickly began to suffer. Revenues decreased as advertisers felt neglected. The best staff members began looking for safer jobs elsewhere.

Finally, the family advised Henni to sell the firm. Since she was not capable of running it, and they had no time to do so properly, she agreed. But the business had suffered much damage already, and this affected its value. The interim financial statements were disheartening, and it was difficult to find a buyer at a fair price. Eventually, Henni sold the enterprise at 50 pfennigs on the Mark. The sale brought a very good sum – more than enough to last Henni and her family until the children finished university. It would probably cover trust funds that would set up each son in business and provide Trude with a handsome dowry. Nonetheless, Henni couldn't help but think how much value the firm had lost in the less than two years since Victor's death. How, she wondered, could she have ruined it like that? 'What would poor Victor think?' she worried obsessively.

What to do with the family fortune? Naturally, Henni relied on advice from her brother, Martin, a bank director. He thought it wise to place some of it, perhaps 30 per cent, in conservative investments such as cash and bonds, another 30 per cent in real estate, and 40 per cent for him to invest in the booming stock markets. As it happened, the late 1920s was one of the best periods in German history for investing. Markets everywhere were soaring to unheard-of levels, and Martin sought to take advantage of this boom on behalf of his sister and her children. He insisted, however, that she invest only the money she had – no borrowing on margin to invest additional funds. As a banker, he was pragmatic enough to realise the huge opportunity, but sufficiently conservative to see the great risk. This recommendation had far-reaching consequences.

The days and months rolled by for Georg at school, and his life fell into a routine. His only concern was a noticeable change in attitudes towards him. Gradually he became an outcast, and he had no idea why. The other boys first started ignoring him. Later, through the winter of 1927/8, and then into 1928/9, even the masters began treating him badly. From being perfectly, though formally cordial, they now became almost gruff. Finally, both students and staff began treating him badly and calling him names. Georg, only ten, did not know or understand what was happening in Germany. He had certainly been aware of, and had studied in school, the political upheavals since 1918. What he did not understand, especially since he was not religiously observant at school, was why the people around him were suddenly calling him 'Jew'.

When he was a baby and then a boy, completely oblivious to politics, his family had shielded him from the birth of the National Socialist German Workers' Party – the Nazi Party. From its beginnings in late 1919, German newspapers had given it an inordinate amount of coverage. Several factors may help to explain this fascination: the Nazis promised to return the country to its pre-war condition; one of their young leaders, Adolf Hitler, seemed charismatic; and the nation lacked strong political leadership. Hitler had gone to jail for his part in the Munich Beer Hall *Putsch* (armed insurrection) of 1923 and had written his manifesto, *Mein Kampf* (My Struggle) in a Bavarian prison. The first of its two volumes had appeared in 1925, and it made very clear that the author would rid Germany of its Jews. Apparently, Hitler's aims found favour with many people. Perhaps Marquartstein – only fifty miles from Munich and ten from the border with Austria (Hitler's homeland) – was ripe for these sentiments.

In any case, in 1929, Georg was ten and still quite unaware of the greater world. Although he had attended Erich's bar mitzvah in December 1928, he did not know what it meant to be a Jew. Being apart from his family for so long, he had had no opportunity (especially at his school) to receive instruction in the religion of his forbears. To all intents and purposes, Georg had no religion. When his classmates and other people started calling him 'dirty Jew', he had no idea of what they meant. All he knew was that his friends had stopped liking him, and that hurt.

At home in the summer of 1929, he asked Erich what was going on and why people were taunting him at school. Erich, almost fourteen, quiet and introspective but observant and intelligent, had remained at home. He had read the newspapers and heard the adults talking, and he was afraid. He told Georg that some new political leaders were blaming the Jews for all of Germany's post-1918 ills. Of course, he added, this was preposterous, but anti-Semites were beginning to gain in numbers. Erich presciently worried what might happen if these fanatics gained power.

In the autumn of 1929, his fellow students treated Georg even worse. Now his teachers hardly ever spoke to him, and usually rudely. He resolved to go about his business and ignore the mistreatment, but late in October disastrous news arrived. On 30 October the news spread like wildfire, reaching even isolated Marquartstein. The previous day, in New York, the American stock markets had taken a huge tumble. Ordinarily Germans, let alone rural Bavarians, would have taken no notice. However, the bubble had finally burst. And it hadn't happened just in New York: stock exchanges around the world had followed suit as they opened. There had been a worldwide sell-off of shares, and every single market had plummeted.

Rich people had become middle class overnight, and members of the middle class who had invested on margin were now poor. It was only over the next few weeks that this became clear. The crash had not affected just individuals. It had hurt nations as well and, most importantly, banks. Even in the 1920s, banks were indispensable. Few individuals squirreled away all their money at home. The world financial system rested on the stability of the banks, and nobody had realised just how vulnerable they were. Banks do not just hold depositors' money and lend it out to individuals and institutions. They also have deposits from other banks and often invest their own excess cash elsewhere.

As soon as the crash occurred, there was a worldwide liquidity crisis. Many investors had borrowed money to invest in the ballooning stock market and had pledged the stock as collateral. They now faced 'margin calls' and had immediately to pay off the loans for the now-worthless shares. Where could they get such huge sums? From the banks, of course. At the same time, depositors wanted their cash, as they feared for the safety of their investments. But the banks never kept such huge amounts on hand. They had to retrieve it from other banks, which didn't have it either. Almost immediately, banks began closing in what was quickly becoming a vicious circle. Soon there was no place to obtain cash, even for people with large balances in their accounts. Many banks were unable to address these demands for hard currency and declared bankruptcy, leaving depositors with nothing at all.

This crisis certainly affected the Hein and Seckel families. While they had been quite conservative with their family fortunes, they were not immune from the banking problems. The value of their blue-chip shares fell dramatically, and they were unwilling to sell at such low prices – and probably would never have seen the cash, in any event. Fortunately for Henni, Martin Seckel had done the best he could for her. When all the dust settled, Henni recovered about a quarter of her investments – a manageable situation. She and the children would not lose the flat or go hungry, but they would have no luxuries whatsoever for the foreseeable future. Martin, as a bank director, had access to limited amounts of cash and ensured that Henni never ran short.

Henni had already paid for Georg's tuition, so she did not need to worry that the school would send him home, as it did some of his classmates. But the crash almost immediately increased the enmity he faced at school. Hitler's Nazis had long proclaimed that the Jews controlled the banking system, and now they screamed that the stock market's collapse had been part of a Jewish plan to dominate the world. The person on the street who didn't know any better might believe this charismatic leader. That meant more and more public mistreatment of Jews. A few months earlier, in August 1929, over 100,000 people had swarmed to a rally to hear Hitler at Nuremberg. By Christmas, Georg could no longer stand the taunts and made his uncles promise not to send him back.

Over the holidays, Georg and Erich again spoke of the situation. Erich, now fourteen and spending more and more time with his uncles, had become politically aware and also nervous. He would educate his younger brother in such matters. He explained more forcefully who and what the Nazis were and what they meant to the family. All this unpleasantness could not help but frighten Georg too.

The uncles found a new school for Georg at Juist, in the Frisian Islands off north-western Germany, near the Dutch border. They felt that the isolation would render politics a non-issue. As well, the family doctor suggested that the North Sea climate would be better for Georg's breathing troubles.

The young fellow didn't mind the new school, but the surroundings were not as pleasant as at Marquartstein. The scenery, for one, was much less to his liking. While the climate was a bit warmer at sea level, Juist really was a backwater and offered no distractions. At least the anti-Semitism was not overt – for the moment.

With every passing month, however, matters worsened. In the German general election of September 1930, the Nazi party received over 18 per cent of the popular vote and elected 117 members to the parliament, out of a total of 577. It thereby became the second largest party, behind only the Social Democrats, with 143 members. The Communist party, with 77 elected members, had finished second in the popular vote, with over 24 per cent of ballots. The Nazis were becoming increasingly powerful, and many of the people on the street might now see them as legitimate.

By the spring of 1933, even Juist had become unbearable for Georg, now twelve. He went home for the summer holidays, never to return.

CHAPTER SIX

High School in London (1934–5)

In the late 1920s, Georg Hein's older brother, Erich, had begun taking an interest in German politics. Though barely a teenager (having been born in December 1915), he seemed to have a fresh eye that his elders didn't. Or perhaps they just refused to see what was quickly becoming obvious: the general mood in Germany towards Jews was changing, and for the worse.

Erich's apparent political naïveté was upsetting to his older relatives. How much could a mere boy understand about world politics? They avoided the subject whenever he brought it up, which he did almost incessantly. He clearly did not have their older, wiser, long-term view of history against which to measure current events. After all, both the Hein and the Seckel families had spent more than two hundred years in Germany and had never experienced mass discrimination or a *pogrom*.

Yet Erich raised the issue at every family gathering. At Friday Sabbath dinner, his uncles would seek to assuage his fears, to no avail. They were very intelligent and reasonable people, and knew that the average German was not a raving anti-Semite. Erich always asked pointed questions and raised some new example from current events. In the end, they told Erich, reason would prevail and everything would go well again. Yet they could not persuade him.

In 1929, he began to speak to his mother, and then to his uncles, about emigration. He had no particular country in mind, but several Seckel cousins lived in England. Henni's sister, Rosa, had a married a French Jew named Willi Wertheimer, who had spent most of his life in Bradford, Yorkshire. When he was about a year old, his family had emigrated to Britain (c. 1871) because of the Franco–Prussian War. The Wertheimers, like many of their forbears, were in the rag trade. Their relatives, the Mosers, lived in a small but well-established Jewish community in Bradford (a maternal great uncle, Jacob Moser, had been Lord Mayor of that city in 1910); hence the family's choice of destination. In the worldwide financial crisis of the late 1920s, Willi's business, while supporting his wife and children, was not a huge success. More important, Willi was genuinely pleasant and would help anyone in need.

Erich hadn't had much contact with his English cousins but knew that they lived comfortably and might be able to assist him. His mother corresponded with them regularly, and he asked her to enquire about conditions in the United Kingdom.

Henni, like her brother and brothers-in-law, advised Erich not to be foolish – there was no need to consider such reckless action, which would also be very expensive. Erich was like a dog with a bone, however, and continued at least to think about the idea. Despite his mother's mild admonitions, he began researching the possibilities himself. His late father, Victor Hein, had travelled to London several times on business before 1914, and Erich remembered him reminiscing about how beautiful and cultured it was – perhaps not as much so as Berlin, but still lovely (and safe). Erich even had, as a memento, Victor's Baedecker travel guide to the British capital, which his father had annotated along the margins. In his spare time, Erich referred to it regularly, partly to commune with his dead father and partly out of curiosity about the greater world outside of Germany. He also remembered his father praising Britain's political system and stable government.

Over time, Erich determined that England would be a safe haven. How to get there he was not sure. He was certain, however, that despite his youth, he had to lead the family to safety. Erich finally found an ally in his uncle Martin Seckel, who agreed that Germany was becoming too unpleasant.

The *Munich Post* had been trying since the early 1920s to focus attention on the evil policies of the National Socialist Party. On December 9, 1931, it finally succeeded.[1] That day it published 'The Jews in the Third Reich', by Fritz Gerlich. The writer detailed with frightening accuracy the Nazis' plans for Germany's Jews. He outlined Hitler's hopes to revoke their civil rights, confiscate their property, and reduce them all to slave labour.

Everyone in the Jewish community had read or heard about Gerlich's article, and a few began to get very nervous. It became a regular point of discussion for Jews in Hanover, especially on Saturdays at synagogue. Martin Seckel took up the cause early in 1932 and contacted his sister Rosa Wertheimer in England. She and Willi indicated that they could not help financially but did offer any other form of assistance within their powers. They found out about the documents that the Heins would need to move to England.

Erich Hein had grown into a very pensive and solitary teenager. He was a good student and had earned the trust of his mother and his uncles. He turned sixteen on 6 December 1931, and, after the Gerlich story appeared three days later, they began to take him much more seriously and to realise that he was indeed wise beyond his years. For that reason, when the opportunity arose in early 1933, Uncle Martin and Erich made a reconnaissance trip to London. Using family contacts from Yorkshire and former business associates of Victor's, they put together a plan and began in London to implement it. They secured a student visa and a modest flat in central London for Erich and arranged for him to attend the Regent Street Polytechnic high school. The headmaster there, a kind English gentleman named Fred Wilkinson, agreed, for a small fee, to keep a special eye on Erich and report back to Henni weekly. 'Wilkie' was married but childless and more than happy to help. With the details in place, uncle and nephew returned to Hanover.

The plan began to unfold, and by late August 1933 Erich was back in London, living in his own flat and attending the Polytechnic. From an early age, he had, at his father's insistence, studied foreign languages, and so his English was competent, if not fluent, and he was able to manage. Of course, at sixteen, he had never lived on his own or cooked for himself, let alone cleaned house. And in order to keep him away from temptations, his family tightly controlled the purse strings. Wilkinson kept an eye on him, dropping by the flat without warning and dispensing him a weekly allowance. Although his English skills hampered his studies, this was not a major concern. Despite being solitary, however, Erich felt overwhelmingly lonely.

At the end of term, Erich went home for the Christmas holidays. It was a joy for him to see everyone, especially his little sister, Trude, who idolised Erich. But there were important issues for them all to discuss, and England was the only topic. Erich was by now certain that that country should be their safe haven, and he easily convinced them.

The situation at home for German Jews was by late 1932 already unpleasant. And it worsened dramatically in the first half of 1933. Adolf Hitler became Chancellor on 30 January. In late February, the Nazi Party began its take-over of German life. It surreptitiously organised and participated in a riot that resulted in the burning of the *Reichstag* (the parliament), so that it could react to the lawlessness by quashing civil rights. Freedom of speech, of the press, and of assembly, as well as from invasion of privacy and from searches of homes without court order all passed into history.[2] Germany quickly became a totalitarian state.

In late March 1933, the Nazis opened their first concentration camp, Dachau, in Bavaria; Buchenwald, Sachsenhausen, and Ravensbrück soon followed.[3] The camps received no official publicity, and if anyone asked about them officials replied that they were to house criminals and other anti-social elements.

On 1 April Hitler declared a compulsory boycott of all Jewish-owned businesses, and the real economic persecution began. The Nazis justified the measure by arguing that Jews owned a disproportionate percentage of businesses and were therefore bleeding the country and its Aryans of their rightful wealth. There was little opposition, as Nazi storm troopers were everywhere, enforcing the boycott with brutality. They would block doorways to Jewish shops and assault anyone who tried to enter. Later, in 1935, the Nazis forced Jewish merchants and business owners to march with signs that read, 'Don't buy from Jews. Shop in German businesses.'

On 11 April 1933, the Nazis issued an official and complex definition of what constituted a 'racially pure Aryan'. Needless to say, it took special care to define what was *not* Aryan, especially who was and who was not a Jew.

For example, if someone had only one 'non-Aryan' grandparent, he or she was not racially Aryan. Just two weeks later, the Nazis created the infamous *Geheime Staatspolizei*, or '*Gestapo*' (Secret State Police). At the same time, they passed a law limiting non-Aryans' entrance into professional schools and universities to no more than their proportion of the population.[4] As a result, 3,500 of 8,000 Jewish students had to leave universities. Evidently the Nazis aimed to encourage Jews to leave Germany – much easier and more profitable than the ultimate 'Final Solution'.

Germany's more than 500,000 Jews (less than 2 per cent of the population) faced what was rapidly becoming a 'no-win' situation. Many Jews insisted that, if they only 'kept their heads down', the terror would blow over and cooler heads would prevail.

At least in the early years of Hitler's rule, anti-Semitic policies aimed primarily to drive Jews out of Germany. There was no overt mention of mass extermination. While busy making covert plans to the contrary, Hitler made a public show of the position that the emigration of the Jews from of Germany would satisfy him. That way, he reasoned, they would become someone else's problem. Many Jews – the lucky ones – would eventually accede to Hitler's wish. Many more stayed, unwilling to leave behind all their possessions or simply lacking money for travel. Many Jews decided to stay because they had faith in the basic decency of the German people. They were sure the Nazi regime could not last, and were hoping for the restoration of 'The good old Weimar Republic' of the 1920s.

The Heins and Seckels were not going to stand by idly and watch the devastation that was likely to come. In very short order, at the end of 1933, they sent young Georg (now fourteen) to live with Erich (now seventeen and a half) in London, and he too enrolled at the Regent Street Polytechnic. Henni did not know what to do about thirteen-year-old Trude. The girl could not live with her older brothers on her own, and Henni could not leave Germany until she had sorted out important financial matters. There was also the problem of obtaining official permission to leave Germany and to enter the United Kingdom.

The Wertheimers had sponsored Erich into England, but they could not afford to extend that coverage to anyone else. Georg had received a temporary student visa from British authorities, and it would last until he finished high school. Trude was too young to go as a student without extensive supervision, and Henni would have to stand in line with everyone else who wanted to leave Germany for the United Kingdom – a group that was growing exponentially.

Immensely complicating a departure from Germany was the financial issue. The Nazi government had made it very difficult for Jews to convert assets into cash or to transfer cash out of the country. Even Henni's brother, Martin, the bank director, could do little to help. The family decided to try Switzerland as a safe haven. They smuggled small sums to Zurich and continued sending the monthly allowance to London, but there were no other legal or official methods to move money that were free from Nazi scrutiny and theft.

The situation in Britain for the reception of German refugees was very uncertain in 1933. England had never considered immigration a problem until the worsening situation in Germany made it clear that many Jews would seek refuge in Britain, which had very few immigration controls until 1933.[5] The requirement for passports to cross international borders had emerged only during the First World War,[6] and then came the complicated system of visas for each country. In 1933, the gathering tide of German Jews was challenging Britain's Foreign Office, and the issue arose even at Cabinet meetings.[7]

Whereas up to the 1930s Britain placed very few restrictions on visitors and immigrants, suddenly the Home Office began limiting how long new arrivals could stay. Most Jewish newcomers were in transit to another destination. This suited the British government, which worried that a massive influx of Jews might cause racial upset and anti-Semitism, and that there would not be enough jobs for them. It was, after all, the depths of the Depression, and work was increasingly scarce.

The government had a two-fold answer. First, it encouraged Jewish immigrants to continue onward to either the United States (which had an open door policy towards Jewish immigrants) or Palestine (which the United Kingdom administered under the auspices of the League of Nations). Second, it asked Jewish charities to provide financial guarantees that no Jewish immigrant who remained in the country would become a burden on the government. These organisations readily made such commitments, thinking such a situation purely theoretical. This action removed any public financial responsibility from the British government and was therefore easily defensible to voters. The Cabinet committee set up to deal with the issue never met again.[8]

The English government decided not to offer political asylum to German Jews, instead granting them a more temporary form of immigration. It admitted many, for example, on condition that they not take employment. It must have assumed that the ever-worsening conditions in Germany would eventually ease and that the newcomers could and would eventually return home. In Cabinet committee discussions, the British were much more willing to consider immigration of German Jews than their co-religionists from elsewhere. They thought of Polish and other eastern European Jews as less desirable immigrants – 'economic refugees' – definitely not of the same class as their German brothers and sisters.[9]

Authorities in the United Kingdom began to note the increasing arrival of German refugees, especially Jews. A seeming trickle in 1932 had become almost a flood by 1934–5. As early as 1933, the government was worrying that this immigration might begin to overwhelm British voters, and it began looking for places to resettle Germans Jews, initially considering both Palestine and Canada. The Canadian government rejected this and most later overtures of the sort. Britain could facilitate Jewish emigration to Palestine, but only to the point where it would not overwhelm the Arabs there. It did not want to provoke an Arab uprising in Palestine.

Senior British officials began formulating a policy that would allow German Jews entry with a view to resettling most of them elsewhere. Their general expectation was that a large, well-educated, professional class of immigrants (typical of most German Jews) would play havoc with the country's professional population. Lawyers, doctors, and dentists constituted the largest group of German Jewish immigrants to England in 1932–3, and a further influx might mean less work for prosperous domestic practitioners, who possessed high disposable income and supported political parties.

And so the government limited the number of entrants from each category. One way for German Jews to avoid the limit was to arrange for a visa into a third country, using Britain as a temporary safe haven en route. British authorities were more than happy to allow almost anyone to enter if they would promise to go somewhere else quickly. A visa from a third country was a valid ticket for admission.

And so it was in late 1933 that the brothers Hein, Erich and Georg, found themselves living on their own in a flat in London. Both were attending Regent Street Polytechnic and coping with the everyday chores that children of privilege rarely consider. They had no extra money to pay for a cleaning lady, so they had to make do themselves. There was no one to buy them food or prepare their meals, and they could not afford to eat in restaurants, so they learned how to cook.

Then there was the culture shock, especially for Georg. He had been away at rural boarding schools for seven years and had never lived in a major capital. But language posed the trickiest issues for him. Georg had studied French and English, but the school vocabulary is not always that of everyday life. Suffice it to say that he experienced major problems. He could rely only on Erich, but they were in different classes.

Erich naturally found himself acting as Georg's substitute parent. He watched over Georg to ensure that he did his schoolwork and kept after him to do his fair share of cooking and housework. But Erich, at eighteen, was not ready to be a parent and did not possess the temperament to deal with a fourteen-year-old's irresponsibility. Eventually, Georg came to resent Erich's constant admonitions and made sure that Erich knew he was upset. After all, Georg had been living essentially on his own since the age of seven. He began to play tricks on his brother, using his superior intelligence and cunning to outwit and outfox Erich. It was good sport for Georg, but Erich did not appreciate it. He let Henni know what was happening in his letters and the occasional long-distance telephone call, but even she was unable to talk sense into young Georg. Henni began to worry that perhaps she had made a mistake sending Georg to live with his brother.

Headmaster Wilkinson imparted at least some structure into Georg's life and, while reasonably kind towards the boys, would not put up with any shenanigans. At school, the teachers gave Erich and Georg special help. Every day after class, the young men would stay an extra ninety minutes to study colloquial English. They both tried very hard and were quite capable, but Erich progressed faster in English than his younger brother did.

Their deficiencies in language also made it difficult for the boys to make friends among their classmates. The inevitable teasing was especially hard on Georg, as he had nobody but Erich at home for emotional support and had to grow up in a hurry. But being away from home for many years at such a young age had prepared him well for that aspect of life in a foreign country. And, while Hanover was a large and cosmopolitan city, it was by no means the equal of London. That was both good and bad. The British capital offered a diversity of distractions, and this lively fourteen-year-old, who lacked evening and weekend supervision (other than his older brother), enjoyed himself thoroughly. On the good side, there was the incredible variety of museums, art galleries, and theatres; on the not so good, gambling clubs, bars, and brothels, which would not admit anyone just fourteen.

Erich's school marks were satisfactory, but Georg's poor English hampered him severely. The one area in which he shone (other than German) was athletics. Since he had never seen a cricket or a rugby match, let alone played either sport, he concentrated on track and field. He had been a star sprinter at boarding school, and his speed and determination helped make him new friends on the Regent Street track team. He competed in the hurdles and earned the respect of his team-mates. Since everyone in English schools participated in sports, his success carried over into his classes and gained him some friends there, too. But his poor English continued to haunt him, and he coped mainly by staying silent.

In the meantime, life for the family in Germany continued to worsen. On 7 April 1933, Hitler had banned Jews from jobs in the civil service.[10] Despite the labour woes of the Depression, Henni's servants voluntarily quit in April 1933. They did not want to appear to be aiding Jewish enemies of the *Reich*. Replacements were difficult to find, but, with only Henni and Trude at home, Henni settled for a single cook/housekeeper and hired a Polish Jew in her early twenties to fill the position.

During the rise of National Socialism in the early 1930s, Hitler's views and policies appealed mainly to young men, the backbone of the workforce and the largest group of unemployed people. Joining the Party's SA storm troopers assured young men of food, clothing, and shelter in the depths of the Depression, when jobs were very hard to find. It wasn't really a difficult choice.

On 10 May 1933, the Nazis held a massive book burning in central Berlin, near Humboldt University. Nazi brownshirts also struck at some thirty other universities across Germany on the same night, burning volumes by such 'anti-German' Jewish writers as Albert Einstein, Sigmund Freud, and the poet Heinrich Heine.[11] The growing sense of unrest in Germany had just become palpable.

Europe had almost nine and a half million Jews in 1933, as follows (numbers are approximate):

Poland	3,000,000
Soviet Union	2,525,000
Romania	980,000
Germany	565,000
Hungary	445,000
Czechoslovakia	357,000
Britain	300,000
Baltic states	265,000
Austria	250,000
France	225,000
Holland	160,000
Greece	100,000
Yugoslavia	70,000
Belgium	60,000
Turkey	56,000
Bulgaria	50,000
Italy	48,000
Miscellaneous	41,000
Total	9,497,000[12]

Henni worried about Trude's fate. She could not send her daughter to London, as there was no place for her there, and she had no English. She was clearly too young to stay on her own with her older brothers. The schools in Hanover were becoming decidedly unfriendly towards Jews, and the thirteen-year-old came home almost every afternoon in tears. The teachers had taken to ostracising all the Jewish children, seating them in a separate row at the back of each classroom, and had begun insulting and demeaning them. If this was an attempt to force the Jewish children to withdraw from schools, it was successful. Henni had to find a new place for Trude soon, preferably outside Germany, but she was far too young to leave the country on her own.

The costs of leaving Germany were just beginning to become clear in 1933–4. The German government had in 1931 instituted a form of 'departure tax' – 25 per cent of assets – for anyone wishing to emigrate. All remaining capital belonging to prospective emigrants went into blocked accounts and became subject to foreign-exchange conversion at predatory, government-determined rates, which caused further losses of between 20 per cent and 95 per cent. Emigration between 1933 and 1937 cost from 30 per cent to 50 per cent of a person's wealth, and from 1938 on, from 60 per cent to 100 per cent.[13]

Germany signed a ten-year non-aggression pact with Poland on January 26, 1934.[14] Later that year, Hitler implemented a secret plan, in violation of the Treaty of Versailles, to re-equip and re-arm his country. While the treaty forbade Germany from building warplanes and manning an air force, the government organised gliding clubs and taught many Nazis how to fly. It also built many dual-purpose aircraft. If anyone from abroad questioned the large numbers of planes, the Nazi government would simply reply that they were for civilian transport. But it could easily convert them to bombers, and Winston Churchill would make issue of this fact in 1937, long before he gained power.

On 23 May 1934, more bad news came to torment Henni. Her dear brother, Martin, fifty-five, her banker and protector since Victor's death, had died. Now all the men in the family closest to Henni had gone – Victor and Martin both dead, Erich and Georg in England. Martin's widow, Irma, and their two children, Georg and Edith, were alone.

Taking her cue from Erich Hein, Irma emigrated to England with Georg and Edith before the war. This action must have virtually bankrupted Martin's family. But all three survived the war, and Martin's grandchildren and great-grandchildren are alive today.

The emigration of Martin's family, despite the huge cost, deeply affected Henni. Her two sons were already in London, and it should have been a natural instinct for her to follow them. But how would they be able to afford to live if she left Germany and had to leave all of her remaining wealth behind to the Nazis? Victor had died before the Depression, and her finances were no longer the best. Martin, in contrast, had survived the worst of the Depression and planned his finances to ensure his family's safety. And so, while his survivors could afford the move, Henni could not.

Martin's death could not have happened at a worse time for Henni and it brought on severe depression. In desperation, she turned to Victor's two younger brothers – Paul, who had the doctorate in chemistry, and Adolf, a lawyer. They both offered her whatever help they could. Victor's younger sister, Sophie, was married to Siegfried Beer, and they lived in Berlin with their three children. Henni cheered herself by taking Trude there for occasional family visits.

On 2 August 1934, President Paul von Hindenburg died. Hitler soon merged his title of Chancellor with that of President. In a plebiscite, 90 per cent of eligible voters cast ballots, and 90 per cent of them approved.[15] Hitler was now supreme commander, *Führer* of the Third *Reich*.

On 2 January 1935, tragedy hit the Heins again, under suspicious circumstances, when both Siegfried Beer and Paul Hein died on the very same day. Was criminal (perhaps Nazi) activity behind their deaths? Current speculation suggests a connection between the two deaths. Were the two just innocent bystanders caught up in a Nazi demonstration that went terribly wrong? Both men were active in the Heins' publishing business. Had they angered Nazi authorities by printing something embarrassing or inflammatory? Was there a deliberate plot to murder them? Whatever the causes (which are today unknown), their deaths hit Henni like a ton of bricks.

One by one, and now two at a time, so many of the family's men were dying. She was forty-eight and becoming used to all the death. She could again have fallen into severe depression, yet she fought on. She still had her daughter to take care of. Henni continued to search for a safe haven, but funds were beginning to run short. Besides, Trude was now fourteen, and Henni would still not let her go to London alone. She again tried the English relatives, but they could do nothing. Emigration to Britain was becoming increasingly difficult, with visa requirements a major issue.

Adolf Hein's body was discovered on 2 September 1935. The lawyer and family patriarch had committed suicide, unable to stand the pressure of Nazi doctrines and violence against Jews. Ever since the mass suicides of Jews resisting the Romans at Masada about 2,000 years ago, their co-religionists have considered taking one's own life an honourable act in the face of overwhelming odds. Adolf's son, Herbert Henry Hein, was deported to a concentration camp in February 1943.

Notes

1. David Aretha, ed., *The Holocaust Chronicle* (Lincolnwood, Ill.: Publications International, Ltd, 2001), 25.
2. *Holocaust Time Line 1933–1945*, Florida Center for Instructional Technology, University of South Florida, www.fcit.coedu.usf.edu/holocaust/timeline/TEXTLINE.HTM
3. *The History Place Holocaust Timeline*, the History Place, www.historyplace.com/worldwar2/holocaust/timeline.html
4. D. Niederland, 'Jewish Emigration from Germany in the First Years of Nazi Rule' (article at www.history-of-the-holocaust.org/LIBARC/LIBRARY/Themes/Jews/Niederla.html, 1988).
5. Louise London, *Whitehall and the Jews 1933–1948*, in series British Immigration Policy and the Jews (Cambridge: Cambridge University Press, 2000), 20.
6. London, *Whitehall and the Jews*, 19.
7. Ibid., 20–30.
8. Ibid., 28–31.
9. Ibid., 31.
10. Aretha, ed., *The Holocaust Chronicle*, 62.
11. Ibid., 53.
12. Ibid., 69.
13. A.J. Sherman, *Island Refuge: Britain and Refugees from the Third Reich 1933–1939* (Ilford, Essex: Frank Cass & Co. Ltd, 1994), 25–6.
14. Aretha, ed., *The Holocaust Chronicle*, 78.
15. Ibid., 75.

CHAPTER SEVEN

Passing the Torch (1935–9)

In September 1935, Henni Hein had just a few close relatives left alive. Beside her three children, there were only her sisters Toni (married to Max Flatow) and Rosa (married to Billy Wertheimer in England), her sister-in-law Irma (Martin's widow) and Sophie (married to Siegfried Beer and living in Berlin), and her first cousins Hedwig Seckel (married to an important Rabbi, Bruno Italiener) and Margaret Seckel (married to Benno Joseph), and Hedwig Baer, widow of her first cousin Richard Seckel. Henni had matured very quickly, however, after her husband died in 1926; she had had her say in all of the family's major financial decisions. She was more than capable of looking after herself, but did she have the determination to go on? The future of her fifteen-year-old daughter still remained uncertain, and she vowed to spend every pfennig she had left to send Trude out of Germany to safety.

Also in September 1935, the German parliament made it illegal for Jews and Aryans to marry (or to carry on 'inter-racial' affairs). As well, Jews could not employ Aryan women under forty-five as domestic servants.[1]

At the Regent Street Polytechnic in London, a student two years older than Georg fell ill and died. Georg had known the boy only by sight, but everyone at the school had to attend the funeral. It was a particularly sad occasion, especially for Georg, who had been unable to attend services after the recent deaths in his own family. The funeral made a deep impression on him, as it was the first he'd attended since his grandfather died in 1927. The name of the dead boy was Peter Stevens.

Georg Hein graduated from Regent Street Polytechnic in April 1936 at age seventeen. His marks were, for the most part, acceptable; he did much better in class than in his final exams. Despite receiving an average of 79 per cent on nine subjects during his last school term (second highest in his class), Georg's final exams averaged only 54 per cent, although he ranked seventh on the exams and fifth overall for the year. His teachers were quite complimentary: 'Is working very hard' from his English master – 73 per cent during the year and 46 per cent on the final exam. His French teacher wrote, 'A splendid worker, but his English is rather a handicap.' The mathematics master reported: 'Every credit is due to him for his splendid effort.' His chemistry professor commented, 'He works well & shows interest & good ideas.' Not surprisingly, his highest marks were in German: 100 per cent during the term and 97 per cent on the final exam.

Would Georg attend university or look for a job? His graduating marks were enough for entrance to a decent university, and he considered the London School of Economics (LSE). Certainly there was money for him to attend the LSE, and he could handle the work, but was he keen?

But there was another issue. Georg Hein had entered the United Kingdom on a student visa, and if he left school he would have to leave Britain as well. The deadline for action was 31 December 1936. Georg, Erich, and Henni had a long telephone conversation. As long as Georg stayed in school, he could probably have renewed his visa, but he could not remain a student forever. Grey clouds seemed to be working their way across the continent. If war came, how would it affect Georg? Erich was safe, as he had entered England early and without conditions.

Erich and Georg came up with a plan: if they could find someone to adopt Georg, he could stay in England. Henni readily agreed, despite her reservations about possibly losing the family and emotional ties to her son. But who would adopt Georg? The obvious answer was Fred Wilkinson, headmaster of the Regent Street Polytechnic. The two boys made an appointment to meet with 'old Wilkie'. Erich had graduated from the Poly three years earlier and had kept in touch with the likeable teacher, whom he regarded as something of a 'Mr Chips' type, with no children of his own.

At the meeting, Erich and Georg carefully explained the situation and gave their family's guarantee that the adoption would, if Wilkinson agreed, be in name only – sort of an 'adoption of convenience'. Henni would place into trust in an English bank sufficient monies to pay for all of Georg's living and school expenses until he was twenty-one.

Wilkie was a decent fellow, with the British sense of fair play, and he had come to like the Hein boys. He readily agreed, and his lawyers, Lake & Sons, drew up the adoption papers by July. But Henni was unable to leave Germany for long enough to sign the papers. The Nazi government was already hampering Jews wishing to travel, and Henni worried that if she left she might lose whatever property and money she still had. Besides, she had no visa to enter England, and officials would probably not believe that she was there for only a few days to sign papers. By 1936, British officials assumed that any Jew leaving Germany for England was on a one-way trip. It would be unsafe to have the papers sent to her at home, as government censors might intercept them and the police arrest her on some trumped-up charge.

Some surreptitious investigation convinced her that she could travel briefly to Italy without arousing suspicions. After all, Italy and Germany were close allies, with Mussolini's Blackshirts being the original Fascists. Henni made arrangements to go by train across Germany and Austria to the northern frontier of Italy, high in the Alps, to the small vacation town of Colle Isarco. There, on 20 July 1936, she found the legal documents waiting for her. She signed the adoption papers, and the manager of the Palace Hotel witnessed them. The papers went back to the lawyers in London.

It was a difficult trip for Henni. She knew that she was doing the best for her son, but she felt anguish at his loss. Even though he was seventeen, and even with all her difficulties raising him, she found the legal parting very hard. She believed to some degree that she had been a failure to him as a mother. After Victor died, when Georg was only six, she had been unable to deal with his outbursts and had sent him away to boarding school. When the rising tide of Nazi persecution forced him to leave school, she had sent him to England. She had given up on Georg, had not provided him with a loving upbringing at home. She had pawned him off on others, and she could not forgive herself. The train trip from northern Italy back to Hanover seemed very long and lonely.

In August of that year, Georg combined a trip home with a visit to the Summer Olympics in Berlin, where he stayed for two weeks with his Aunt Sophie, widow of Siegfried Beer. Adolf Hitler tried to use the Olympics to show the world how perfect was the German master race, but Jesse Owens, the black American sprinter, won four gold medals, and Hitler, who considered blacks even more menial than Jews, shunned him.

The Olympic Stadium in Berlin was a masterpiece, but it made full use of Nazi symbolism. A massive stone German eagle stood watch above it from a podium overlooking the *Führer*'s private box. Hitler proudly presented the gold medals to most of the victorious athletes, especially to exemplars of Aryan perfection. Germany was the games' leading medal winner (thirty-three gold, twenty-six silver, thirty bronze), beating the United States (twenty-four gold, twenty silver, twelve bronze).

The changes in Germany since he had emigrated shocked Georg. Whereas in 1933 Hanover he would see occasional mass gatherings of Nazis and hear the odd story of roving gangs of fascist thugs beating up someone, 1936 Berlin was militaristic and Nazi to the core. There were black-uniformed troops at every turn, goose-stepping and giving the raised right-hand salute while bellowing '*Heil* Hitler!' at every opportunity. Georg found that both ridiculous and revolting, but knew enough not to admit it to anyone outside the family. These developments terrified his Aunt Sophie, who was making plans to leave Germany as soon as possible, regardless of the cost.

After the games, Georg returned to Hanover to see his mother and sister. He still blamed his mother for what he perceived as her lack of love for him, and she was unable to comprehend his ingratitude. After a week of bittersweet silence, Georg left for England.

Back in London, Georg took the signed adoption papers to his lawyer, who would file them with the British government, ensuring that the authorities would not arrest Georg and deport him to Germany for overstaying his visa. In due course, the Foreign Office would reply that it had revoked all previous conditions of his visa and that he could remain in Britain unconditionally and accept employment.

During summer 1936, while Henni was in Italy in July and Georg in Germany in August, Spain had blown up like a powder keg. Earlier that year, national elections had resulted in a Communist coalition, which angered the right-wing military. On 18 July, General Francisco Franco, Spain's military Chief of Staff, commanded a widespread revolt by troops. The Republican Communists initially retained Madrid, the east coast, and most of the Basque border territories in the north. The military-led Nationalist rebels captured the main southern cities of Seville and Cadiz, and counted among their supporters many western and northern Spaniards. In September, the conflict drew international attention: the Soviet Union sent arms to communist sympathisers to put down the rebellion, while Hitler and Mussolini volunteered men and equipment to aid Franco's *coup d'état*.[2]

Henni Hein finally found a way to get Trude out of Germany. After scouring Europe, she had located a school for childcare workers in Zurich. The school had agreed to take Trude, now sixteen, into its two-year program but would guarantee no more than that. At the end of the course, she would have to leave Switzerland. Henni was ecstatic about the acceptance and hoped against hope that the situation would change, and that the Swiss would eventually let Trude stay. In the meantime, she paid handsomely for twenty-four months of breathing room for her daughter.

In autumn 1936, Georg entered his first year at the LSE. He enjoyed his classes but did not work hard enough to succeed. In Germany, he had never tried terribly hard at school. His good memory and his ability to quickly grasp complex issues and ideas had always stood him in good stead academically. The occasional teacher would accuse him of laziness. For the first few years in England, however, he had had to push himself, mainly because of his poor English. Once he mastered the language, he began to revert to his old habits of working just enough to pass, but never sufficiently hard to shine.

After a couple of months, Georg realised that this was not the life for him. But he had difficulty in broaching the subject with Erich. He knew that failure would reflect badly on him and might really upset their mother. So he ignored the problem, hoping that it would just disappear.

In the spring of 1937, after final exams, Georg had to admit to both Erich and Henni that he had wasted his year – he would not return to LSE. What would he do? Now that school did not hold his future, what would? He spent two months during spring 1937 asking himself that question while making a show of looking for employment.

Meanwhile Nazi Germany, sensing a potentially valuable ally in Spain should Franco succeed, began pouring in military men and materiel. This was the perfect opportunity to test the Third *Reich*'s armed forces and equipment. With Hitler quietly planning his conquest of Europe, he and his

High Command could obtain some serious practice. Despite the Treaty of Versailles forbidding Germany from re-arming, the *Luftwaffe* now had more – and better – combat-ready aircraft than did England. In Spain, German pilots did General Hermann Göring proud, showing how devastating air power had become. The battle-worn and tested German pilots who bombed Guernica and Almeria in April–May 1937 would later lead their squadrons in the *blitzkrieg* of 1939–40.[3]

In London, Lake & Son, Solicitors, eventually wrote to the Aliens Department at the Home Office on behalf of Georg Hein to request permission for him to accept a job offer in a London advertising agency, as a space buyer and market researcher: 'in view of the boy's specialised study of economics such a position will afford better opportunities for the full development of his talents.'[4] The work turned out to be interesting and challenged Georg's language skills. He enjoyed the challenge and, even more, the pocket money that he earned. Now he could afford a few luxuries and begin to enjoy life the way he never had. There had always been a governess, or a parent, or a schoolmaster, or an older brother watching over him. Now, with money to burn, he vowed to go out and have fun!

Would someone who had known a very regimented life manage on his own? Very gradually, Georg began to experiment. In February 1937, he turned eighteen. Whatever Erich said or did seemed ridiculous to Georg, and eventually even his mother's advice in letters and telephone calls fell on deaf ears. His income, however, was quite small, so he couldn't get into too much trouble.

When he was younger, Georg had looked up to Erich. Erich had always been quiet and reserved, and as he grew up he retreated inwards. He had stayed in school and continued to attend synagogue regularly. He had asked Georg to go along with him, but his brother had no interest. As Georg's independence grew, his reliance on Erich declined, and he became increasingly unable to understand or relate to his older brother. He began to wonder if there was something wrong with Erich.

Over the winter of 1937–8, Georg gradually made new friends. People from the advertising agency, especially the younger, less inhibited ones, took him under their wing. They would go out for a pint of beer most nights after work and party seriously at weekends. Georg enjoyed the life and often returned to his and Erich's flat in the wee hours of the morning, somewhat the worse for wear. He would sleep until noon on Saturday and Sunday, disgusting Erich, who reserved most Saturday mornings for temple. One Saturday night early in 1938, Georg and his usual gang went to a new place. It was his first visit to a gambling club, and the glitz and opulence appealed to him. All of a sudden, Georg thought he'd found his place in life.

On 12–13 March 1938, Hitler announced the *Anschluss*, Germany's annexation of Austria. Without consulting the Austrians, Hitler had made them citizens of the Third *Reich*. Austrian Jews were now subject to the worst of the Nazi citizenship laws and could expect treatment no better than that of German Jews.

In May 1938, seventeen-year-old Trude Hein finished her course in early childhood education in Switzerland. The Swiss, while preaching neutrality, were reluctant to upset the Nazi regime in Germany, on which they relied for millions of Francs in banking fees. So Trude was forced to return to Hanover. The situation there was dangerous, and Henni resolved to help her tiny daughter (only four feet ten but almost an adult) leave the country, whatever the cost.

In November 1938, Henni sent Trude to England. The exorbitant fees for exit papers and travel used up much of the family's remaining wealth. Henni cried herself to sleep the night Trude left, all alone in the family apartment. Irma Seckel, Martin's widow, arranged for her own departure from Germany in November and also her entry into the United States, where she settled in Poughkeepsie, New York, and died in 1967.

Henni's first cousin Hedwig Seckel had married a prominent rabbi, Bruno Italiener. Because of a last-minute sponsorship from the Jewish community in England, the Italieners and their two daughters (nineteen and twenty-seven) obtained special permission to leave Germany. This left in Germany Henni; her sister, Toni (wife of Stern Flatow), and their four children; and Hedwig Baer, widow of Richard Seckel, the lawyer. None of these was able to escape, and all eventually perished in the holocaust. Sophie Beer remained in Berlin, but she was not of Jewish birth. Her husband, Dr Erich Beer, was able to escape to the United States.

When Trude Hein arrived in England, Erich met her at the train station, guided her off the incoming train, and placed her on an outgoing one. That took her to look for a job on the south coast of England. She found work, using her Swiss training, in the Hants and Dorset Babies Home in Parkstone (about thirty miles west of Portsmouth on the south coast).[5] There she was subject to a highly regimented existence and life in a dormitory. Trude felt bewildered and completely alone but eventually settled in. It was certainly a decent existence, and she was exceedingly grateful to be safe in the United Kingdom.

In the summer of 1938, an international conference dealt with the pressing 'Jewish Refugee Problem'. US President Franklin Roosevelt had called for the symposium, which took place at Evian-les-Bains, France, 6–14 July. Costa Rica and the Dominican Republic each announced willingness to accept Jewish immigrants in return for large fees; the other thirty countries in attendance proclaimed that they would not take in large numbers. On 23 July, the German government ordered Jews to obtain special identity cards that they had to show whenever the police asked.[6]

On 16 September 1938, a police inspector filed a report on Georg Hein at Hampstead Station, London. It reviewed his living arrangements with Erich and stated:

Since April, 1937 Georg Hein has been employed in the Market Research Department of Coleman, Prentise and Varley, Ltd., Advertising Agents, ... at a wage of 30/– (30 shillings a week), plus travelling and subsistence allowances. He informed me that his wages are to be raised to 40/– per week at the end of this month.

His work consists chiefly of travelling to provincial towns, organising squads of girls to distribute advertisements in leaflet form from door to door.

The alien appears very respectable and as his employers pay for most of his meals his circumstances are satisfactory.

He has been warned to attend the Aliens' Office, Bow Street, to notify change of occupation.[7]

Germany's aid to Franco in the Spanish Civil War in 1936 had only increased Hitler's appetite to display his military prowess. Using the Sudetenland as a bargaining chip, he threatened in summer 1938 to attack Czechoslovakia and reclaim that border region, where ethnic Germans predominated.

British Prime Minister Neville Chamberlain hastened to Hitler's Bavarian mountain lair, Berchtesgaden, to beg him not to invade the Sudetenland. During September 1938, several meetings between the two leaders culminated with the Munich Conference, at which Britain and France agreed to allow Germany's illegal annexation of the Czech territory. Deplaning on his return from Munich, Chamberlain held up a copy of the agreement and proclaimed: 'Peace in our time.' On 15 October, Germany went ahead and unilaterally annexed the Sudetenland.

While the Munich Conference was taking place, Germany made it illegal for Jewish lawyers to practise. Only two months earlier, in July, it had cancelled the licences of all Jewish doctors. On 5 October 1938, at the request of the Swiss police, Germany recalled all passports belonging to Jews and issued them new ones marked with a large 'J' – the Swiss wanted no German Jews seeking asylum in their country.[8]

In November, all hell broke loose. On the seventh, an angry German Jew named Herschel Grynszpan walked into the German embassy in Paris and shot the first official he could find – Ernst vom Rath – who soon died. German authorities had just deported Grynszpan's family to Zbaszyn, a refugee camp across the border in Poland, and he was furious.

Two nights later, using the murder as justification, gangs of Nazi hoodlums set out to take revenge on Jews in Germany and Austria. They destroyed windows in all Jewish homes, businesses, and synagogues. In some cases, they dragged Jews out into the streets and beat them. Ninety-one Jews died, and fire destroyed some buildings, including over 250 synagogues. Authorities arrested 30,000 Jewish men and sent them to concentration camps in Germany but later released most of them. '*Kristallnacht*' (the Night of Broken Glass) – 9 November 1938 – in effect unofficially launched the Holocaust.[9]

Many German Jews who were still able to buy their way out resolved to leave the country as soon as possible.

On 11 September 1938, the Hampstead station of the Metropolitan (London) Police Force reported that Georg Hein had claimed that his brother, Erich, had just said that he was about to commit suicide. The police inspector visited their flat and interviewed Erich. He wrote: 'His conversation was quite rational, and except that his condition was obviously neurotic, I could trace no evidence of insanity calling for action by me.' The authorities consulted two physicians. Dr Rosenthal (whom Georg called) thought that Erich was 'certifiable and should be detained'. Dr Rees (whom the police engaged) found no cause for such action.[10] Had Georg simply tired of Erich's constant disciplining, or was Erich actually *in extremis*?

After Trude's emigration, her mother took stock of her finances and decided how much of her declining fortune she could send to England to support her children. She reasoned that this would probably be her last chance to send money out of Germany before the Nazi government simply nationalised all Jewish assets. Already, its confiscatory fees had made the export of funds prohibitively expensive for Jews. Henni decided how much she would need for herself and arranged for her bank to transfer the balance to England.

Complicating matters, the police again received a call to Erich and Georg's home on 19 October 1938. This time, they doubted Erich's sanity, took him into custody, and remanded him to the St Pancras Hospital, pending his appearance before the 'Justices in Lunacy'.[11] No disposition of the case is available, but no committal took place at that time. Later in life, Erich suffered from fully fledged schizophrenia, right up until his death in 1960.

Unfortunately for Erich and Trude, when the funds from their mother arrived in London, nineteen-year-old Georg made a beeline to the bank branch. There he withdrew the entire amount – some six hundred pounds (about three years of a labourer's wages in London) – and deposited it at a different bank, where he opened a new account in his own name.

Erich had immediately expressed his fury when he grasped what was happening, but Georg simply avoided him. Erich contacted Henni in Germany and informed her of Georg's actions, but neither had any influence on Georg or could recover the remaining funds before they all disappeared. On 7 February 1939, Henni wrote to her younger son:

You indicated that you were glad and thankful that I didn't abandon you because only next of kin would help you to … [?] I have tried everything in my power to lead you the right direction. You had a childhood which perhaps few people have had and now you have brought great disappointment to your mother and siblings. Shouldn't you have insight about what you should do now to bring us more sorrow? Improve yourself before it is too late. There might be a time when you would like to get help from your relatives and you would be sorry that you were estranged from them.[12]

Within three months, Georg had exhausted his family's fortune. Georg didn't know what to do. He could not very well go back to Erich, cap in hand, begging for his help. And so, in his increasing desperation, he turned to crime to support himself. Police records show that they charged Georg Franz Hein, of no fixed address, with the following crimes in 1939:

1. January 20–25. Theft of a vacuum cleaner from his employer, Electrolux Ltd. (Georg admitted having taken his salesman's sample machine and pawning it for the sum of £2.)
2. Failing to report his change of address to authorities, as was required of a German citizen.
3. June 10–12. During his employment as a shop assistant at a tobacconist's, Hein stole £40 from the till during the illness absence of the shop manager.[13]

The court found Georg guilty of all three offences and remanded him in custody until sentencing. On 18 July 1939, the magistrate sent him to Wormwood Scrubs Prison for Boys for concurrent sentences of three months on each of the two larceny charges. The court learned at that time that Georg had been living in common rooming houses, had pawned most of his clothing, and was practically destitute.[14]

Georg's older brother actually attempted to contact him in prison. The Warden of His Majesty's Prison at Bristol (where authorities had transferred Georg) replied to Erich's letter, advising him that Georg 'says that he does not see that any useful purpose can be served by your visiting him'.[15]

As Nazi persecution of Jews in Germany worsened, one would assume that Britain would have made it easier for German Jews to emigrate there. Yet, despite increasing publicity about the horrendous conditions for Jews in Germany, the United Kingdom was making entry more and more difficult for them; by 1939, it was all but impossible, except for children.

But Britain had already done a great deal to help. It took in many German and Austrian refugees in the 1930s. Some 225,000 Jews left Germany between 1933 and 31 August 1939, and 140,000 or so quit Austria. Probably 90 per cent or more of those immigrants passed through Britain on their way to safety, whether there or elsewhere.[16] While some people within the British government loudly proclaimed their fears of Jewish refugees overrunning the country, many bureaucrats whose job it was to curtail refugee immigration turned a blind eye for as long as they could. There were over three million Jews in Poland, and Britain alone could not have received that large a group, nor its economy sustain such numbers. Nobody in the 1930s outside senior Nazi ranks could possibly have known what Hitler was planning for

European Jews. No sane person could envisage the horrors that were about to take place.

In 1938 and 1939, the British government was starting to prepare for war. Winston Churchill kept reminding the government during the 1930s that, if war came, Britain could not afford to lose it. If the country had spent all of its time worrying about refugees and none readying itself for war, it would have lost the Battle of Britain and Germany would have invaded England. If that had happened, what good would it have done for the Jews to have found safe haven there during the 1930s?

In March 1939, Hedwig (Baer) Seckel received an unusual but welcome telephone call in Hanover. The speaker identified himself as being with the Kinder Transport agency and told Hedwig to ensure that her son, Peter, fourteen, was at the central train station at a certain time, ready to leave Germany. A group of charitable Christian Germans, who could not bear to be responsible for the deaths of Jewish children, had set up the furtive organisation. Through their remarkable and dangerous efforts, thousands of Jewish children left their parents for freedom just months before the war. Had the Nazis caught wind of what was happening, they could have faced recriminations. Fortunately, most of the German border guards turned a blind eye, in many cases as a result of being offered a financial incentive to do so. Some of the children were unable to cross by train and had to actually cross the frontier on foot. Peter Seckel's two older sisters, Gertrude and Erika, had departed Germany by Kinder Transport a bit earlier, but Peter was too young to go on his own at that point. Fortunately, this train had room for him, and hundreds of children had received permission to enter England. As the train pulled slowly out of the station, the lonely boy waved good-bye to his sobbing mother, unable to understand her equal feelings of grief and joy at his impending liberation. The two were never to see one another again. Peter eventually resettled in the United States, where he raised a family of his own.

By July 1939, Henni Hein had her three children safe in England. Despite her grief at not having her children close by, where she could see and touch them, this gave her great satisfaction and a sense of peace in a world collapsing around her. For her, the future grew constantly bleaker. She had exhausted her savings on the children's safety and security and had no money left. No longer a lady of wealth and privilege, she had had to give up her beautiful home, which she could not afford to maintain. She was now fifty-three and almost completely alone. Her husband and her parents were long gone, and her closest ally – her brother, Martin – and her brothers-in-law had died. Only her older sister, Toni, and her sister-in-law, Sophie Hein, a widow of sixty-five, remained.

Henni had done everything she could to ensure her children's survival and now lost all hope for herself. On 21 July 1939, she took an overdose of sleeping pills and slipped away, ensuring that the pain for her at least would end there and then.

Notes

1. Sherman, *Island Refuge*, 58.
2. Dupuy and Dupuy, *The Harper Encyclopedia of Military History: From 3500 B.C. to the Present*, 4th ed., 1,127–9.
3. Dupuy and Dupuy, *The Harper Encyclopedia of Military History: From 3500 B.C. to the Present*, 4th ed., 1,129.
4. National Archives, Kew, document HO 405 / 20069. Home Office Alien file on Georg Franz Hein, Lake & Son to E.N. Cooper, Esq., Aliens Department, Whitehall, 29 April 1937.
5. National Archives, HO 405 / 20069, on Georg Hein, draft of letter from the Home Office to Mr Shiff of the German Jewish Aid Committee.
6. Aretha, ed., *The Holocaust Chronicle*, 130–31.
7. National Archives, HO 405 / 20069, on Georg Hein, Metropolitan Police report of 16 Sept. 1938.
8. Aretha, ed., *The Holocaust Chronicle*, 132–9.
9. Ibid., 140–41.
10. National Archives, HO 405/20069, file on Georg Hein, Metropolitan Police report of 11 September 1938.
11. Ibid., report of 19 October 1938.
12. Letter from Henni Hein to Georg Hein, 7 February 1939.
13. National Archives, file HO405 / 20069, London Metropolitan Police Report.
14. Ibid.
15. Letter of F. Townsend, HM Prison Bristol, to Erich Hein, 16 August 1939.
16. Sherman, *Island Refuge*, 269–71.

Part Three: Peter Stevens in the RAF (1939–41)

CHAPTER EIGHT

From Airman to Pilot Officer (September 1939–March 1941)

In late August 1939, the British government knew that war was certain. It would need space to hold enemy aliens. The only space ready and available was prison facilities. And so the authorities asked the governor of each prison to identify petty criminals who had almost completed their sentences or who seemed no threat to the public. The government issued an emergency order, which would allow release of such people on 1 September 1939.

Twenty-year-old Georg Hein, an inmate in Bristol, received a railway ticket to London on Friday 1 September and an order to report to a police station in London on his arrival.[1] He followed the first instruction, but not the second. He was now a fugitive, as well as an enemy alien.

At dawn on that same day, a million and a quarter highly trained and well-equipped German soldiers crossed into Poland. With no advance warning, and not even a declaration of war, Hitler had begun the Second World War. The *blitzkrieg* was unrelenting and very quickly overran the token Polish defences.

The German-Jewish poet-philosopher, Heinrich Heine, had written some 105 years earlier:

Watch out! I mean well with you and therefore I tell you the bitter truth. You have more to fear from a liberated Germany than from the entire Holy Alliance along with all Croats and Cossacks.

A drama will be enacted in Germany compared to which the French Revolution will seem like a harmless idyll. Christianity restrained the martial ardour of the Germans for a time but it did not destroy it; once the restraining talisman is shattered, savagery will rise again, ... the mad fury of the berserk, of which Nordic poets sing and speak ... The old stony gods will rise from the rubble and rub the thousand-year-old dust from their eyes. Thor with the giant hammer will come forth and smash the Gothic domes.

The German thunder ... rolls slowly at first but it will come. And when you hear it roar, as it has never roared before in the history of the world, know that the German thunder has reached its target.[2]

Georg Hein, knowing that this was the inevitable result of the megalomaniac's rise to power, had already made his plan for private retaliation. He had chosen a name that was typically English, yet nondescript – one that he had learnt at Regent Street Polytechnic. It was the name of an older student who had taken sick and died. The entire school had attended the funeral of Peter Stevens.

Hein wasted no time. On his arrival in London, he went to the cemetery where the boy lay and made a note of his date of birth on the headstone – 13 April 1917. Hein then went to the appropriate government office and requested a copy of the boy's birth certificate. This was an early instance of 'identity theft', though perhaps with a slightly more altruistic purpose.

Britain reacted swiftly to Hitler's ruthlessness. It issued an ultimatum to Germany to cease and desist but received no reply. On Sunday 3 September at 11.15 a.m., Prime Minister Neville Chamberlain, who had so recently returned from Munich and proclaimed 'Peace in our time', announced over BBC radio the declaration of war. France and Britain had signed a mutual defence pact with Poland and had to honour it.

That afternoon, Georg Hein went to the RAF enlistment station in central London, presented 'his' birth certificate, and introduced himself as Peter Stevens. He declared, in an Oxford-sounding accent, that he wanted to be a fighter pilot. The induction form asked for his religion, and he listed 'Church of England' (Anglican). Georg Franz Hein was unofficially dead; Peter Stevens was alive again.[3]

Peter Stevens signed the appropriate documents, took the oath of allegiance to the King, and passed his physical examination. He was now Airman 900146 in the Royal Air Force Volunteer Reserve. As candidates were inundating the RAF, Stevens's processing took several days. He eventually arrived at No. 1 Depot at Uxbridge, where he received a uniform and began his military training in earnest. To a twenty-year-old, war may seem nothing but glorious. Peter Stevens would come to know at first hand that it is anything but.

Unbeknown to Peter Stevens, his aunt Hedwig Seckel (née Baer), mother of Peter Seckel (whom the Kinder Transport had saved) chose 5 September to emulate Henni Hein: like Henni, she had been unable to escape Germany, and she took her own life.

In early September, in an attempt to help put Georg Hein back onto the 'straight and narrow', the Home Office wrote to Otto Schiff, head of the German Jewish Aid Committee in London. The letter detailed Georg's legal troubles and asked for the committee's help in providing 'mature guidance to secure that he does not continue his present mode of living'.[4]

Schiff replied on 12 September, thankful for the 'sympathetic terms in which [the letter] is written'. He added that:

> …under ordinary circumstances we would be only too delighted to take over the care of Georg Hein. Unfortunately, however, under the present

circumstances, I really feel that it is impossible for us to give the necessary care to this young man, and for his own sake as well as for that of other people I candidly think that for the time being much the best solution would be for him to be detained after the expiry of his prison sentence as an enemy alien.[5]

On 17 September, the Soviet Union (in accordance with the Treaty of Non-aggression between Germany and the Union of Soviet Socialist Republics dated 23 August 1939), invaded Poland from the east. By 5 October, Poland ceased to exist as an independent political entity. Between this date and early April 1940, the Germans actually rested their military might during the so-called 'Phoney War'.

On 18 September 1939, the Home Office wrote to the governor of HM Prison Bristol as well as to the Bristol police and instructed them to detain enemy alien Georg Franz Hein under a restriction order. Each office responded separately that the prison had released Hein and sent him to London on 1 September.

While Stevens found the RAF initial training physically demanding, it was quite boring. He longed for something more interesting but knew enough not to draw attention to himself. On 11 November (Armistice Day) 1939, the RAF sent Stevens to a training base in northern England called RAF Finningley. It was near Doncaster, in South Yorkshire.

Meanwhile, the British authorities searched in earnest for Georg Hein. While they did not seem to think him a threat to the war effort, they worried about his potential for criminal behaviour. The assistant commissioner of the Metropolitan London Police at New Scotland Yard wrote to the Under Secretary of State, Home Office Aliens Department, on 24 November:

… exhaustive enquiries have been made to trace this man but without success. He is the subject of the circulation in Supplement 'C' of the Police Gazette of 15th November, 1939, case No. 3. In the circumstances the Restriction Order is being retained at this office until he is traced.[6]

On 5 December, the RAF sent Aircraftman 2nd Class Peter Stevens to its No. 5 Initial Training Wing at Hastings. The town, on the English Channel in south-east England, about thirty miles east of Brighton, had been a popular pre-war tourist destination. Along its lovely seafront promenade, Stevens and his fellow RAF volunteers practised their formation marching daily. This was to be the full basic training course, and Stevens learned well the appropriate body of knowledge and the requirements of military life. His test marks on both military basics and general intelligence were exceedingly high, and the authorities eventually singled him out for pilot training. The unpleasant years in private schools in Germany had finally paid off.

By 5 January 1940, Peter Stevens had shown sufficient promise for formal selection for pilot training and promotion to leading aircraftman. Because of the large numbers of volunteers, however, he would wait several months before beginning his pilot training. In the meantime, there was a good deal of classroom time, during which he and the other raw recruits learned the theory and physics of flight. Their instructors tested them early and often. But knowledge of this information does not guarantee good piloting skills.

In spring, the Germans advanced again. On 9 April 1940, they launched their next major offensive. Simultaneous ground assaults on Denmark and naval and air attacks on Norway led to the defeat and occupation of both countries in relatively short order.

On 10 May, the Germans rolled across the border into France, putting at risk the entire continent. The Third *Reich* had amassed approximately two-and-a-half million men on its western borders, with about two million French troops opposing them. As well, the British Expeditionary Force had stationed about 400,000 men in France, and the RAF had some 500 aircraft there. The Belgian army stationed some 600,000 men on that country's eastern border.

The French government had relied for the republic's defence on the strength of its Maginot Line fortifications, which dated from the 1930s. The Germans, however, took little heed of the Maginot Line and barrelled across the Dutch and Belgian frontiers, bypassing a large part of the French lines. They did attack France, but mainly via the Ardennes forest of Belgium. The resistance melted away completely, and the German Panzer tanks overran Belgium and Holland in less than a week. Despite the many Allied troops, the Germans' equipment, training and experience were too good. By 15 May, their tanks had crossed into France from the north and were rapidly winning territory.

Amazingly, Hitler ordered his armoured divisions to stop their attack on 26 May. This allowed bewildered Allied troops to regroup and make for Dunkirk on the English Channel. From that port took place one of the great military rescues of all time. The Germans had surrounded almost 220,000 British soldiers and another 112,000 French and Belgians on French soil, and Britain sent an armada – almost every one of its vessels still afloat – to their aid between 28 May and 4 June. Even so, the Germans took many Allied soldiers as prisoners.[7]

Also on 10 May 1940, Neville Chamberlain's government lost a vote of no confidence in the House of Commons, and the King invited Winston Churchill to form a new government. The former First Lord of the Admiralty (during the Great War), who had entered the House of Commons in 1900, had been a lonely Tory backbencher during the 1930s. He had tried valiantly (but in vain) to stir the Conservative government to action over Hitler's surreptitious and massive rearmament of Germany. Finally, Churchill's forecast had come to pass, and German hordes had overrun much of Europe. Now his mission was to save Britain – and the rest of the still-free world – from the Nazi menace. On first addressing the nation as Prime Minister on 13 May, he promised: 'I have nothing to offer but blood, toil, tears and sweat.'

At the end of his basic training, on 21 May 1940, the RAF shuffled Peter Stevens off to its No. 33 Maintenance Unit at Lyneham for a course in aircraft familiarisation. He spent only two weeks there and transferred to No. 3 Elementary Flying Training School at Hamble on 9 June.

There he took his very first, twenty-five-minute flight as a passenger in an Avro Cadet biplane. In his new RAF pilot's flying logbook, Leading Aircraftman Stevens proudly recorded four items from the training syllabus: 1) Air Experience, 1a) Familiarity with cockpit layout, 2) Effect of controls, and 4) Straight & level flight. After another thirty-five-minute flight that same day, he added to his list of instruction items 3) Taxying and 5) Climbing, gliding & stalling. There was to be a lot of classroom time as well, in the theory and mechanics of flight. This was it! Stevens finally was a pilot! Or at least training to become one…

The Avro Cadet was an early-1930s biplane trainer with a 150-hp Genet Major radial engine. Its very forgiving landing gear allowed low-time student pilots to produce a reasonable landing. As with most post-1918 biplanes, it was relatively docile and easy to fly. On it, a new pilot could build confidence quickly.

Several days earlier, on 4 June, Churchill had risen again in Parliament and had told the British:

We shall not flag nor fail. We shall go on to the end. We shall fight in France and on the seas and oceans; we shall fight with growing confidence and growing strength in the air. We shall defend our island whatever the cost may be; we shall fight on beaches, landing grounds, in fields, in streets and on the hills. We shall never surrender and even if, which I do not for the moment believe, this island or a large part of it were subjugated and starving, then our empire beyond the seas, armed and guarded by the British Fleet, will carry on the struggle until in God's good time the New World with all its power and might, sets forth to the liberation and rescue of the Old.

Italy entered the war on the side of Germany on 10 June. During the first half of that month, the Germans, with inspiration from their overwhelming victories, continued to roll across France. They entered Paris as conquerors on 14 June. By 21 June, the French government realised that it had lost and offered its capitulation.[8]

The British Expeditionary Force had lost almost 70,000 of its men, and the RAF had left behind in France the ruins of more than 200 fighter aircraft, including half of its Hawker Hurricanes.[9] Lord Dowding, chief of Fighter Command, had given up far more than he thought prudent, realising that he would need every possible plane to defend England. When Churchill, regretting the German destruction of the French, had ordered him to send another ten squadrons to France, Dowding had correctly and wisely responded that his job was to defend Britain, not France. Churchill, in this rare instance, deferred to one of his military commanders.[10]

During his first week of flight training, Stevens spent just under six hours in the cockpit of the Avro Cadet. On the tenth day of instruction, 22 June, after only eight-and-a-half hours of training, Stevens flew his first solo – a grand total of ten minutes in the air! But at least he had made it! Many trainees didn't reach even that stage. Anywhere from one-third to one-half typically left after each phase of pilot training.

Over the next month of training, Aircraftman Stevens completed the entire initial flying course. On 22 July, with twenty-three hours and fifteen minutes of student dual time (i.e., with an instructor) and twenty-four hours and thirty minutes of solo time in the Cadet, his instructor rated him 'Average'. Not good enough to satisfy Stevens, and probably not good enough for fighters, but at least he had passed! And many colleagues did not.

After the *Wehrmacht* had rolled so easily over most of western Europe, the Germans now turned their sights onto the region's only remaining bastion of freedom: Britain.

On 18 June, the Prime Minister told the Commons:

What General Weygand called the Battle of France is over. I expect that the Battle of Britain is about to begin. Upon this battle depends the survival of Christian civilisation. Upon it depends our own British life, and the long continuity of our institutions and our Empire. The whole fury and might of the enemy must very soon be turned on us. Hitler knows that he will have to break us in this Island or lose the war. If we can stand up to him, all Europe may be free and the life of the world may move forward into broad, sunlit uplands. But if we fail, then the whole world, including the United States, including all that we have known and cared for, will sink into the abyss of a new Dark Age made more sinister, and perhaps more protracted, by the lights of perverted science. Let us therefore brace ourselves to our duties, and so bear ourselves that, if the British Empire and its Commonwealth last for a thousand years, men will still say, 'This was their finest hour.'[11]

The Battle of Britain did indeed begin, and it was almost entirely a contest of wit and will between the two nations' fearsome air forces. Fortunately, the British, through technical innovation, had the upper hand. In the mid-1930s, their scientific establishment had begun research into a so-called death ray but soon realised that such an invention was far beyond its technical capabilities. Its research did develop, however, the capability to detect at long range the presence of aircraft – radar.

The Air Ministry soon built the world's first chain of early-warning radar sites all along England's southern and eastern coastlines. But it did not stop there. It also connected each radar station directly to the Command and Control headquarters of RAF Fighter Command. In this way, the British could see the *Luftwaffe* massing its bomber raids over France, long before the aircraft would appear over England. Using this information, they could prepare adequate defensive reaction, guiding the appropriate number of fighter aircraft against the invaders. At the same time, the *Luftwaffe* had its fleet of *Stuka* dive-bombers target the array of radar antennae dotting the English coast. It destroyed several such stations during the Battle of Britain, but the British substituted mobile replacement stations and quickly repaired the permanent posts.

The fight began in earnest on 16 July 1940, when Hitler announced plans for Operation *Sea Lion*, the invasion of the United Kingdom. The island nation relied economically and militarily on imports. Since the war's outbreak, food and materiel had arrived continuously by convoy from Canada, and the *Luftwaffe* initially targeted these supplies as they entered the English Channel and the Thames estuary. The Germans hoped thereby to draw out the RAF so that they could test its abilities. German bombers made regular sorties, usually by daylight, from the north-west coast of France, taking with them squadrons of Messerschmitt Bf 109 fighters for protection. Losses mounted on both sides, but there was no clear winner.

At the outset of the Battle of Britain, Fighter Command had 650 aircraft, a good number. As well, Lord Beaverbrook, in charge of aircraft production, was delivering almost 100 new planes per week. The Germans, however, had along the French coast some 2,500 fighters and bombers.

How must Peter Stevens have felt? He knew that he was capable of becoming a pilot and was learning about the Battle of Britain – both good news and bad – while stuck in training. Like most young pilots, he must have been anxious to enter the fight and was likely feeling completely useless doing what he was doing.

On 29 July 1940, Stevens transferred once again, this time to No. 9 Elementary Flying Training School at Ansty, near Coventry. This airfield was also home to the Armstrong Whitworth aircraft factory. Here he moved 'up' to the venerable de Havilland Tiger Moth biplane. The training schedule was similar to that for the Cadet but included some cross-country flight, adding navigation into the piloting equation. Through to 16 August, he completed eighteen hours on the Tiger Moth, seven and a half of them solo. He passed his course, again as 'Average'. At least his instructor on the Link trainer (instrument flying simulator) noted that Stevens, who had had seven hours on the Link, was 'Very good on full panel'.

The famous Tiger Moths actually had less power than the Cadets – their de Havilland Gypsy Major inline engine produced only 130 horsepower. None the less, with their huge wing area, they could perform aerobatics and climbed well (635 feet/minute). Even at their maximum speed of 109 mph, they could hardly cause a pilot trouble. Britain built over 8,800 of them, and they remained the RAF's primary *ab initio* training aircraft until 1947.[12]

The *Luftwaffe* anti-shipping missions continued into August but did not destroy the RAF's fighters, as the Germans had hoped. Hermann Göring, a First World

War fighter pilot in charge of the German air force, changed tactics in early August. If he could not destroy the RAF in the air, he would try to do so on the ground. *Luftwaffe* bombers targeted RAF fighter stations non-stop during most of August and the first week of September. While this made life very difficult for the heroes of RAF Fighter Command (the 'Few'), they kept on fighting.

Britain's two primary fighter aircraft in the Battle of Britain were the Supermarine Spitfire, a very fast and elegantly agile all-metal aircraft with a beautiful and instantly identifiable elliptical wingplan, and the Hawker Hurricane, a cloth-and-metal workhorse that could absorb terrific amounts of battle damage and remain aloft. Both had the famous twelve-cylinder Rolls-Royce Merlin engine and were capable of good speed.

The *Luftwaffe*'s primary fighter was the Messerschmitt Bf 109. It had a slightly more modern Jumo powerplant and had undergone battle-testing and proven itself in the Spanish Civil War. But it had a very cramped cockpit, and its narrow landing-gear track caused many ground-handling accidents on take-off and landing. As well, the Bf 109 had very limited endurance. It took thirty minutes to take off, climb to altitude, and cross the Channel and carried only eighty minutes of fuel, which allowed it just twenty minutes over England.[13]

Believing his own press, Göring reported to Hitler that he had crippled the RAF fighters in the Battle of Britain. In reality, RAF Fighter Command had almost enough aircraft but was losing pilots faster than it could replace them. Also, two of its two senior commanders developed a tactical disagreement. Keith Park was in charge of the south-easternmost part of England (11 Group), and Trafford Leigh-Mallory, the central part of England as far north as Scotland (12 Group). As 11 Group bore the brunt of the *Luftwaffe*'s attacks in the air and on the ground, Fighter Command detailed 12 Group to act in reserve and to go to 11 Group's aid whenever that was necessary.

How best to apply this tactic? Whenever Park's pilots in the air needed help, they were usually desperate. Leigh-Mallory, however, thought that the best way to confront the Germans was to have his squadrons take off and form large airborne forces that he called 'big wings' to go on the attack. However, while 12 Group formed up and flew to the site of the fighting, the battle wound down. Again, because the Bf 109s had so little time over England, it was imperative to engage them quickly. In addition, since 11 Group usually scrambled its squadrons early, it left its airfields defenceless. Park requested that 12 Group stay in reserve to defend those bases while 11 Group was on patrol.

But Leigh-Mallory and one of his right-hand men, Douglas Bader, commander of 242 Squadron, couldn't see it.[14] Lord Dowding intervened and forced Leigh-Mallory to request that his pilots stop wasting time forming up, and enter the fight quicker. Dowding did not do so early or forcefully enough, however, and it almost cost Britain the war.

On 19 August 1940, Aircraftman Stevens moved to No. 11 Flying Training School at Shawbury (near the Welsh border, about thirty-five miles north-west

Beach July 1924 – The Hein family with the governess. (*Trude Hein artefacts*)

Georg Hein immediately before emigration to England. (*Author's collection*)

LAC Peter Stevens enjoying free time at the seashore.
(*Author's collection*)

Modelling his first RAF uniform.
(*Author's collection*)

Practising marching on the front at Hamble. (*Author's collection*)

Pilot Officer Peter Stevens (front row left), graduating from a Pilot's course (others unknown). (*Author's collection*)

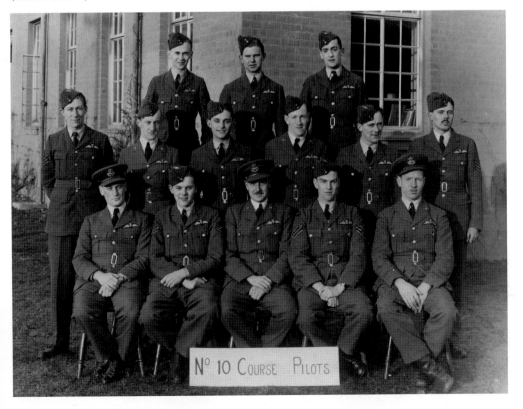

Pilot Officer Peter Stevens, displaying his new officer's uniform and Pilot's wings, November 1940. (*Author's collection*)

ACB) I form recd
6/June
30/9/46

(24.9.46). Letter from Air Ministry:
Copies am C/4837. and

Applicant's pre-war history is not a happy one. He was arrested in July '39 on two charges of larceny, and sentenced to 3 months HL. On release he was ordered to report to Paddington Police station where a R.O. was waiting to be served on him. He disappeared completely however, and was not traced until 1941 when it was revealed that he had enlisted in the R.A.F. under the pseudonym of Peter Stevens (for the use of which name he has no authy) and was at that time a P.O.W. in Germany – the R.O. was consequently revoked. The pps also reveal that he "appropriated" £600, intended for the joint use of his brother (a mental case) and sister, from whom he is consequently estranged. It is ∴ apparent how he earned the description of a thoroughly undesirable alien, but one must give full credit for his 22 operational flights over Germany, in which his gallantry culminated in his capture, to which his award of the M.C. testifies. His service record is described by ISNB as magnificent, and the conclusion is that he has lost his former waywardness with more advanced years. The appln is sponsored by the Air Ministry in view of alien's present occupation as ADC. and interpreter to Air Vice Marshall Davidson.

Alien is of German naty and 27 years of age. He has served over 7 years in H.M.F. reaching the rank of S/L., and is graded A(i) [Aii] by ISNB. No M.5 report as yet.

I grant, subject to favourable M.5 report.
Note:- (a) Service index. ✓
(b) Nominal index
& form N6YA to 88219 S/L. P. Stevens, M.C., (home address)

17 OCT 1946

Handley Page Hampden Mk I

1 De Havilland three bladed, constant speed propeller
2 Spinner
3 Bristol Pegasus XVII, 9 cylinder radial engine
4 Engine cooling air gills
5 Oil cooler intake
6 Flame suppression exhaust pipe
7 Engine bearer struts
8 Undercarriage retraction struts
9 Shock absorber undercarriage leg struts
10 Port mainwheel
11 Inboard fuel tank
12 Wing lattice ribs
13 Fabric covered flaps
14 Wing joint ribs
15 Landing and taxying lights
16 Slot guide ribs
17 Port leading edge slots
18 Port fabric covered aileron
19 Wingtip fairing
20 Port navigation light
21 Engine nacelle
22 Aerial mast
23 Oil tank
24 Dinghy stowage
25 Nacelle tail fairing
26 Wing outboard fuel tanks
27 Nose compartment glazing
28 Bomb aiming windows
29 Spare ammunition drums
30 Folding chart table

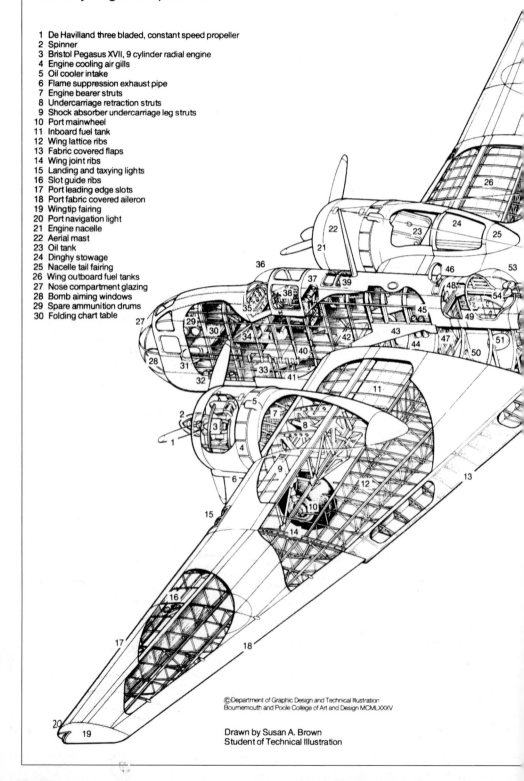

Drawn by Susan A. Brown
Student of Technical Illustration

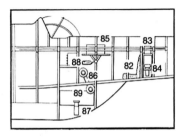

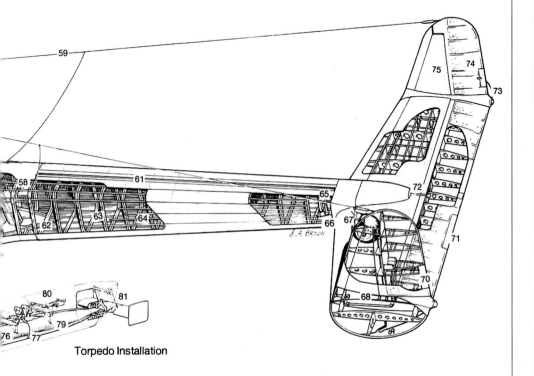

Torpedo Installation

31 Front gunners/bomb aimers seat	53 Upper gun hatch	75 Tail fin
32 Flame floats	54 Twin Vickers K-type machine guns	76 Adjusters
33 Parachute stowage	55 Radio equipment	77 Attachment cable and slip
34 Engine throttle and propeller controls	56 Twin Vickers K-type machine guns	78 Front crutch
35 Instrument panel	57 Flare chutes	79 Rear crutch
36 Windscreen panel	58 Radio control bench	80 Depth setting dial
37 Pilots seat	59 Aerial leading cables	81 Drum control attachment to air rudder
38 Control column handwheel	60 Fuselage skin plating	82 Operator's seat
39 Centre cabin roof hatch	61 Tail boom skin joint flange	83 Receiver
40 Access to lower deck level	62 Tail boom joint frame	84 Camera
41 Bomb stowage	63 Tail boom frame	85 Receiver and indicator
42 Wing spar carry through structure and seat	64 Stringer construction	86 Tailing aerial winch
43 Wing attachment joint plate	65 Tailplane control linkages	87 Flame float stowages
44 Lavatory	66 Retraction jack	88 Operator's dinghy stowage
45 Oxygen bottles	67 Tail wheel	89 Drum control gear
46 Retractable D/F loop aerial	68 Rudder control linkage	
47 Parachute stowage	69 Rudder mass balance	
48 Rear gunner's mirror	70 Rudder tab	
49 Controls	71 Elevator tabs	
50 Wing attachment ribs	72 Elevator hinge control	
51 Rear gunner's seat	73 Tail lights	
52 Trailing aerial winch	74 Fabric covered rudder	

Flight Lieutenant Peter Stevens at the command of an Anson, post-war (top). Peter Stevens' POW Identity card (bottom). (*Author's collection*)

| 1 | 2 | 3 | 4 | 5 | 6 | 7 | 8 | 9 | 10 | 11 | 12 | 13 | 14 | 15 | 16 | 17 | 18 | 19 | 20 | 21 | 22 | 23 | 24 | 25 |

Personalkarte I: Personelle Angaben   *Stevens*

Beschriftung der Erkennungsmarke

Nr. *3786*

Kriegsgefangenen-Stammlager: **Stalag Luft 3**   Lager: *Oflag X C*

Name: *STEVENS*

Vorname: *Peter*

Geburtstag und -ort: *13.4.17*

Religion: *C.O.E.*

Vorname des Vaters: *verweigert*

Familienname der Mutter:

Staatsangehörigkeit: *England*

Dienstgrad: ~~P/O~~ ~~F/O~~ *F/Lt*

Truppenteil: *R.A.F.* Kom. usw.:

Zivilberuf: *Reklameagent* Berufs-Gr.:

Matrikel Nr. (Stammrolle des Heimatstantes): *88219*

Gefangennahme (Ort und Datum): *Amsterdam 8.9.41*

Ob gesund, krank, verwundet eingeliefert: *gesund*

Lichtbild

Nähere Personalbeschreibung

Grösse	Haarfarbe
1,72	*d'blond*

Besondere Kennzeichen:

Fingerabdruck des rechten ! Zeigefingers

Name und Anschrift der zu benachrichtigenden Person in der Heimat des Kriegsgefangenen

Mutter der Braut:
55 Footseday Road
Elthean S.E.9

Des Kriegsgefangenen

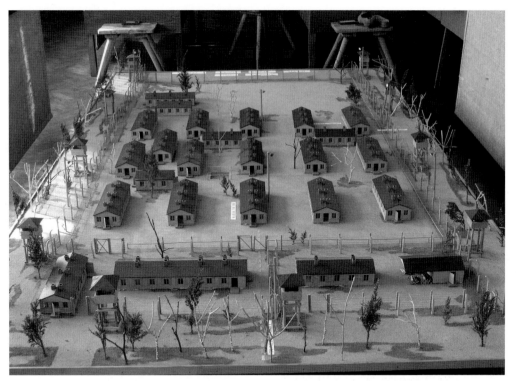

A model of North Compound, Stalag Luft 3, on display at the Stalag Luft 3 Museum, Zagan, Poland. Hut 104 is the centre building in the first row of five, and the path of Tunnel Harry lead from Hut 104 towards the front bottom of the photo. (*Author*)

Model of a typical 'Goon box' observation guard tower, Stalag Luft 3 Museum, Zagan, Poland. (Author)

An original caricature of Peter Stevens drawn by Tom Slack, found on the reverse of the 1944 Stalag Luft 3 Christmas Menu. (*Author's collection*)

1944 Stalag Luft 3 Christmas Menu, hand-drawn, probably by Tom Slack. The selection of dishes is undoubtedly more fantasy than reality. (*Author's collection*)

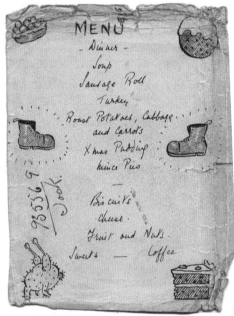

A hand-drawn caricature of Peter Stevens, by Tom Slack (Stevens' roommate and a very talented artist), Summer 1944. (*Author's collection*)

Squadron Leader Peter Stevens, wearing the ribbon denoting the Military Cross, 1946/47. (*Author's collection*)

Unnamed official of 401 Squadron (RCAF Reserve) and Peter Stevens presenting a 401 Squadron tankard to Douglas Bader during a 1950's visit by Bader to Montreal. (*Author's collection*)

Wedding of Squadron Leader Peter Stevens to Claire Lalonde, Montreal, 1953. (*Author's collection*)

Schloss Marquartstein, the Bavarian boarding school where 6-year-old Georg Hein was sent when his father died in 1926. (*Author*)

Author, Peter Stevens and Peter Stevens Jr., Ottawa, circa 1961. (*Author's collection*)

Wing Commander H.M.A. 'Wings' Day, one of the leaders of the Great Escape, taken by the author at Day's London home in 1967.
(*Author*)

Peter Stevens and Hermann Glemnitz arm-in-arm at the Stevens family home (Toronto, 1970), taken during the 25th reunion of the Ex-RCAF POW Association. Glemnitz had been the Chief Guard at Stalag Luft 3 and had played a key role in the Great Escape. He was invited to the reunion as a guest of the Association, and stayed in our home.
(*Author's collection*)

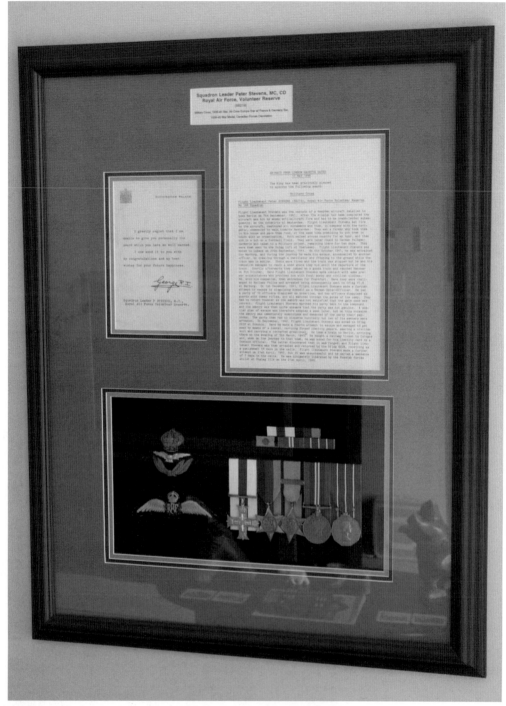

Medals awarded to Peter Stevens (Military Cross, 1939–1945 Star, Aircrew Europe Star with France and Germany Bar, 1939-1945 War Medal, Canadian Forces Decoration). (*Author*)

of Birmingham), for training on the twin-engined Airspeed Oxford aircraft. At this point, it was clear that the RAF had chosen him to fly bombers. Sadly, there would be no Spitfire in his future. The transition from a single-engine biplane to a twin-engine monoplane is not easy. Things happen much more quickly at higher airspeeds, and the many more and complex systems and controls require memorisation. As well, loss of the engine in a single-engine makes it a glider, and not much changes in the handling, but in a twin it will quickly turn the aircraft towards the side of the failed powerplant. Only immediate corrective action by the pilot can avert disaster.

The Airspeed Oxford was the simplest possible twin-engined aircraft and was a trainer. It had a pair of either Armstrong Siddeley Cheetah engines of 375 hp each or Pratt & Whitney Wasps, producing 450 hp each. Its maximum speed was 188 mph, and its service ceiling, 19,500 feet. It could carry just three people, but its bomb bay could hold up to twelve small practice bombs of twenty-five pounds each.[15]

Peter Stevens received five hours and twenty minutes of dual instruction on the Oxford before he obtained permission to fly solo on 24 August. He spent much of this practising forced and precautionary landings – a skill that he would need more than once.

Hitler had set 13 August as a deadline for his invasion – *Adler Tag* (Eagle Day). As it drew near, he asked his *Luftwaffe* commander about the necessary air superiority over the English Channel. Göring kept promising it but never delivered it. Hitler postponed the assault.

On August 20 Winston Churchill congratulated the RAF:

The gratitude of every home in our Island, in our Empire, and indeed throughout the world, except in the abodes of the guilty, goes out to the British airmen who, undaunted by odds, unwearied in their constant challenge and mortal danger, are turning the tide of the world war by their prowess and by their devotion. Never in the field of human conflict was so much owed by so many to so few.

All hearts go out to the fighter pilots, whose brilliant actions we see with our own eyes day after day; but we must never forget that all the time, night after night, month after month, our bomber squadrons travel far into Germany, find their targets in the darkness by the highest navigational skill, aim their attacks, often under the heaviest fire, often with serious loss, with deliberate careful discrimination, and inflict shattering blows upon the whole of the technical and war-making structure of the Nazi power. On no part of the Royal Air Force does the weight of the war fall more heavily than on the daylight bombers who will play an invaluable part in the case of invasion and whose unflinching zeal it has been necessary in the meanwhile on numerous occasions to restrain.[16]

Until late August, Hitler had refrained from bombing London. For some reason, that directive now changed. Some accounts suggest that the first bombs fell there through navigational error at night – easy to happen with the era's primitive navigational instruments.

In any case, the *Luftwaffe* now made London one of its primary targets, beginning the 'Blitz', whereby Germany hoped to undermine British morale. East London, with its dockyards and factories, was a good target, and the Germans started huge fires there almost every night. In reality, the strategy backfired: Germany had provoked the British bulldog, which was not in a mood to roll over and play dead.

The RAF retaliated in kind on the night of 25/6 August 1940, sending more than sixty bombers to Berlin. Because of bad weather, most of the bombs fell on farms and forests south of the capital, and the British lost several aircraft through fuel shortages on the long trip. The Germans joked that the RAF, by dropping bombs on farms, was trying to starve them out.[17] Yet the raid greatly embarrassed Göring, who had promised the Germans that if the RAF ever bombed Berlin they could call him 'Meyer' (a typically Jewish name).

RAF bombers were also flying regularly against closer targets as well. The Germans were gathering invasion barges at most French, Belgian, and Dutch ports, and RAF Bomber Command attacked these facilities at every available opportunity.

At the end of August, Peter Stevens had recorded eighty-two hours and forty minutes in his logbook, including almost forty hours solo – roughly the amount of time in the air for a typical successful candidate for a single-engine private pilot licence in Canada or Britain today.

During the first half of September 1940, the Germans greatly intensified their bombing raids, both by day and by night. Scores of Dornier and Heinkel bombers, along with *Stuka* dive-bombers and the ubiquitous Messerschmitt fighters, roamed the skies over England. The critical day of the Battle of Britain was 15 September. The *Luftwaffe* threw everything it had into the air over England. The RAF claimed to have destroyed 179 enemy aircraft, along with another forty-two probable 'kills'; it lost only twenty-five planes (with thirteen pilots missing or killed).[18]

The situation was becoming more and more difficult for the RAF, but it did not let that show, especially to the enemy. Göring now made a critical error: he reduced the number of raids on Fighter Command airfields. Aircraft losses had become almost crippling, but the RAF repaired battle- and bomb-damaged aircraft and put them back into service as quickly as possible.

During September, Stevens continued pilot training, still flying the Airspeed Oxford. He passed his fifteen-hour solo test on 3 September and a CFI (chief flying instructor) test on 6 September. More cross-country work led to night flying – crucial for a bomber pilot. On 19 September, Stevens was an observer for seven night landings and then completed three on his own.

On 25 September he had his cross-country instrument flying test – i.e. flying without reference to the horizon, or 'blind'. This is a very complicated skill, hard to master. Many pilots are unable to cope in instrument flying conditions (either in cloud or at night) and lose control of the aircraft. Certain instruments on the dashboard enable a pilot to maintain the plane's attitude; of course, aircraft instruments in 1940 were nothing like the computerised systems available today.

So, to a new pilot, passing the instrument flying test was a significant milestone. At the end of September, Stevens had a total of 123 hours in the air, of which fifty-seven were solo. In addition, he spent four hours and twenty-five minutes in the Link trainer between 29 August and 24 September.

After 12 October, Hitler ordered his invasion barges and troops to stand down. There would be no invasion of England in 1940. The Battle of Britain continued until the end of October, but at a reduced pace, and with the threat of invasion ended.

During October, Stevens continued his training on the Oxford, concentrating on cross-country and instrument flying. On 24 October, he passed another CFI test and an instrument flying test. He completed his work on Oxfords on 28 October, with 140 hours, including seventy-two solo. At this point, his piloting and instrument flying skills were again 'Average', but his air navigation skills were rated 'Above Average'. He had also used the Link trainer for five hours and thirty-five minutes.

On 31 October 1940, England, for the first time in months, dawned quietly. It took some time before the RAF realised that the skies overhead devoid of German aircraft signified that it had won the Battle of Britain.

Fighter Command had lost 915 planes, and 733 pilots had died or sustained wounds.[19] The RAF's website claims that, between 10 July and 31 October 1940, Fighter Command destroyed 2,378 enemy aircraft and counted 974 'probables'.[20] These numbers seem high, but even if one reduces the total by a third, Britain's victory was decisive.

And on 2 November 1940, the Royal Air Force Volunteer Reserve released Leading Aircraftman Peter Stevens, 900146, and immediately remustered him as probationary Pilot Officer Peter Stevens, 88219. That organisation had judged him capable of serving as an officer. To mark this sombre but proud occasion, Stevens arranged for a portrait of himself in his new officer's uniform. Undoubtedly the Officers' Mess celebrated a new member. But, anxious to avoid discovery, he remained reticent in social situations, fearful of drinking too much and showing his fluency in German or, far worse, his true identity. To have that discovered would have meant immediate arrest.

Also on 2 November, the RAF posted Pilot Officer Stevens to No. 2 School of Air Navigation at RAF Cranage, about twenty miles south-east of Liverpool. Between mid-November 1940 and 2 January 1941, he attended an advanced course in navigational skills. During this period, he flew only as a passenger in the Avro Anson, learning what he had to, while watching an experienced pilot accomplish the requisite tasks. An air navigator required such training, which involved Stevens acting as navigator for fourteen long-distance flights over England.

The Avro Anson looked ungainly. It was eight feet longer than the Airspeed Oxford and had a continuous row of windows along each side, with a round gun turret on top of the central fuselage. While it had engine pairings, power levels, and airspeed potential similar to the Oxford's, it was actually armed, and could undertake maritime reconnaissance in combat. The RAF acquired more than 11,000 models, and this very useful aircraft type served in the force until 1968.[21]

Meanwhile the Home Office had not forgotten about Georg Hein. On 27 December 1940, it received a tip! Mrs E.F. Bell lived at 7 Fairwood Court in east London (which was in the middle of enduring the Blitz), and she worked for Lake & Son, Hein's solicitors. She called the Home Office to report that the firm had received a Christmas card from Hein and that it had apparently come from someone in the RAF. The postmark was from Shrewsbury (not far from Cranage). Undoubtedly a patriot who thought she was helping the authorities apprehend a dangerous enemy alien fugitive, Bell mentioned that she was calling without her firm's knowledge and requested that the Home Office keep the information confidential.[22]

A report to the file stated:

> …exhaustive enquiries were made by the Shropshire Police in co-operation with Flight-Lieutenant Bruce, D.A.P.M., Royal Air Force. Officers Commanding RAF stations throughout the County were supplied with copy photographs of Hein but unfortunately, efforts to trace him have so far been unsuccessful.[23]

Stevens passed his air navigation course and on 4 January 1941, received a posting to No. 16 Operational Training Unit (OTU) at Upper Heyford, ten miles north of Oxford. An OTU exposed new pilots to their final training prior to their first combat operations. There are no flight entries in his logbook for the balance of January, so he must have spent that period either in the classroom or on leave.

In February 1941, Stevens did more air work in the Avro Anson, primarily in long-distance navigation. Finally, on 21 February, he flew a real combat aircraft. He received a one-hour demonstration flight in the Handley Page Hampden, a twin-engined medium bomber. Since the plane's fuselage is only thirty-six inches wide, there is no room for a co-pilot's seat. In practice, the student simply sat or stooped behind the pilot, looking over his shoulder.

As soon as this inaugural flight ended, Stevens took control of the Hampden and completed a ninety-minute solo flight, getting accustomed to handling the plane and practising take-offs and landings. Wing Commander W.J. ('Mike') Lewis, later a close friend of Stevens, considered the Hampden 'a good performer and a reliable aircraft ahead of its time':

> The Hampden was a gorgeous aircraft with two extremely reliable 980 hp Bristol Pegasus engines. The weight/power ratio was excellent, and it embodied features unique at the time. It may have been the first aircraft in the world to have slotted flaps and under-wing refuelling – even a retractable tail wheel.
>
> And the Hampden was a great aircraft to fly – the flaps and slats functioned beautifully. It had an H-control for the undercarriage and flaps. When the wheels were down you selected 'flaps down' and they would come down about 15 degrees. As you eased off the speed, the flaps lowered automatically until you got down to approach speed. Eventually they came down to about 30 degrees. Then you rounded out, touching the ground just before the stall – the slats came out, the flaps went to full down (45 degrees), the operation was fully automatic.[24]

But the Hampden's controls were complicated. As it was a single-pilot aircraft, that one pilot had to do everything, and its pilot notes showed no fewer than 111 items in the cockpit.

As Stevens began to accumulate time in the Hampden in February and March 1941, he began to love the aircraft as much as Lewis did. Even if it wasn't the Spitfire for which he had longed, it was a joy to fly. Quite fast for a bomber of the period, it could reach a maximum speed of 265 mph.[25] Although this velocity was unobtainable with a lot of weight on board, it approached fighter speeds. And on training flights it typically had a light load.

Pilot Officer Stevens used his OTU time well, learning how the plane handled in all sorts of configurations. With and without instructors, he practised cross-country and instrument flights. During the last half of March, he was navigator for seven practice bombing runs at Otmoor.

In a Hampden, the navigator didn't just navigate; he was also the bombardier and nose gunner. He sat in an odd-shaped Plexiglas-and-metal dome, below and forward of the pilot. Once over the target area, he removed the bombsight from its case and installed it in its mount, above an area of flat glass. In this way, the navigator/ bomb aimer could adjust the sight for airspeed, wind speed, and direction and altitude and obtain as accurate as possible a sighting on the target. Once he had lined up all the needles, he merely pressed the 'tit' on the bomb release, and away the device fell. In practice, it was a black art to place bombs anywhere near the target, so Stevens took these training runs seriously and did his best to learn the method.

A squadron leader of No. 16 OTU signed off Stevens's logbook on 30 March 1941. To that date, Stevens had had 196 hours and forty minutes in the air, including ninety-one hours and thirty minutes as pilot in command; he had had thirty minutes of night flying and six hours and fifty minutes of instrument time.

On 31 March, the commanding officer signed off Stevens's logbook. His ratings were 'Above Average' as pilot and navigator and 'Average' in bombing. Somebody had added: 'Worth earmarking as a First Pilot at an early date.'

Pilot Officer Peter Stevens was now officially combat-ready, and on 1 April 1941, the RAF posted him to 144 Squadron, Bomber Command.

Notes

1. National Archives, document HO 405 / 20069, Home Office Aliens file on Georg Franz Hein. Governor of HM Prison, Bristol, to the Home Office, 21 September 1939, confirms this. The government sealed this file until the year 2051, but the author of this book petitioned in November 2006 for its early opening, which was granted on 8 December 2006.
2. Amos Elon, *The Pity of It All: A Portrait of the German-Jewish Epoch 1743–1933* (New York: Picador, 2002), 143–4.
3. This is the description of Georg Hein's name change as he told it to his family. It explains the change from his actual birth date (15 February 1919) to the date on his RAF Record of Service (13 April 1917). 'Mike' Lewis later said that Peter Stevens had told him that he had taken the name from a former London co-worker in his fifties whom the authorities would never have conscripted. This account does not explain the birth date in the RAF records.
4. National Archives, document HO 405 / 20069, Home Office Alien file on Georg Franz Hein. Copy of draft letter from the Home Office to the German Jewish Aid Committee.
5. Ibid. Letter from the German Jewish Aid Committee to J.C. Grant of the Home Office.
6. National Archives, HO 405 / 20069, file on Georg Hein.
7. Dupuy and Dupuy, *The Harper Encyclopedia of Military History from 3500 B.C. to the Present*, 4th ed., 1,159–62.
8. Ibid., 1163.
9. David E. Fisher, *A Summer Bright and Terrible: Winston Churchill, Lord Dowding, Radar, and the Impossible Triumph of the Battle of Britain* (Emeryville, Calif.: Shoemaker & Hoard, 2005), 125.
10. Ibid., 117–24.
11. www.bartleby.com/73/2055.html
12. Bowyer, *The Encyclopedia of British Military Aircraft*, 107–8.
13. Adolf Galland, *The First and the Last: The Rise and Fall of the Luftwaffe 1939–1945* (New York: Henry Holt and Company, Inc., 1954), 18.
14. Fisher, *A Summer Bright and Terrible*, 201–3.
15. Bowyer, *The Encyclopedia of British Military Aircraft*, 92.
16. www.winstonchurchill.org/i4a/pages/index.cfm?pageid=420
17. Middlebrook and Everitt, *The Bomber Command War Diaries: An Operational Reference Book 1939−1945*, 76–7.

18. www.raf.mod.uk/bob1940/september15.html

19. Paul Brickhill, *Reach for the Sky: The Story of Douglas Bader* (London: Collins, 1954), 233.

20. www.raf.mod.uk/bob1940/calendar.html

21. Bowyer, *The Encyclopedia of British Military Aircraft*, 62. Peter Stevens was later to fly the Anson extensively in Germany after the war.

22. National Archives, HO 405 / 20069, file on Georg Hein, Home Office Memorandum of Enquiry, 27 December 1940.

23. Ibid., Report to the Chief Inspector, May 1941.

24. W.J. ('Mike') Lewis, 'Hampden Ops with 44 Squadron RAF' (Markham, Ont.: *Journal of the Canadian Aviation Historical Society*. 44, no. 4 (winter 2006), 124–8.

25. Moyle, *The Hampden File*, 12.

CHAPTER NINE

144 Squadron: Hemswell and North Luffenham (April–7 September 1941)

B efore reporting in April 1941 for duty with 144 Squadron at his new base at RAF Hemswell, Pilot Officer (P/O) Peter Stevens had an important errand in London. British military officers were traditionally required to buy their own uniforms. To that end, Stevens visited a top-quality bespoke tailor in Vigo Street, just off Savile Row, and picked up a new uniform that he had ordered previously. Above all, he wanted to make a good first impression at the squadron!

Unfortunately for Stevens, someone who knew that he was a wanted man spotted him there. That person visited Scotland Yard, which filed a report:

> On 2nd April, 1941 a Mr. Roy Escott, 4, Carew Road, Mitcham, an employee of Messrs. Colman, Prentis and Varley, Advertising Agents, 1, Old Burlington Street, W1, called at New Scotland Yard and stated that he had seen Hein in Vigo Street on 31st March, 1941, when he was wearing an R.A.F. uniform. Mr. Escott was unable to supply any further information but promised to speak to Hein if he saw him again and endeavour to find out where he was stationed. To date, Mr. Escott has not seen Hein.[1]

During the first half of 1941, the home of 144 Squadron of Bomber Command was RAF Hemswell, in the Midlands, about ten miles north of Lincoln. The base, as was typical during the war, housed more than one squadron – 61 Squadron also flew Hampdens. When he arrived there, P/O Stevens received directions to the officers' quarters, directly across the road from the base. He obtained a room and met his new batman.

144 Squadron did not have a high profile, but it did make a significant contribution to the war effort. It finished the war as the RAF squadron with the most Hampden operations and the most Hampden losses.[2]

In due course, Stevens met the squadron's commanding officer, Wing Commander G.S. Gardner, who welcomed him on board. Gardner inspired confidence and assured Stevens that he would do very well. He then instructed the adjutant to take Stevens over to the Officers' Mess and introduce him around. Stevens had already received assignment to a bomber crew as navigator on one of the Hampdens.

Because of the Hampden's unusual design and layout, the RAF decided on an unusual crewing system. There was room for only one pilot's seat, but what would happen if anything incapacitated the pilot? Senior officers felt that an uninjured crew's going down in an aircraft with an unconscious or dead pilot would harm morale. A Hampden bomber had a crew of four: the pilot, the navigator (in the nose of the plane, below and forward of the pilot), a wireless operator/air gunner (rear upper), and an air gunner (rear lower).

Since the navigator had to know a fair bit about flying, and since the pilot also had to be able to navigate, senior officers decided that all Hampden navigators should also be fully qualified pilots. Thus pilots new to combat could enter the world of operations in stages, which eased the transition to real war. In the event of the pilot's incapacitation, the navigator could take control of the plane. In theory.

With the Hampden's design, a man could move from the plane's nose up to the pilot's position only by crawling through a narrow tunnel up and under the pilot's seat, surfacing just behind the pilot. The navigator could then lower the pilot's seatback, pull out the injured man, climb into the seat, raise the seatback and strap himself in, and take over flying duties. Nobody asked how all of this could happen while the aircraft was in a high-speed vertical dive. In practice, it was virtually impossible. But at least the possibility existed, and that was good enough to satisfy the crews.

Stevens took his place in his crew, along with a new rear lower air gunner. The system for pilots also applied to air gunners. So, as new pilots and air gunners arrived at a Hampden squadron, they would join a new crew with an experienced pilot and wireless operator/air gunner. Thus each crew consisted of two experienced men and two rookies. A tour of duty in Bomber Command consisted of thirty combat operations, and for the first ten the men would be rookies in a new crew. After about ten ops, they would form a new crew of their own with fresh replacements, and they themselves would become the 'old boys'. In this way, the navigator would become first pilot after ten missions.

Stevens didn't have much of a chance to settle in before going on operations. On 3 April 1941, his baptism came. He had already met his new crew but had not had much time to get to know them. His aircraft commander and pilot was P/O Roake, with Sgts Daniels and James as air gunners. Their bomb load consisted of a single 1,500-pound magnetic sea mine. The target was the harbour at the French port of Brest.

Laying a mine at sea or in a harbour was a regular event for Hampdens. In practice, the action had the nickname 'gardening', and each target area earned a code name, usually the name of a vegetable, flower, or animal. Brest was well defended, with a good deal of flak (anti-aircraft artillery fire) as standard. It was a major U-boat base and the refuge of two German battleships, the *Scharnhorst* and the *Gneisenau*.

The post-op debrief to the squadron intelligence officer at Hemswell on 4 April (presumably by telephone) reported that the Hampden had taken off at 7.29 p.m. and, thanks to visible moonlight, they had been able to:

> ...plant our vegetable in the correct position from 500 feet at A.S.I. [air speed indicated] 155 [miles per hour]. We had no wing bombs, as it was our first trip. We were held by single searchlights for short periods, and had some tracer fired at us...The flare path at St. Eval (Cornwall) was laid out downwind, we made four attempts to land before touching down, at our fifth attempt, early enough to pull up in time. Two other aircraft overshot.[3]

The aircraft landed at 12.33 a.m. The 'Duty' column records the operation as 'Gardening – Jellyfish Area' but gives no reason for its diversion to a different airfield on its return to England.

Stevens recorded this operation, like all other combat ops, in his logbook in red ink. All others were in dark blue or black, but clearly combat was special. We know nothing about how Stevens responded to his first taste of combat. Such initiation was a rude awakening for many men, who had envisioned combat as much more glorious than it turned out to be.

After a safe return from an op, a wonderful meal awaited crewmembers who still had an appetite. In the middle of the night, the fully decked-out Mess awaited the conquering heroes. The kitchen staff was wide awake, proud to serve whatever the returning warriors wanted, despite strict rationing of food in Britain during and after the war. As many eggs as one cared to eat were on offer. For civilians, the variety and quantity of food would have evoked memories of a pre-war Christmas. And yet no one complained; these men had *earned* it.

Most airmen would return to base completely 'wired' – exhausted but unable to sleep because of all the adrenaline coursing through their veins. It was often daylight before anyone was able to nod off.

Usually, a crew that landed at an airfield other than their own returned to base the next day (assuming their aircraft was still safe to fly). Stevens's logbook, however, shows that he flew on 4 April from St Eval to Boscombe Down (home of the Ministry of Defence's aircraft test facility) and on 5 April from there to Upper Heyford. On 6 April, Stevens was a passenger (along with Sgt Douglas Wark) on another Hampden flying from Lindholme to Hemswell.

On 7 April, Stevens (along with Roake, James, and a Sgt Dorman) took part in his first 'real' bombing operation aboard Hampden AD 846. The same crew carried bombs instead of a sea mine, and this was his first trip to bomb his home country, Germany. At 8.06 p.m., the aircraft took off for the port and U-boat base of Kiel on the north coast of Germany, carrying two 500-pound bombs plus two small bomb containers (SBCs) holding a larger number of small bomblets such as twenty or forty pounders. The Operations Record Book (ORB) for 144 Squadron reported:

> Set course from BASE at 20.11 hrs, and flew at 1500 feet below the cloud base and crossed the ENGLISH COAST on track. Shortly after, we saw a gap in the clouds and climbed through, steadily climbing to 11,000 feet. After flying for about an hour we were completely clear of any clouds, above and below us. We crossed the enemy COAST on track and E.T.A. We arrived in the target area at 23.15 hours and immediately started our run up from south to north. After the bombs had been dropped the rear gunner saw one bomb burst in the target area. When we arrived over KIEL we saw one large fire situated in the target area, which appeared to be a long row of warehouses burning furiously, the roofs and walls of which were seen to collapse. Five other fires were seen in the dock area, north, south and west of the target. The Flak was concentrated and appeared to be shooting mainly at flares. The searchlights were very intense and operated mainly singly. We left the target area at 20.23 hours [sic] and set course for home, and at a point 54°09′N. 09°30′E. a large concentration of searchlights were operating in groups of eight and ten, there was no Flak, but an aircraft was seen about 200 feet below us, flying in the opposite direction, and was identified as a twin-engined aircraft. We crossed the ENGLISH COAST at SKEGNESS and landed at BASE at 03.05 hours.[4]

This raid was quite large and a major success, as it included 229 bombers and lost only four of them. It lasted five hours (i.e., there were planes over the target bombing for five continuous hours) and inflicted significant damage at naval and industrial zones. Two yards building U-boats – Deutsche Werke and Germania Werft – closed during the attack and were out of commission for several days. A fire in the naval ammunition dump took two full days to burn itself out.[5]

The crew of Hampden AD 846 had been in the air for seven hours and ten minutes, according to Stevens's logbook. How did it feel to Stevens to drop bombs on his own country for the first time?

Crews rarely flew combat missions on consecutive nights, but it did happen occasionally. On 8 April, Roake, Stevens, Daniels, and James went back to Brest for more 'gardening'. A German flak ship fired on them as they crossed the English Channel, but they completed the mission without further incident, landing back at Hemswell after six hours airborne.

Since he wasn't piloting the combat trips, Stevens kept current by flying local trips of an hour or two whenever possible. He volunteered or was detailed to go and obtain replacement aircraft and return them to Hemswell.

Another operation on 10 April targeted Düsseldorf, in what the crew called 'Happy Valley', the heavily defended Ruhr River valley: industrial centre of the Third *Reich*. The bomb load comprised one 1,900-pound bomb plus two 250-pounders. Crewmembers reported no trouble finding the target, as it was on the Rhine River. They dropped their bombs from an altitude of 11,000 feet, but all three exploded short of the target. Anti-aircraft artillery fire was 'intense and very accurate', and there was more flak at Rotterdam on the return trip, but the Hampden landed safely at RAF Coningsby after five hours in the air.[6] Its crew was lucky: five of the twenty-nine Hampdens attacking that target did not return.[7]

For the next week or so, 12–21 April, Stevens saw no combat duty but made fourteen Hampden flights (twelve as pilot), again to remain current. Practice was always welcome, both as a diversion from the stress of combat and to keep one's navigational and piloting skills sharp.

On nights when there was no mission to fly, most officers spent the evening in the Mess, having a few pints, singing around the piano, or telling stories. Stevens had already come to realise that men who were there when he arrived three weeks earlier had gone missing. And so, even with the singing, the mood was not exactly joyful. Occasionally there would be a movie or a trip to the local pub in the nearby village. Some men drank too much; others didn't.

It wasn't until 23 April that Roake, Stevens, and James, along with a Sgt Woolnough, went back to Brest, but this time carrying a load of real bombs, not a mine. With four 500-pounders in the bomb bay and one 250-pounder under each wing, they set course for France. They dropped the high explosives in the target area and saw all six devices explode, but no fires were burning when they departed.[8]

The same crew carried a sea mine to Aalborg, Denmark, on the night of 25 April. The town, near the northern tip of the Jutland peninsula, required a long return flight over the North Sea. Fortunately, the crew encountered no flak; the trip took seven hours and twenty minutes and was relatively uneventful – unusual for combat operations!

Another 'gardening' expedition set out from Hemswell on 3 May 1941, but this time with a new crew. The pilot was Flight Lieutenant Rawlins, with Stevens as navigator and Sgt Taylor and P/O Vaughan as air gunners. The target was Borkum ('Nectarine' area), one of the Frisian Islands in the North Sea belonging to Germany, near where Stevens had spent his last years at boarding school. It took the crew some time to pinpoint the target area, during which one or more German flak ships engaged the crew. After laying the mine, the airmen returned to base.[9]

Two days later, Stevens flew as navigator for Sgt Gibson, with Sgts Adam and Dorman as air gunners. The target was Mannheim, about fifty miles south of Frankfurt. The bomb load consisted of one 1,000-pounder in the central bomb bay and one 500-pounder under each wing. Leaving base at 10.15 p.m., the crew flew eastwards on course for Germany. Out over the North Sea, it was standard procedure to test the bomb doors and the bomb fusing.

This test led to major problems. The bomb bay doors would not open electrically, and so the crew manually opened and re-closed them using hydraulics and hand pumps. At every attempt, the aircraft's electrical system refused to operate properly. The pilot decided to jettison the wing bombs and drop the 1,000-pounder on the nearby Belgian port city of Ostend, but, despite every action, the bombs would not leave the plane. It was highly dangerous to return to base with bombs on board, but in this case there was no choice. Many times during the Second World War, aircraft landing at base with bombs still on board had them fall off the plane as they touched down, blowing up the aircraft. Fortunately, this time the Hampden made a very nervous but safe landing at Hemswell at 1.30 a.m. An examination showed an electrical fault in the bomb arming system.[10]

This marked Peter Stevens's eighth and final operation as navigator. His combat flight time on those missions amounted to forty-five hours and thirty-five minutes. It was time for him to move up to aircraft commander and to form his own crew. He had a grand total of 127 hours as pilot-in-command.

To become a combat pilot, however, one had to pass certain tests. Between 10 May and 13 June, Stevens was at No. 14 OTU to upgrade himself to first pilot. He flew eleven trips in the old Anson, plus another twenty-two in the Hampden, practising various skills to regain his piloting proficiency. While retraining, he flew no combat ops. On 14 June 1941, the commanding officer signed off his logbook; his piloting skills were 'Above the Average'. P/O Stevens was ready to form his own crew and to command an aircraft into combat.

On 17 June, P/O George Girardet became Stevens's navigator, and Sgts Daniels and Crowe his air gunners. Stevens and Daniels were now the 'old boys', and presumably Girardet and Crowe were the rookies. The target for that night was Wangerooge, another Frisian island, about twenty miles north of the port of Wilhelmshaven. The mission was to lay a magnetic mine in German shipping lanes, and the return trip took six hours.

Three days later, Stevens again flew with George Girardet as his navigator but took Sgts Dorman and Wark as air gunners. The target was Cologne, another major centre across the heavily defended Ruhr River region (Happy Valley). The crew took off at 11.23 p.m. The plane was climbing through 8,000 feet near the English coast when the lower rear air gunner announced over the intercom that his hatch cover had blown open and he was unable to close it! Stevens realised that the five-hour flight over water and enemy territory would be very dangerous and decided to land and repair the hatch. He announced to the crew that he would land at the nearest airfield, RAF Mildenhall, for immediate repairs before continuing the operation. During the landing at 12.45 a.m., the hatch fell off completely and destroyed an important navigational antenna on the fuselage. The mission ended there and then.[11]

Some unexpected and surprisingly good news arrived. On 22 June, Hitler abrogated his alliance with Stalin and, under the guise of Operation *Barbarossa*, attacked the Soviet Union. While this had no direct bearing on the British, it did allow them a significant bit of breathing space. Hitler, planning to occupy all of Europe, made the same mistake as Napoleon – invading Russia. During the first month of the campaign, German storm troopers made impressive progress; for the first six or seven months, the Germans were almost unstoppable. But they were attacking the Soviet Union on a front 2,000 miles long! It would eventually become impossible for the *Wehrmacht* to maintain such a pace, and then to properly supply such a lengthy front.

On 23 June, Stevens, Girardet, Wark, and Dorman took off at 11.12 p.m., carrying four 500-pounders, bound once more for Düsseldorf. Their target was the railway marshalling yards. They crossed the Dutch coast at 10,000 feet and headed for the target. Once again, anti-aircraft fire was very heavy. Because of heavy haze, the crew could not pinpoint the plane's exact position, and Stevens dropped his bombs into 'intense A.A. [anti-aircraft fire] and searchlights'. To be as accurate as possible, he had flown around the target area for twenty-five minutes, attracting continuous flak. The Hampden made it safely back to base at 4.18 a.m., and once on the ground, the crew discovered shrapnel damage to the port flap.[12]

The four men did not fly during the next week, although other squadron members did. But on 2 July they took off from RAF Coningsby for Duisburg, smack in the middle of 'Happy Valley'. Their bomb load consisted of two 500-pounders plus two SBCs. Fortunately, their trip was relatively uneventful, and, despite their attack on a heavily fortified target, they reported no altercations.[13] Only eighteen of the thirty-nine Hampdens that went to Duisburg that night reported dropping their bombs in the target area.[14]

Three days later, on 5 July, a new man joined the crew. Sgt John 'Math' Matthews, quiet but intelligent, took Dorman's place as lower rear air gunner. The target was Osnabrück, about eighty miles west of Hanover and only some fifty miles across the Dutch border. Stevens took off at 11.15 p.m. and proceeded to the target area unimpeded. Once again, the railway marshalling yards were difficult to pick out in the darkness. The crew dropped its bombs and later commented on the poor defences.[15] This mission involved thirty-nine Hampdens, and three did not return.[16]

Next, Stevens reported to No. 7 BATF (beam approach training flight) for instruction in the new 'Lorenz' radio navigational system – a forerunner of the instrument landing system (ILS) in use today – which allowed for more accurate approaches during low visibility. Stevens spent ten hours from 8–12 July learning the system on an Airspeed Oxford training aircraft, plus seven in the Link trainer.

On 14 July, Stevens led an operation that included air gunners Wark and Matthews and a new navigator, Sgt Hemmings. Their target was the only one that Stevens really feared, his hometown: Hanover. The aiming point was the main railway station near the city centre, quite close to his boyhood home. Thoughts of his mother and his aunts, uncles, and cousins must have flooded into his mind. But he could not bring himself to avoid the mission. He flew a warplane that carried 2,400 pounds of high explosives to the town where, as far as he knew, his mother still lived.

They took off at 10.34 p.m. and flew mostly over the North Sea, turning south and crossing the enemy coast near Borkum. The Hampden passed through belts of searchlights, and several flak batteries targeted it. It dropped its bombs slightly north of the aiming point, and the men spotted a huge fire when their 1,900-pounder hit the ground. They saw many other fires as they departed, and they returned to England via the same route. When the plane neared home, the pilot's attention focused on the weather. There was significant low cloud over most of south-central England, and he decided to stay to the north, where skies were clear. He landed at RAF Driffield, just ten miles from the North Sea, about sixty miles north of what was about to become No. 144 Squadron's new base.[17] Stevens shut down the engines and made sure that his crewmen were all right. But how was he?

In mid-July 1941, both 144 and 61 Squadrons transferred from Hemswell south to RAF North Luffenham. This was a new base (it had originally opened as a training field in 1940) about seventy miles straight north of London, close to Peterborough and Leicester. In practical terms, the move did not significantly change how 144 Squadron went about its business.

North Luffenham was a typical RAF base, with one- and two-storey dark brown brick buildings. The closest village was Edith Weston, almost outside the front gates, but 'RAF Edith Weston' might have sounded odd. The village's pub, The Wheatsheaf, became the pilots' local.

Throughout the summer of 1941, the Home Office and the Metropolitan Police continued to hunt for Georg Hein. On 17 July, the RAF Record Office reported to the Home Office that it had consulted the commanding officers of No. 27 Maintenance Unit at RAF Shawbury and No. 11 Flying Training School at RAF Shrewsbury. It stated, 'replies have been received from both units to the effect that they have no trace of the person concerned having served as an airman or a civilian'.[18]

On 19 July, Stevens, Hemmings, Wark, and Matthews learned that their target that night would again be Wangerooge, on a 'gardening' mission to the 'Yam' area. In addition to their magnetic mine, they carried two 250-pound under-wing bombs. They took off at 11.05 p.m. and followed the specified route. They arrived at 1.33 a.m. and dropped their mine from 600 feet. In the target area, light guns fired on them. After laying the mine, Stevens climbed to 2,000 feet, from which altitude he dropped his bombs on a searchlight emplacement near the German seaplane base at Norderney. After a long over-water flight home, the Hampden crossed the English coast a full seventy miles north of its planned track, indicating higher-than-expected winds from the south. It landed back at North Luffenham at 5.15 a.m., an hour and ten minutes after sunrise.[19]

For their next operation, 22 July, their old navigator, P/O George Girardet, rejoined Stevens, Wark, and Matthews. Girardet, something of a playboy, was dating a famous American actress who had taken the English stage and cinema by storm, Frances Day. George often showed up back at North Luffenham driving her large Rolls-Royce touring car.

Douglas Wark was more of a musician than a fighter. A talented professional trumpeter, he played with both the London Symphony Orchestra and the London Philharmonic but saw war service as 'the right thing to do'. John Matthews was the quiet, intellectual type. He and Wark roomed together in the Sergeants' Mess. Both were qualified radio operators, but the senior Wark had the official duty – and the upper rear gunner's position, much roomier than that in the 'Tin', immediately below his feet.

The target for this operation was difficult: Frankfurt. One had to fly over 'Happy Valley' (or travel a great distance to bypass it) to reach Germany's second city. The bomb load that night was a single 1,000-pounder plus two 500- pounders. Stevens and his men took off from Stamford at 10.47 p.m. and reached the target without incident, within five minutes of the planned time. Gliding in over the city, they attracted a great deal of attention from a number of searchlights, but no flak. George Girardet dropped the bombs from 7,000 feet, and the crew witnessed several fires around the city.

On the return trip, the plane encountered dangerous thunderstorms at 13,000 feet. As it flew through the cloud tops at that altitude, the Hampden's wings accumulated quite a bit of ice, which can bring down a plane. The ice added a great deal of weight to the now-much-lighter aircraft. But Stevens worried about the ice's degradation of lift as it formed on the leading edge of the wings and altered their shape. This might be enough to cause the plane to stall and crash. Also, ice on the propeller blades would greatly reduce their efficiency, leaving less power to convert into airspeed. The obvious solution was to move away from the clouds as quickly as possible and to descend into warmer air, where the ice would melt. This was the textbook solution, and it is exactly what Stevens did. The Hampden landed back at North Luffenham at 6.07 a.m.[20] Amazingly, all sixty-three aircraft detailed to bomb Frankfurt that night returned safely.[21]

On 27 and 29 July, Stevens went on night flying tests (NFTs) with Douglas Wark but flew no operations. Another NFT on 30 July *did* result in a mission. The target that night was Cologne, another large and well-defended city, famous for its huge gothic cathedral. Again, the Hampden carried a 1,000-pound bomb, plus two under-wing 500-pounders. Stevens and his crew took off at 11.30 p.m. and climbed through cloud and bad weather as they headed south-east. The Hampden reached the target and dropped the bombs from 7,000 feet at 2.24 a.m. On the return flight, crewmen observed large fires in the border town of Aachen.

Once again, severe thunderstorms hit hard over western Belgium and the English Channel, producing a great deal of lightning and the always-dangerous icing. Stevens tried to climb to escape the storm but at 16,000 feet found himself still in the middle of it. Discretion being the better part of valour, he decided to descend instead and finally left the clouds at 4,000 feet. The weather back at base was extremely bad, so Stevens landed at Wyton instead, albeit with a hung-up 500-pounder still on his port wing! The men had tried to jettison it twice, but it simply would not budge. Luckily, it stayed in place as the plane touched down and rolled out on the landing field at 6 a.m.

At 10.34 on the evening of 6 August 1941, the now 'official' crew of Stevens, Girardet, Wark, and Matthews took off from North Luffenham. On this operation, they flew Hampden AE 122, code-marked 'PL-W'. Their target was the railway workshops at Karlsruhe, in south-western Germany about eighty miles south of Frankfurt, and the bomb load consisted of one 1,000-pounder and two 500-pounders – just half of the Hampden's maximum. Total flying time for their roughly 900-mile trip would be over seven hours, and they could expect heavy flak en route, especially over the target.

The Hampden's range while carrying 4,000 pounds of bombs was 870 miles, so Karlsruhe was near the extreme edge of its range. Bomber Command detailed thirty-eight Hampdens for that target.

On the first part of the operation, the aircraft experienced severe icing in cumulonimbus (thunder) clouds at 8,000 feet. Climbing above the clouds to 12,000 feet, it was able to avoid the icing and continued on course at that altitude.

In the general target area, the cloud cover was 9/10 (i.e. 90 per cent of the sky was obscured), with tops at 10,000 feet. Gliding through the clouds to pinpoint their position, the Hampden broke out into the clear at 8,000 feet. After identifying the Rhine River and various canals, they dropped their bombs 'in the target area' from 7,000 feet on a compass heading of 310 degrees at 2 a.m. Flak over the target was indeed heavy. Searchlights caught the bomber, and one or two pieces of shell hit it, but it was able to leave the area safely.

Flying back above the clouds, the Hampden had just crossed the Moselle River near Namur, Belgium, when searchlight cones caught it again. The lights held it for a few seconds and then went out, indicating that they were working in concert with German night fighters. Sure enough, one of the air gunners in the rear of the fuselage soon reported a fighter approaching at a range of about four hundred yards on the starboard quarter. German pilots knew that the Hampden was not well armed and was particularly vulnerable to attacks from abeam and from below. Stevens immediately threw the aircraft into a steep corkscrew-diving manoeuvre to the same side, and the German Ju 88 opened fire. After the Hampden had pulled out of the dive, the Ju 88 pulled alongside on its port beam, then crossed above it to begin another attack from the starboard quarter. As Stevens again used the evasive corkscrew, the Ju 88 approached from below and latched onto its tail. Firing a cannon burst, the German pilot put about fifty holes in PL-W and injured all three non-flying crewmen. There was damage to the radio receiver, the intercom, the TR 9, the IFF (Identification – Friend or Foe), and the hydraulic system and the pressurised air bottle that backed it up. The attack also hit the rudders and tailplane, as well as the starboard engine and fuel tanks.

At first, the Hampden's rear guns froze, but as the Germans approached to a range of 100 yards the guns miraculously came to life. In the midst of a steep dive, the injured Wark reached up and grabbed his gun trigger, firing a short burst, which hit home. The Ju 88 exploded into flames and fell to earth in burning pieces.

After further evasive action, Stevens levelled the aircraft at low altitude and set a course for England. As the intercom was now out of service, and he was forced to stay in his seat and fly the plane, he was unable to witness the damage, both human and mechanical. One of the rear gunners jettisoned a burning ammunition tin, and Matthews put out a small fire in the rear of the fuselage using the coffee from Wark's thermos!

The human toll was even worse than the damage to the aircraft. Flying shrapnel had injured both rear gunners, who each bandaged their own wounds. John Matthews took hits in both face and thigh and had lost his right earphone completely. Douglas Wark had received two bullet wounds to the thigh, and he told Matthews to bale out of the stricken aircraft. Matthews was unable to don his parachute, however, because one German bullet had knocked the buckle off the harness. Girardet, however, was much worse off. 'Math' Matthews came forward through the tunnel under the pilot's seat to check on him and found blood spattered all over the aircraft's nose. Girardet had taken a German 20-mm cannon shell through his thigh and was bleeding profusely. The rear gunner immediately applied a tourniquet high up on Girardet's leg, at least slowing the bleeding somewhat. It was clear, however, that the navigator was in great pain and needed urgent medical attention, and someone apparently thought briefly of dropping him from the plane and opening his parachute for him on the way out. When it became clear that the aircraft remained airworthy, and that the flow of blood had been staunched somewhat, this idea was discarded.

Using dead reckoning to head for home (i.e. navigating without reference to instruments other than a compass and airspeed indicator), Stevens quickly realised that the most direct course would take them close to the Thames estuary. He had no IFF or radio for communications, and the British would probably shoot first and ask questions later. Despite flying slowly with a damaged starboard engine, he made a difficult decision. He would turn northwards over the North Sea and stay well clear of the Thames before heading westwards to cross the English coast. Though adding perhaps fifteen to thirty minutes to the journey, Stevens reckoned that the additional time might just save all their lives. He finally headed north for a full hour before turning inland.

Wark managed to repair the radio transmitter and began sending the SOS signal. Rather than heading for North Luffenham, Stevens decided to land at the nearest airfield. Approaching RAF Coningsby (home today to the Battle of Britain Memorial Flight), Wark was unable to raise anyone on the radio to warn of PL-W's impending arrival. At this point, Stevens learned for certain the rest of the damage: no flaps and no undercarriage.

In preparation for what could easily be a very dangerous and difficult manoeuvre, 'Math' Matthews muscled the near-dead Girardet's heavy form rearward through the access tunnel and up onto the 'D' spar of the main wing. This spot, just behind the pilot, was the safest place to endure the coming crash.

And so Stevens used the plane to practise his first belly landing by the early light of dawn. After a mission that lasted almost seven-and-a-half hours, the fuel tanks were just about dry, so the risk of fire was minimal. As the badly damaged aircraft came to a quiet rest back on English soil, an amazed Stevens took stock of his injured crew and waited for the ambulances. The pilot and Wark climbed out through the fuselage's top hatches, and standing on the port wing, helped Matthews get Girardet out of the stricken plane.

Coningsby had not been expecting any arrivals so early – at 5.50 a.m. – and virtually the entire base was asleep. After five minutes, a very angry Stevens ran off to find medical assistance. He finally located some ground crew members with a truck, which he commandeered to act as a makeshift ambulance and pick up his crew.[22]

Each of the two wounded air gunners was in hospital for more than a month before discharge back to active service, and both survived the war. On Stevens's recommendation, Wark received the Distinguished Flying Medal for his decisive action in shooting down the Ju 88 and repairing the radio. Girardet nearly died from blood loss but spent about six months in hospital and also survived the war.

Shortly afterwards, Stevens received a letter dated 23 August:

My son, John Matthews has expressed such admiration for you in his letters, for the masterly way you brought your 'plane and crew back safely from Ops on the night of the 6th Aug., that I feel I must congratulate you on a great performance.

After such an eventful trip to land without an undercarriage was really wonderful.

John says it is entirely due to you that he is still here. My wife and I warmly thank you.

Wishing you the best of luck always, I am

Sincerely,
J.W. Matthews

Peter Stevens wrote back on 26 August:

> In reply I can only say how proud I was to have John in my crew and I am looking forward to flying with him again when he returns from his sick-leave. Fortunately his injuries were not of a very serious nature and he was able to render some most valuable assistance without which I think our return would have been very doubtful.

Matthews later took part in another very dangerous mission. As the Hampden's strategic usefulness declined (and losses rose), top British officials decided to 'give' a number of them to their new ally, the Soviet Union. In September/October 1942, they dispatched two squadrons of Hampdens, converted to torpedo-bombers, to the north Russian port of Murmansk. The aircraft took off from northern Scotland to fly 1,000 miles, at the very extreme limit of their potential. Soviet authorities learned late about the arrival date and fired at many of the aircraft as they flew in. Several Hampdens ran out of fuel and crashed, and Soviet forces shot down a number, with great loss of life. Six of the destroyed planes were from 144 Squadron.[23] Matthews survived the expedition and spent a very cold time on board a ship back to the United Kingdom.

Wark had had to leave his experienced crew and join a new 'sprog' (rookie) crew with Stevens and Matthews; he later said that he had been quite apprehensive. He had already survived a good number of operations and didn't appreciate having to break in a new crew. He bonded fairly quickly with Matthews but wrote that Stevens 'was a rather reserved man – perhaps shy'.[24] After he had recuperated from the events of 6–7 August, the RAF offered him a commission, but he refused. As he later explained, he didn't want to be responsible for the life of anyone else. He was offered his choice of postings and heard about a course up in Scotland, quite close to St Andrews. He applied for a spot there and spent almost six months in Scotland, honing his golf game!

Characteristically, Stevens in his logbook noted simply about the harrowing events of 6–7 August: 'Crashed on return at Coningsby.' Nothing more.

And while he had been flying a badly damaged aircraft back to England, British authorities continued their manhunt for Georg Hein. On 22 August, Scotland Yard wrote to the Home Office: 'He is still circulated as wanted … and enquiries are still proceeding in an endeavour to trace his alleged enlistment in the Royal Air Force.'[25]

As a result of the events of 6–7 August, Stevens received a two-week break from operational flying. He had proven himself under fire and was almost two-thirds through his first tour of duty (thirty operations). While it was not usual for airmen to receive such a reward, Stevens welcomed it. It undoubtedly took him at least a week just to calm down and for his legs to stop shaking.

It was clear that he would require a new crew, and its members were to be Sgt Alan Payne (navigator) and Sgts Ivor Roderick Fraser and H. Thompson (air gunners). Oddly, while Payne had begun pilot training, he had been unable to complete it and was therefore *not* a qualified pilot. Apparently the RAF had tacitly stopped putting two pilots in each Hampden.

The new crew flew its first operation together on 25 August. The target was the main post office in Mannheim, halfway between Frankfurt and Karlsruhe. The Hampden carried one 1,000-pound explosive device in the bomb bay and two 500-pounders under the wings. It took off from North Luffenham at 8.15 p.m., extremely early for that time of year. Stevens later reported to the squadron intelligence officer that it was light enough when they crossed the enemy coastline that German fighters and flak batteries would have had no trouble at all seeing them. Fortunately, there were none of either in the vicinity. Crossing Belgium, Stevens again encountered bad weather and attempted to climb above it but found the aircraft so heavy that he could not. His oil pressure dropped to 45 PSI, and the cylinder-head temperature rose to 105°C. Not wanting to lose any more engine performance, he ordered Payne to release the two 500-pounders. The Hampden was then able to climb again, and the starboard engine parameters returned to normal.

Because of cloud cover over the target area, one crewman dropped a flare, which illuminated the city centre. The crew dropped the 1,000-pounder, and one member reported having seen a dummy fire to the south-west of the town. The Germans often set these as decoys, far from the true target area, hoping that the bombers would attack them. In this case, Payne had realised the ruse and dropped the bomb on target. Severe weather impeded the trip home, but the aircraft returned to base at 3.15 a.m.[26] Three Hampdens out of thirty-eight on the trip did not return.[27]

Two days later, on 27 August, the crew was to bomb Mannheim a second time, but this time their target was the railway station. The bomb load was four 500-pounders and two SBCs. On the outward leg, again over Belgium, Stevens was unable to climb higher than 9,500 feet, still low enough to be within flak range. He again ordered Payne to drop the two wing bombs unfused, so that they would not explode on a civilian target. Despite this lessening of weight, engine performance continued to deteriorate, and Stevens informed the navigator that they would attack a 'last resort', or target of opportunity. The closest German town was Trier, where the plane dropped the rest of the bombs. The crew reported the results as 'extremely gratifying' – two large fires, which soon merged into one huge conflagration. The men saw five very large explosions, and many smaller ones, as they departed the target area. Finally, with the aircraft's operating weight way down, the engines began acting normally. Bad weather over the English Channel blew the Hampden off course, but the plane landed safely at Bircham Newton at 4.15 a.m.[28]

It was a very busy week for Stevens and his crew: two days later, on 29 August, they set course for Frankfurt at 9.50 p.m. Carrying a single 1,900-pounder in the bay and one 250-pounder under each wing, they identified the target, dropped their munitions and returned to base safely at 5.10 a.m.[29]

The crew received orders to bomb Cologne on the night of 1 September. This time, the Hampden carried one 1,000-pounder plus two 250-pounders under the wings. Take-off occurred at 8.15 p.m. The crew dropped the bombs on target from 7,000 feet and returned to Horsham at 2.10 a.m.[30] Of the thirty-nine Hampdens on the mission, three did not come home.[31]

On 3 September, Stevens flew his crew on its fifth operation in nine days – an inhuman amount of stress on the men. One day of rest between trips was insufficient to allow an airman to catch up on sleep and to recover his nerve. And tired men make mistakes. The target this night was Brest, with one 1,000-pounder and two 500-pounders. The RAF dispatched 140 planes but recalled most before they reached France, when terrible weather threatened to envelop most of England and create havoc for the returning bombers.[32] Stevens and his crew had been in the air about seventy-five minutes when they received the recall message over the wireless, and Stevens decided to land at Boscombe Down.

After this mission, Stevens had accumulated 140 hours and ten minutes flying combat operations. He had been pilot and aircraft commander for ninety-four hours and thirty-five minutes of that time.

And then it came, the news for which they had all hoped, yet at the same time dreaded. On 7 September 1941, their target was the Big City, the home of evil: BERLIN!

Notes

1. National Archives, document HO 405 / 20069, Home Office Alien file on Georg Franz Hein, Report to the Chief Inspector, Metropolitan Police, May 1941.
2. Mark Postlethwaite, *Hampden Squadrons in Focus: A Photographic Album of the Units That Went to War in the Handley Page Hampden* (Walton on Thames, Surrey: Red Kite, 2003), 56.
3. National Archives, document AIR 27 / 981 – 144 Squadron Operations Record Book (ORB), Report of 3/4 April 1941, 50.
4. National Archives, 144 Squadron ORB. Report of 7/8 April 1941, 52.
5. Middlebrook and Everitt, *Bomber Command War Diaries*, 142.
6. National Archives, 144 Squadron ORB, Report of 10/11 April 1941, 54.
7. Middlebrook and Everitt, *Bomber Command War Diaries*, 143.
8. National Archives, 144 Squadron ORB, Report of 23/24 April 1941, 59.
9. Ibid. Report of 3/4 May 1941, 69.
10. Ibid. Report of 5/6 May 1941, 71.
11. Ibid. Report of 20 June 1941, 105.
12. Ibid. Report of 23/24 June 1941, 108.
13. Ibid. Report of 2/3 July 1941, 123.
14. Middlebrook and Everitt, *Bomber Command War Diaries*, 170.
15. National Archives, 144 Squadron ORB. Report of 5/6 July 1941, 127.
16. Middlebrook and Everitt, *Bomber Command War Diaries*, 172.
17. National Archives, 144 Squadron ORB, Report of 14/15 July 1941.

18. National Archives, HO 405 / 20069, file on Georg Hein. Letter of 17 July 1941, from the RAF Record Office to the Under-Secretary of State, Home Office, Bournemouth.

19. National Archives, 144 Squadron ORB, Report of 19/20 July 1941, 137.

20. National Archives, 144 Squadron ORB, Report of 22/23 July 1941.

21. Middlebrook and Everitt, *The Bomber Command War Diaries – An Operational Reference Book 1939–1945*, 183.

22. National Archives, 144 Squadron ORB, Report of 6/7 August 1941, 156–8.

23. Moyle, *The Hampden File*, 44–5.

24. Letter of Douglas Wark to the author, undated but received in November 1989.

25. National Archives, HO 405 / 20069, file on Georg Hein, Assistant Commissioner of the Metropolitan Police to the Under Secretary of State, Home Office Aliens Department, 22 Aug. 1941.

26. National Archives, 144 Squadron ORB, Report of 25/26 August 1941.

27. Middlebrook and Everitt, *Bomber Command War Diaries*, 196.

28. National Archives, 144 Squadron ORB, Report of 27/28 August 1941, 179.

29. Ibid., Report of 29/30 August 1941.

30. Ibid., Report of 1/2 September 1941.

31. Middlebrook and Everitt, *Bomber Command War Diaries*, 198.

32. Ibid., 199–200.

CHAPTER TEN

Abandon Aircraft! (8 September 1941)

'Pilot to crew, abandon aircraft! Bale out, bale out!' Quietly to himself, Stevens gave them his blessing, 'Thanks chaps, you've done everything you could. Now, go while you still can. Good luck to you all, and be safe.'

With the badly damaged Hampden clawing to stay airborne after bombing Berlin, and with searchlights dancing all about the sky, Stevens had made the fateful intercom call to his men. Two of the three followed his order. Sgt H. Thompson, one of the rear gunners, baled out successfully. The Germans captured him, and he spent the rest of the war as a prisoner.[1]

Sgt Ivor Roderick Fraser (serial no. 649384), the other rear gunner, was not so fortunate. Reports surfaced after 1945 that he too had baled out, but no one knew whether he did so with or without his parachute, or if perhaps he had sustained serious injuries and had lost consciousness. If he was wearing a parachute, it failed to open. He did not survive. No one ever found his body, and he has no known grave.[2] At Runnymede, a quiet spot on the Thames near Windsor Castle, where King John signed Magna Carta in 1215, the Commonwealth War Graves Commission maintains the beautiful Runnymede Memorial to honour fallen soldiers with no known final resting place. Among the more than 20,000 names on the monument, Fraser's appears on wall panel no. 43. A tiny but uplifting tribute to such a magnanimous sacrifice of a human life.

Not knowing what was happening to his two rear gunners, Stevens flew his Hampden as best he could. He realised that the plane's weight had changed with their departure, but was too busy trying to maintain control to think about their fate. Little by little, as the seconds passed, he realised that he could, indeed, fly the kite. His concentration was total, and so a tap on his shoulder a minute or two later shocked him. Looking over his shoulder, expecting to see a ghost, he recognised his smiling navigator, Sgt Alan Payne. Asking him what the devil he was doing there, Stevens learned that flak had damaged the nose compartment, rendering Payne's escape hatch inoperable. Stevens asked if him if the flak had injured him, and Payne confirmed that he was still in one piece.

Payne asked whether the aircraft was flyable. When Stevens replied that it seemed to be, Payne said that he would much rather take his chances in a perfectly good (!) aircraft than with a parachute! Everyone in the crew had heard about Stevens's successful belly landing a month earlier, and the navigator assumed he must be an expert!

Stevens now sought to move Payne and himself as far from Berlin as he could. Flak shells were bursting and searchlights burning holes in the sky, looking for a target such as Hampden AD 936. Stevens headed roughly north towards the Baltic, but that was almost a hundred miles away and no closer to home.

Before the two men could take stock and make crucial decisions, the *Luftwaffe* intervened. Two German night fighters had spotted the Hampden in the cone of a searchlight and made strafing passes. With tracer bullets lighting a path back to the fighters and giving Stevens a clue as to their location and angle, he instinctively dived away. Praying that the now-dark sky would obscure their plane, Stevens watched his altitude indicator unwind as he neared the ground in a steeply banking descent. Sensing that he was approaching terrain, he gently pulled back on the control yoke, praying that his damaged elevator would have enough surface area remaining to stop the Hampden from ploughing into the ground. Fortunately, he had pulled out early enough that the aircraft could level out just a hundred feet above the trees. He seemed to have evaded the Germans.

Stevens decided to try to make it back. Doubting that the aircraft could cover the 500 or so miles to England and safety, his attention turned towards the gauges in his cockpit. The engine temperatures and oil pressures seemed acceptable, but fuel remained low in the portside wing tank. All he could do was attempt to steer the most direct course for home. It was now about 1 a.m., and about 375 miles remained to the Dutch coast, plus 140 to the English coast.

Stevens admitted his doubts to Payne, who ran the numbers around his head and reached the same conclusion. At least they should try and run as far as they could, he suggested, and then take events as they came. Stevens agreed. And so the Hampden headed westward over Germany, trailing a thin stream of aviation fuel from its port wing. A normal speed with no bomb load might have been 200 mph or more. Without the weight of the missing two rear gunners, they might have neared the Hampden's maximum speed of 265 mph. But with serious damage and the need to conserve fuel, Stevens slowed to the most economical speed, about 170 mph. This would lengthen the journey but save the two engines a great deal of fuel, and the remaining high octane might get them home. At that speed, however, reaching the sea would take more than two hours and crossing it almost another hour.

They spent the next two hours in several ways. Although Payne was not qualified to fly a Hampden, he had received a certain amount of flight training, and was eager to help. But the extremely narrow cockpit stopped from giving any direct aid to the pilot and he spent his time doing whatever he could to lighten the aircraft. Payne jettisoned the five portable machine-guns in all three locations (two rear upper, two rear lower, and one nose), the portable toilet behind the main wing spar, and the remaining ammunition tins and personal gear. Stevens had to concentrate intensely to maintain his very low altitude without hitting anything. At the same time, he kept listening to the drone of the two Bristol Pegasus radial engines, waiting for the pitch to change, indicating a more serious emergency. The seconds ticked away as if in slow motion.

Requiring human presence and regular reassurance, the two young men huddled together and hoped that the miles of darkness would pass by more quickly. The engines' droning was not as reassuring as it should have been. Both men were aware that they did not know how long the motors would keep them in the air. And they were flying at 170 mph only 100 feet above the ground – not exactly safe. In an emergency, they would have precious little time to react. They were already far too low to use their parachutes. And if one or both engines sputtered and died, Stevens would have to land straight ahead and hit whatever might be in front of them, be it trees, or a building, or a farmer's field. Especially dangerous in the pitch black of night.

And so, as two hours had dragged by since the anti-aircraft artillery hits, the fuel-gauge readings over Holland showed England was indeed unreachable. An external compartment in the port wing root had a built-in life raft, but that wing had sustained the most battle damage, and the raft might be unusable. Besides, Stevens could not swim and somewhat feared the water. The North Sea might not prove as benign for a belly landing as the field at RAF Coningsby had the previous month. Calling to Payne, Stevens announced his decision: they would find a cleared field and attempt a landing.

Just as Stevens was becoming comfortable with his decision, the port engine began to sputter and cough. He instantly turned to the port fuel gauge – 'Empty.' The starboard side still had as much as thirty minutes' fuel left. Later-model Hampdens could cross-feed fuel between tanks, but AD 936 was an earlier version. Any remaining flight would take place on a single engine. 'No choice now,' he informed Payne. 'We'll have to do a crash-landing!'

With his port engine about to cut out completely, Stevens decided to give them an additional 'out' and climbed to 3,000 feet. If anything went badly wrong now, they could at least use their parachutes. The Hampden did not have feathering[3] propellers, so Stevens could only cut the port ignition switch and steady himself for the coming landing. The port propeller caused a huge amount of drag, making the aircraft yaw to the left. Stevens had to counter that adverse yaw by commanding almost full right rudder pedal, adding to the workload. The additional drag from the unpowered propeller also meant that the plane needed full power from the remaining engine to remain airborne, dramatically increasing fuel consumption. Stevens knew that little time remained and that he had to land quickly! Descending would not be a problem, as the aircraft in this configuration would drop like a stone.

Stevens started searching the ground by available ambient light and ordered Payne to do the same. Looking down, he caught a glimpse of water, but it was clearly a river or canal, flowing perpendicular to their course. Stevens guessed that it must be the River Ems, bordering Holland and Germany. Another thirty minutes of flying on a single engine took them to the outskirts of Amsterdam. Many Dutch were farmers, and so the Hampden might find a suitable field there.

Knowing that time was short, Stevens decided to land as quickly as possible. Aligning the Hampden to fly directly into the wind, he spotted an open field directly ahead. He reduced power on the remaining engine and deployed the landing flaps to lower the wing's stalling speed. This last action would allow him to touch down at a lower groundspeed, reducing the severity of the impact and the length of skidding on the ground. As he couldn't be sure of the suitability of the surface, he deemed it wiser not to lower the landing gear.

Should he illuminate his landing site? Stevens thought for a moment and realised that the landing light in the leading edge of the port wing would help him to see the landing surface. But it would also expose him to anyone nearby and make him a target. The only people awake and outdoors there at this hour were probably carrying automatic weapons. A difficult choice, but he decided to stay under cover of night and use what little ambient light there was.

Despite the plane's being very low on fuel, Stevens did not want to chance a fire. Just before touching down, he tightened his seatbelt and shoulder straps and began his emergency-landing checklist. He slid back the pilot's canopy to the full open position, in case he needed to escape in a hurry and the canopy jammed in the tracks. At the last possible moment, he cut the ignition switch to the good engine to minimise any sparks resulting from the landing and the risk of a post-crash fire. Stevens was now piloting a very balky glider.

The subsequent landing was in effect a crash. It was actually fairly good, but without wheels aircraft decelerate much more quickly. As the plane came to rest back on terra firma, both men grasped how quiet things had become so quickly. Checking for injuries, they noticed nothing major and began laughing quietly. After all, they were both alive, albeit on the ground in occupied territory.

Stevens's typically serious demeanour soon returned, and he started issuing orders. First on the list was to take the fire axe and destroy the bombsight, the radio, and any other bits of secret gear that might be of use to the Germans. After that, they would gather together all documents and use them to set the fuselage on fire before making a run for it. Stevens looked around, half expecting to see German soldiers rushing towards them, but saw no signs of life; it was still dark, and nobody appeared to have noticed their arrival. He looked at the aluminium RAF-issue Longines watch on his left wrist and noted that it was just after 3.30 a.m. It was still the middle of the night, and darkness continued its temporary reign. Dawn arrives at about 6.30 a.m. in Amsterdam in early September, and so the two English flyers had a bit of time to depart the area.

After almost seven hours with 2,000 horsepower droning feet away from them, the airmen found the silence deafening. In fact, both were now loath to believe their own ears.

Undoing his safety belts, Stevens climbed out onto the port wing and surveyed the situation, despite the darkness. He saw several holes in the wing and damage to a good part of the port aileron, rudder, and elevator. He kept a watchful eye on the horizon in all directions, expecting to see vehicles, troops, or dogs. He called quietly to Payne: they needed to destroy things and move out on the double.

Wiggling through the tunnel under the pilot's seat and into the nose, Payne used the fire axe and smashed the highly secret bombsight. Crawling back to the centre of the dead Hampden, he pulled together all the flammable papers, charts, and manuals remaining and formed a small pile. Stevens stuck his upper body back into the fuselage, pulled out a lighter and flicked it to life, starting a small bonfire just behind the pilot's seat. Climbing over the pilot's seatback, Payne followed Stevens out onto the wing and then slid down its trailing edge to the ground. Deciding that they would no longer need their flying gear and that it might actually be a hindrance, the two climbed out of their flying suits and tossed them back into the cockpit, hoping that that additional fuel would help the fire to spread.

As the fire grew, the two *Luftgangsters*[4] chose a direction and together ran several hundred yards. When they stopped under a tree to catch their breath, Stevens spoke first. He suggested that they look for a farmhouse and see if the Dutch occupant might be willing to hide them or, even better, put them in contact with the Dutch Resistance.[5]

Stevens then proposed that they head for nearby Amsterdam and look for help. Perhaps they could steal a boat or, even better, find someone from the Resistance who would assist them to get to a neutral country. If they could reach such a territory (Spain, Sweden, or Switzerland), it would quickly repatriate them back to England.

With the adrenaline of the crash still coursing through his veins, Stevens found it difficult to think – but the few thoughts that came to him were not pleasant ones. While Payne worried about capture and becoming a prisoner of war, Stevens was deeply fearful. In Holland, things might stay reasonable for him. But if the Germans captured him, matters might quickly become extremely serious. Any German soldier might take one look at him, spit '*Jude!*' and send him to a concentration camp, or worse. After all, Germany still regarded him as a citizen, albeit a Jewish one – both marks against him. He was, in effect, guilty of treason against his own country. If he were captured and his true identity discovered, he could expect no mercy. Stevens tried to bury those thoughts and deal with the more pressing issue.

Finding the closest road, the pair began walking. Soon a figure appeared out of the gloom, and Stevens, seeing a solitary Dutchman in civilian clothes, decided to confide in him. He told Payne that he would ask for help in English; if the man could not understand, he would try German. Payne looked quizzical at his alleged ability in German but said nothing.

Approaching the fellow, Stevens whispered and asked if he understood English. The man nodded, and Stevens explained that they were Allied flyers who had just crash-landed. Could he help them to escape? The farmer quietly motioned for the two to follow him. Quickly they made their way to a farmhouse, and their host gestured for them to follow him through the door. Once they were inside and had closed the door, they could talk.

While the Dutchman gave the airmen some food, he explained that his house was too close to their crash site and not a safe place to hide. Once they had eaten, he asked them to leave, hide somewhere else, and return the following evening. He did not ask their names, and they did not ask his – which left the Dutchman safer. He promised to try to contact the Resistance and set up a meeting.

Leaving the house, Stevens checked his watch: 6 a.m. on 8 September. Although it was still dark, dawn would soon arrive. Walking for an hour, Stevens and Payne came on a wooden hut beside a soccer field. Breaking the lock, they saw that it was some sort of clubhouse, with space to store equipment and a small snack bar. Hoping that they could hide here safely, they settled in for the day and, nearing exhaustion, lay down to sleep. Two hours later, however, the barking of dogs awakened them. As the noise increased, they prepared to make a run for it.

Notes

1. Oliver Clutton-Brock, *Footprints on the Sands of Time* (London: Grub Street, 2003), 418.

2. Peter Stevens visited the Commonwealth War Graves Commission War Cemetery in Berlin with his family in 1967 and, to his horror, could find no reference to Fraser. He firmly believed that he alone was responsible for Fraser's death, having commanded him to bale out.

3. Propellers on newer aircraft have hydraulic feathering; rotating each individual blade faces its sharp edge directly into the air stream. This minimises drag and allows the plane to fly further without power.

4. German term for 'air criminals', which civilians called Allied airmen who were destroying the Fatherland night after night. Ordinary Germans sometimes beat and/or attempted to injure downed Allied airmen.

5. The author learned in 2001 that they had landed on the farms of the Abbring and Vlieger families, near Zunderdorp, just north-east of Amsterdam

Part Four: Prisoner of War (1941–5)

CHAPTER ELEVEN

Learning Escape: *Dulag Luft*, Lübeck, Hanover (September–October 1941)

Before Stevens and Payne could move, the door opened, and several German soldiers yelled to them to drop their weapons and come out with their hands up. Having no weapons, both men raised their hands over their heads. There was a lot of yelling going on, but Payne couldn't understand a word of it. Stevens, however, acting quite calm, told him to relax and follow his instructions. In what sounded to Payne like rudimentary German, Stevens yelled that they had no weapons and were coming out.

When the two Brits emerged with their hands in the air, the senior German non-commissioned officer (NCO) in charge proudly spoke the only English words he knew, 'For you, the war is over!'

After a quick search of the hut, several German soldiers came out smiling: they had captured dangerous enemies of the Third *Reich*. As the Germans marched the airmen off to a waiting truck with their hands still reaching for the sky, Stevens spied a boy of about ten watching them from a distance.[1] Stevens smiled sadly and waved at the boy.

The captors searched the two Englishmen and then directed them to climb onto the back of a troop-carrying truck. Several armed men climbed in after them to stand guard. After a drive of about thirty minutes, the truck halted outside a building flying a large Nazi Swastika flag. Soon the soldiers prodded the airmen to disembark and led them into Amsterdam Military Prison. They rudely shepherded Payne and Stevens into individual cells beside one another, where they could at least talk.

The official German record of the incident survives from the military headquarters at Bloemendaal:

At 0500 hours an enemy aircraft crashlanded 2 kms Northeast of Nieuwendam. Aircraft set on fire after landing. Crew on the run. Type Hampden. Commanding Officer of [the German seaplane base at] Schellingwoude got orders for search and guarding. Further report to Lg.Kdo.Ic.

Between Nieuwendam and Zunderdorp 1 enemy aircraft crashed.

C 103/XI got order to take care of things.

C 103/XI reports: Search action from Nieuwendam to Zunderdorp with three parties. The aircraft is being guarded. All people on the roads on their way to Nieuwendam Amsterdam are being controlled, farmhouses are being searched. In command of these actions Hauptmann Prossel.[2]

In Amsterdam guards again searched Stevens and Payne, but no one interrogated them. The airmen received reasonably good treatment, and, during visits to the bathroom, Stevens exchanged names with several other prisoners. Survivors of the same mission to Berlin, they were airmen from a Vickers Wellington twin-engined bomber from 12 Squadron, serial number Z8328: Squadron Leader S.S. Fielden, Pilot Officer W.J. Peat (Royal Canadian Air Force, or RCAF), and Sgt A.H. Smith (Royal Australian Air Force).

At seven o'clock in the morning two days later, 10 September, guards removed the five Allied prisoners from their cells and loaded them onto a bus, again under heavily armed guard. Stevens was coming to realise that he did not like having loaded submachine-guns pointing at him so regularly. After a twenty-mile trip south to Utrecht, the Germans unloaded the five prisoners and put them on a passenger train. A contingent of guards accompanied them and placed them in two compartments, each with several German guards. Stevens asked, in poorly accented German, where they were going. The response was simple: '*Dulag Luft*.'[3]

Every Allied airman had, by 1941, heard about *Dulag Luft*, the German interrogation centre for all Allied aircrew prisoners of war. Located in a suburb of Frankfurt called Oberursel, it was to be the first taste of life as prisoners of war for Stevens and his colleagues. The RAF was regularly bombing major German rail centres, and rail lines needed constant repair. While Frankfurt was only about 225 miles from Utrecht, but the train did not reach its destination until about 7 p.m. The prisoners then boarded a much smaller tram for the hour-long trip to Oberursel. Guards marched the five prisoners a couple of miles to the camp.

Arrival at *Dulag Luft* was the last time in their lives that Peter Stevens and Alan Payne saw each other.[4] Guards searched the men completely, escorted each to his own cell, and placed them in solitary confinement for the duration of their stay, which could last from ten days to two weeks.

Dulag Luft was not typical as a German prisoner-of-war camp. It only interrogated newly captured Allied airmen. A single block of between one hundred and two hundred individual cells, it used all kinds of psychological tricks to pry out secret information. Of course, the Geneva Convention required that prisoners give their captors only their name, rank, and serial number.

The most obvious trick of interrogators at *Dulag Luft* was the use of a fake Red Cross form. Interrogators told nervous captives that their relatives would worry terribly until they knew that their family members were alive and prisoners of war. The Germans claimed that if the prisoner would complete the form, the *Luftwaffe* (which operated prison camps for all Allied airmen) would immediately notify the Red Cross in Switzerland, which would send word to the man's family. Yet the so-called Red Cross form had questions relating to all sorts of military secrets:

Aircraft type and serial number
Names and ranks of the other crewmembers
Squadron number
Home airfield
Mission target
Base and squadron commanding officers
Location, reason and time of crash or bale out
Pay rate

Most British and Commonwealth prisoners figured out that this was a trick, and almost all of them refused to complete it. Their interrogators would become much less friendly in a hurry. Treatment from this point on might include any combination of sleep deprivation, threats of violence, bugging of cells, and the withholding of food.

After five to ten days, each prisoner moved out into the general part of the camp, where he received temporary accommodation under the control of a so-called permanent group of prisoners. This brief period allowed for indoctrination into the life of a *Kriegie* (German for prisoner of war).[5] Prisoners in transit obtained whatever uniform clothing and kit they were missing (depending on supplies) and learned what to expect, and how to manage, at a permanent prison camp.

Stevens found the initial solitary confinement and continuous interrogations tough. He had to steel himself to the possibility of unmasking himself, while trying not even to hint that he was German. He frequently sat alone in his cell, reminding himself that his name was Peter Stevens and that he should say nothing in his native tongue. He sometimes had awful thoughts of what might happen if he slipped up. He had heard horror stories of how nasty the *Gestapo* could be, and he wasn't keen to confirm these.

On release into the camp's general population, one first presented one's bona fides to the Senior British Officer (SBO) thereby proving that one wasn't a German 'plant', or stooge. This also happened whenever a prisoner transferred to a new camp. Of course, the easiest way to prove oneself was to meet a friend or acquaintance from Britain who would vouch for you.

While Stevens was wandering through the camp, he came upon a tall, gaunt officer who spoke with an odd accent and asked him where to obtain some clothing 'kit'. The officer introduced himself as Flight Lieutenant W.J. ('Mike')

Lewis, a Canadian from the Toronto area. They began chatting, each one holding back, as the other might be a German 'plant'.

They asked each other questions that only someone who had spent recent time in Britain might know. 'Mike' Lewis had known a pilot named Bob Barr, who had joined 144 Squadron just as Lewis signed up with his first combat squadron, and the two had kept in touch. Over the following two years, Lewis had learned the names of several Hemswell and North Luffenham locals (i.e. pubs). In fact, only a month earlier, the base commander of RAF North Luffenham had himself been shot down, which had provoked much discussion at Lewis's base. Stevens and Lewis accepted each other's bona fides within about ten minutes. They figured out too that they had both been on the 7 September mission to Berlin and had both reached occupied Holland before capture.

'Mike' Lewis, twenty-three, had been the pilot of an Avro Manchester, the twin-engine precursor of the four-engined Lancaster bomber, one of the war's most famous aircraft. He had an interesting but typical story. He had just completed his rare *second* full tour of duty[6] and was about to go away on a week's leave. In his 207 Squadron Mess at RAF Waddington, his squadron's commanding officer informed him that he was missing a pilot for that night's operation. Would Lewis mind doing just one more, to help out?

Lewis had flown his first tour of thirty-six operations in Hampdens with 44 Squadron, and he enjoyed handling the aircraft, despite its odd shape and undeservedly bad reputation. He later said that, of all the thirty or so planes he flew during his long career in the Royal Canadian Air Force, the Hampden was his favourite. His second tour, with 207 Squadron, had been a nightmare. The Manchester had arrived unproven and suffered from a long list of teething troubles. Rather than working these out in the prototype stage, Bomber Command had rushed the aircraft into production and had forced it on the unlucky 207 Squadron.

The Manchester's new Rolls-Royce Vulture engines (the odd mating of two Peregrine V-12 motors into one large X-24) were underpowered, unproven, and unreliable.[7] Their motors' poor performance made them almost unflyable (the fully loaded aircraft was just too heavy for the available power), and many airmen soon died as a result.

On the night of 7/8 September 1941, 'Mike' Lewis and his Manchester crew had taken off for Berlin, and a German night fighter had attacked them inbound over the Frisian Islands, near the northern Dutch coast. Lewis was able to lose the German but later realised that the enemy had hit his port fuel tank. Fortunately, there was no fire, and the self-sealing fuel tank had worked as it should. For thirty minutes everything seemed fine, but then the port engine's temperature went off the gauge, and Lewis realised that a bullet must have also pierced his port radiator.

Since the two-engine Manchester had way too little power, Lewis knew that flying on one engine was impossible. He had to ditch his badly damaged plane near the beach in ten feet of water off the north shore of the Dutch island of Ameland. Once the aircraft had become a boat, Lewis instructed his crew to take the fire axes and destroy all the secret equipment on board.

Going ashore, the six men hiked across the narrow island to the south shore and spotted a large, motorised lifeboat on the beach, which proved far too large for them to move. They crawled into the boat to spend the night, but the next morning a German sentry discovered and arrested them. Their captors ferried Lewis and his crew to a *Luftwaffe* base at Leeuwarden and then to the prison in Amsterdam. The airmen spent two days there before being transported to *Dulag Luft*.

In some crucial matters, however, Lewis and Stevens had more questions than answers: where will the Germans send us, what will we eat, how do we secure more clothing and gear, and, most important, how can we escape?

The prisoners on the 'permanent staff' were able to answer many of their questions. The Germans would send them to one of several prisoner-of-war camps in Germany and/or Poland – either an *Oflag* (*Offizier Lager*, or Officers' Camp) or a *Stalag Luft* ('*Stammlager Luft*,' or Air Main Camp, under control of the *Luftwaffe*). Apparently the Germans always showed a great deal of respect or deference to officers, regardless of nationality. Later these newcomers would apply this lesson and take the high ground of authority *vis-à-vis* lowly German guards. On occasion, one could order German privates and corporals to go away, just because one was an Allied officer. The correct tone helped immensely, as did a few choice words in German.

As for food, this was to become the bane of existence of all prisoners of war. Food became preoccupation number one, and the meagre rations provided by the Germans were far from adequate. The newcomers soon learned about manna – the heavenly Red Cross parcels. The International Red Cross occasionally delivered them – theoretically a week's supply of goods. They included such luxuries as margarine, tinned meats, cigarettes, chocolate, and various and sundry other staples. The prisoners would soon come to realise how crucial was food, which they had previously (as privileged aircrew) taken for granted.

Clothing and gear (blankets, toothbrushes, and so on) would be available from supplies that came from home or neutral countries. Newcomers obviously arrived without forethought or luggage, with nothing more than the clothing on their backs. Everything for day-to-day living they had to beg, borrow, or steal (preferably from the Germans).

How to escape? That subject was to occupy many minds over countless hours for a very long time. While the RAF was pounding occupied Europe nightly, in September 1941 Britain was not winning the war. Hitler had invaded the Soviet Union in June 1941 – horrifying news for Soviet citizens, but giving Britons some breathing room. *Luftwaffe* bombers, however, remained just thirty miles across the English Channel. While Germany dispatched much of its air force to the Russian front, it periodically reminded England of its enmity, sending unmanned weapons, the German V-1 'buzz bomb', and later the V-2 guided missile. In September 1941, British prisoners of war had little reason for hope. The conflict might last another year – or another decade.

Stevens and Lewis became partners in the project of escape. They knew that 'forty and eight' railway cattle cars (the outside of each car proclaimed: '40 *hommes* & 8 *chevaux*' – 40 men and 8 horses) would soon ship them north-east to their permanent prison camp. Somehow, they decided, they would figure out a plan, and would make good an escape.

Early on at *Dulag Luft*, Stevens had been paranoid about speaking German, guessing that it would be better for him if German officers and guards did not know he could. He could accordingly eavesdrop very effectively, learning about German plans in advance. If he escaped, he could easily revert to his former role: a German citizen in Germany. The difficult part would be to find civilian clothes and realistic identity papers. If he could address those details, he might well reach a neutral country and return thence to England.

Over the next few days Stevens hatched his plan but, trusting no one, kept the details to himself. Members of the permanent staff, already as many as twenty-five by mid-1940,[8] tried to dissuade all newcomers from attempting to escape *Dulag Luft* itself, advising them to await a better opportunity at a permanent camp.

British officers on the permanent staff who appeared to have accepted their relatively comfortable lot and settled in for the duration upset some new inmates. But the new arrivals did not know that those same 'wet blankets' were busy planning their own escape, and their seeming acquiescence lulled the guards into a false sense of security.

The early permanent staff represented a nucleus of men who became some of the RAF's most ardent and successful escapers. The Senior British Officer (SBO) was Wing Commander Harry ('Wings') Day. He had been a pilot in the Great War, and was shot down flying a Blenheim bomber on a photoreconnaissance mission on Friday 13 October 1939. Also in the group were the newly arrived Wing Commander 'Hetty' Hyde; Major John Dodge, an American-born cousin of Winston Churchill's serving in the British Army; and Lieutenant Commander Jimmy Buckley, of the Royal Navy's Fleet Air Arm.

Perhaps most remarkable of all was the irrepressible South African playboy, Squadron Leader Roger Bushell – a brilliant lawyer who had studied at Cambridge, had travelled all over Europe in the 1930s, enjoying the good life, and was a skilled linguist. Bushell would later become 'Big X', head of the escape organisation in the North Compound of *Stalag Luft* III and the brains behind 'The Great Escape'. Bushell was so eager to escape that he enlisted the aid of the commandant of *Dulag Luft*, Major Theo Rumpel! At a dinner party for six senior British officers on the permanent staff, he lured Rumpel into a conversation about escaping. He told Rumpel in his best German what he would say to a German policeman if he found himself on the Swiss border. Rumpel actually stopped him several times to correct his German or to suggest more effective wording! [9]

This seemingly respectable cadre had orchestrated a tunnel escape from *Dulag Luft* in early June 1941 (three months before Stevens arrived). At the last minute, Bushell had decided to use a different plan.[10] The tunnel break was to take place at 9 p.m. Thinking that he should aim to catch an early-evening train from Frankfurt to the Swiss border, Bushell hid under a false floor in a goat shed on the recreation field and broke out an hour or two earlier. He would reach the border early the next morning, before camp authorities discovered the mass escape and alerted all German police.

His colleagues later learned that Bushell had indeed reached the Swiss frontier, where a suspicious German border guard detained him. Bushell realised that his false papers would not stand up to any close scrutiny and gave himself up as an escaped British prisoner of war.[11] It was later suggested that if he had only attempted to cross 200 yards away he would have succeeded. This was the first of several escapes for him and launched his reputation among the Germans as an incorrigible. The Germans had quickly recaptured the eighteen escapees in the main party.

Stevens saw that escape was in fact possible. The camp was still buzzing about the individual escapers, and this constant talk steeled his resolve. He *would* escape! But how and from where?

After about ten days at *Dulag Luft*, the move to a permanent camp was imminent. All the new boys wondered where. The permanent staff could name one or two possibilities, but only the German captors knew for sure.

On or about Sunday 21 September, a group of Allied officers transferred by train to the hellhole of *Oflag* X C, near the Baltic seaport of Lübeck. The group included Peter Stevens and his newfound friend 'Mike' Lewis.

Lübeck was a relatively small camp, with about ten or twelve huts for prisoners inside a fenced compound, along with a hospital, a storage facility, and a separate dining hall/canteen. Besides a parade area, where the prisoners assembled morning and afternoon for *Appell*, or roll call (when the German guards counted them), there was also a sports field. Outside the fence were buildings for the German guards and offices.

Oflag XC already held the nucleus of the 'X' (escape) organisation. Wing Commander Noel 'Hetty' Hyde, the Senior British Officer, and Roger Bushell (later 'Big X') were both veterans of the escape tunnel at *Dulag Luft*.[12]

The worst thing about Lübeck was the inadequate food supply. Very often the 'next meal' was no such thing – perhaps a half-rotten potato or a slice of 'bread' no more than two or three millimetres thick. The new inmates soon began to feel constant and continuous hunger.

The reality of day-to-day existence was horrific. Breakfast consisted of mint tea, a slice of bread (each man received the equivalent of 200–300 grams of black bread per day, to eat as he saw fit), perhaps a bit of margarine, and one tablespoonful of canned meat or horsemeat and another of jam or cheese. Lunch consisted of a bowl of thin cabbage soup and perhaps three or four small boiled potatoes. For supper, the men had mint tea and any leftovers from earlier rations or something from a Red Cross parcel.[13]

Consuming so few calories, men began to lose weight at an alarming rate (up to a half-pound per day). Although a camp store sold sundry goods such as combs, razors, bowls, and cutlery purchasable with camp 'money' (a type of allowance from the Germans), cigarettes soon became the universal currency for barter.

The International Red Cross became the lifeline for all Allied prisoners of war in German-occupied territory. The Geneva Convention forced each power to allow distribution of such parcels to its prisoners. The accepted allowance was a half-parcel per man per week, but there was no guarantee of availability. After all, during war the Germans would hardly give priority to delivery of these life-saving packages. The number of prisoners of war was growing almost daily, and parcel distribution was far from simple. Red Cross organisations in the Allied countries sent parcels, so the contents of each differed slightly. A typical one might include:

1 bar of Cadbury's nut-and-fruit chocolate or something similar
1 tin of Klim (Canadian dried milk powder), or Carnation evaporated milk, or Nestle's condensed sweetened milk
1 tin of cigarettes (fifty) or of pipe tobacco
1 tin of Irish stew
1 tin of rice pudding
1 tin of Fray Bentos corned beef
1 tin of sardines
1 small tin of cheese
1 tin of jam or marmalade
1 packet of cream cracker biscuits
1 tin of butter
1 tin of coffee[14]

Again, this was meant to be two weeks' supply for one man! But it could sustain someone only if it reached the camp and the Germans allowed distribution. Occasionally, camp authorities withheld parcels as punishment. Later, most camp *Kommandants* agreed to place Red Cross parcels at the disposal of the Senior British Officer, and he and his underlings decided whether and when to distribute them. Often, senior Allied officers kept some parcels in reserve, in case of delays with the next delivery.

Because tobacco can suppress appetite, smoking became a virtual necessity. In time, the addiction increased cigarettes' value, and men often gambled using them as currency. One could buy poor-quality German ones made with

Balkan tobacco, but everyone preferred the 'real' thing from Red Cross parcels. A prisoner could become 'rich' (in cigarette terms) and gain power over fellow inmates.

The men fell into a daily routine. Some would sleep as much as possible, although *Appell* intruded twice each day. Others read books from the camp library, visited friends, or exercised. The constant hunger sapped the men's energy, so sports were not a top priority. Later, educational courses would emerge under men who felt qualified to teach a given subject. As the Germans began to realise that these studies were good for the men and took their minds off escape, they began to support and encourage them.

'The Circuit' was a well-worn path around the inside of the camp fence. Named after the tried and true rectangular pattern of airborne approach to an airfield, it allowed airmen to stretch their legs and chat with their mates. It also enabled men a way to avoid anyone they found irritating.

Privacy was scarce. Men lived eight or more to a room, sleeping in bunk beds, and sharing a common lavatory, often with communal toilets, with no dividers. And so they jealously guarded their privacy. After all, most of them were in their twenties, young and active. They needed to expend their energy yet remain healthy psychologically. Each had cheated death, and that reality dawned perhaps only weeks or months later. During combat operations, they either didn't think about dying or accepted it as the cost of freedom. Now that their 'war was over', they had lots of time to think, and several had difficulty. Most had seen one or more comrades die, and there was also guilt at play. Why had they survived while their buddy had died in mid-air?

Only one or two places offered real privacy – the hospital or the cooler (solitary confinement in the camp jail). One could fake one's way into the former, but the latter took more work. Misbehaviour could land one in the cooler for anywhere from a few to thirty days. Insulting a German officer might earn a light sentence; recapture after an escape, fourteen days. The cells were usually quite Spartan, with a bed (usually uncomfortable) and a bucket. Of course, the guards delivered food, but only strict German rations, with no access to Red Cross parcel additions. True privacy came at a cost.

Also present in Lübeck were the irrepressible Brits Wing Commander Douglas Bader and Gilbert ('Tim') Walenn, and the Canadian Eddie Asselin. Bader's story has been the subject of both a book and a movie.[15] He was an RAF pilot who crashed while doing an unauthorised stunt in England in 1931 and lost both legs above the knee. He soon left the RAF but reapplied in 1939, despite the RAF's serious misgivings. Bader was able to show sufficient proficiency for re-admittance as a pilot, and went on to become a highly decorated and successful fighter ace with twenty kills to his credit.

But some prisoners of war came to feel that his accident had embittered him, and destroyed his instinct for self-preservation. He goaded his captors whenever possible – his fellow prisoners debated whether he did it deliberately or not, but many thought him reckless, even dangerous. It was they who would intercept the crossfire generated by Bader's wilful acts of spite.

Tim Walenn had no business whatsoever being in such a camp. A banker, he had joined the RAF Volunteer Reserve in 1937. He trained as a bomber pilot but in 1941 was an instructor at an RAF operational training unit, teaching new pilots how to fly heavy bombers in combat. His Wellington bomber had inadvertently veered off course while he was instructing a new group of pilots at night, and flak hit him over Holland. Walenn and his crew had to bale out, and the instructor found himself a prisoner of war.[16] He would later direct all forgery operations of the 'X' Committee of North Compound at *Stalag Luft* III. He would leave that camp through the tunnel 'Harry' during 'The Great Escape', but recapture followed, and he sadly became one of fifty Allied prisoners whom the *Gestapo* murdered in cold blood as retaliation for that mass escape.

Eddy Asselin, a Canadian fighter pilot who had flown with Bader's famous 'Big Wing', would later mastermind an ingenious mass tunnel escape from *Oflag* XXI B at Schubin, Poland. The tunnel's entrance was below a toilet seat in the communal lavatory, just above the cesspit. Asselin later developed an unpleasant reputation as an inveterate gambler and callous black marketeer. Some people have alleged that after the war he looked up former prisoners of war and attempted to collect on their cigarette and chocolate-bar debts.

Walenn and Stevens, along with 'Mike' Lewis, ended up in the same overcrowded room at Lübeck, sharing it with nineteen others. The two men became friends, and Stevens later became active in the forgery department of 'X'. His fluent German was of course of great use in this type of work.

Having settled into camp routine, Stevens made enquiries about escape. The method was important, but so was the type of assistance one could expect from the 'X' Organisation. For example, a young man wandering around Germany in an RAF uniform might attract unwanted attention. So, one needed some type of disguise. And if an escapee obtained some sort of civilian clothing, the obvious question asked by other Germans was, why wasn't he in the armed forces?

This was to be a major issue for all escapees – how to explain their lack of a uniform? Obviously, they needed a believable explanation, a complete, valid, and foolproof legend, and appropriate (false) papers. How could an Allied officer know what official documents and identity papers he would require to travel through the Third *Reich*?

The 'X' Committee at Lübeck was already working on such important questions. The 'X' groups at the various camps would become expert in these matters. How to gather this type of information, especially from *inside* a camp?

Not only the prisoners suffered. Life was neither pleasant nor easy for those Germans who worked in the camps. While guards received more food than prisoners, it was still not very good. And life was relatively boring for them too, but they had to be alert. Sleeping on duty or losing official property brought penalties close to a death sentence, such as redeployment to the Russian Front, and guards would do almost anything to stay out of harm's way. Prisoners could use this anxiety strategically against weak guards.

The trick was to befriend a guard and compromise him. Then it was relatively easy to blackmail that soldier into doing something seemingly harmless, but valuable to the 'X' Organisation. Whether that meant obtaining supplies from outside or access to documents for copying, the job was a delicate one for only a few tactful prisoners. While most guards had some rudimentary English, a German-speaking prisoner could corrupt them using their native language to put them at ease.

In practice, starting such a useful relationship was fairly easy. The gift of a 'real' (i.e. British or Canadian) cigarette or chocolate bar might do the trick. After a pattern of small gifts emerged, the 'scrounger' would ask a certain favour – shoe polish, a map, a railway timetable, or a length of material (to make civilian clothing). After the guard agreed once, usually in exchange for more gifts, the prisoner 'had' him. In this way, one could prod a guard into providing ever more incriminating goods, such as a 35-mm camera, film, and photographic paper (to print photos for passports and other documents), and even parts for short-wave radio receivers. If the guard balked at a new request, the inmate would threaten him with blackmail, suggesting that the *Kommandant* might not approve of his guards' actions supplying prisoners, and the Russian Front would be a relatively benign fate compared to execution by firing squad. Even though the Germans were winning the war in the Soviet Union, bullets and artillery shells were still flying in both directions, and home soil was much safer.

Stevens was eager to contribute to the escape efforts, especially since he was also anxious to escape. He knew of his huge advantage and was keen to prove his theory. He tried not to think about discovery of his identity, when the Geneva Convention's protections would become useless for him.

Stevens initially offered his services to the 'X' Committee as a native German speaker and also announced his intention to escape as soon as he could. He explained his valuable German linguistic skills by telling a half-truth: he had been sent to boarding school in Bavaria in the mid 1920s. He inquired about support *vis-à-vis* clothing and identity papers. The committee welcomed his approach, but for help he would have to join the queue.

Day-to-day life went on, however, while boredom and hunger ravaged the mind and body. The pace of new arrivals continued at a steady rate. Soon the overcrowding was unbearable and needed addressing. Most inmates were unable to think about much other than their ever-present hunger, and one event brought that issue to a head.

The *Kommandant*, a certain *Oberst* (Colonel) von Wachtmeister, particularly unpleasant, had a cat that often roamed the camp at will. With a large number of ravenous men growing steadily weaker and meaner, someone realised that the pet might make a tasty, if unappealing, meal. And so, one day in the autumn of 1941, that cat disappeared into a prisoner's cooking pot.[17]

Finally, the overcrowding reached a crisis point, and on 6 October 1941, guards loaded Stevens, Lewis, and many other inmates onto cattle cars for transfer to another permanent camp, *Oflag* VI B at Warburg. Immediately before loading them, guards searched everyone and took from each prisoner the second blanket from the Red Cross. All in all, the men were quite happy – any time outside the camp offered potential escape, and no other camp could possibly be as bad.

Stevens and Lewis stuck close together and boarded the same cattle car. Two armed Germans stood guard in the wagon, which carried about twenty-five prisoners, but distracting them, which most veterans could do, would be easy. Stevens and Lewis huddled in a corner near the ventilator screen and quietly hatched their plan.

While the guards' view of them was poor, Stevens took out his dining spoon and started loosening the screws holding the screen over the ventilation opening, which was just big enough to allow a man to pass through. In a few minutes, the four screws were 90 per cent out. The two then enlisted their comrades, arranging for a distraction across the railcar when they gave the signal. They decided to wait a couple of hours, as there were too many German soldiers in and near the camp. An escape might go better if they could jump out in an uninhabited area.

When the train slowed somewhat about eight o'clock in the evening (about an hour past sunset), a peek out through a small gap in the wallboards showed nothing but forest. Lewis gave the signal for the disturbance, and the men began unpacking and shaking out blankets, as if to bed down for the night. Stevens had removed the screen and was already halfway through. Lewis saw him go out and jump. Then Lewis jumped through the gaping hole and narrowly missed the rails.

Unfortunately, another airman who dived through the floorboards, Pilot Officer Robinson, died instantly when a train wheel severed both of his legs.[18]

Robin Beauclair had schemed with John Denny to try another attempt from the same freight car. Using a makeshift hacksaw, they cut a hole in the floorboards at the far end of the car.[19] As Beauclair exited, he inadvertently stepped on the air hoses for the pneumatic brakes. His weight broke the connection between the two hoses, and the emergency brakes engaged. The train came to a screeching halt, and the guards immediately peered outside. Spotting figures running in the twilight, several opened up with their rifles and machine-guns.

Just before the train stopped completely, 'Mike' Lewis had rolled heavily as he hit the ground roughly. Lewis scraped his face, and came up looking a bit the worse for wear. Coming to a halt in the ditch beside the tracks, he looked back and saw Stevens making a dash for the darkness of the woods about twenty yards away. Lewis jumped to his feet, but the guards saw him. More shots rang out in their direction, then whistles, and finally more automatic gunfire.

Several guards disembarked from the front and the rear, but all four prisoners reached the woods and kept on running. After ten minutes of fruitless searching, the guards returned to the train. Slowly, it began moving again, leaving Stevens and Lewis at large, hiding in a forest in northern Germany.

On the ground, in the middle of a thick forest deep inside Germany (near Uelzen, about sixty miles north-east of Hanover),[20] after dark on the cool evening of 6 October 1941, Peter Stevens and 'Mike' Lewis huddled together in the underbrush. They had just jumped off a train moving at about 10 mph, and German guards had fired many bullets in their direction. And not only with rifles, but also with automatic weapons. The two realised how incredibly lucky they had just been, and the adrenaline once again flooded through their bodies. Each had now cheated death twice within the past two months.

But soon, that adrenaline rush from surviving a near-death experience gave way to mind-numbing dread. For while the train had continued on and no guards would be tracking them immediately, their troubles had only just begun. They had no civilian clothing, no German money, and no identity papers. How in the world would they travel any distance and avoid arrest? 'Mike' Lewis was relatively certain that they wouldn't go far. After all, he couldn't speak more than about ten words of German.

Comparing notes, the two airmen realised that neither one had the cache of food that they had hoarded since they left the camp. They returned to the tracks for a quick search. It must have fallen as they were jumping and might still be there. Unfortunately, there was no sign of it; presumably the guards had seen it and taken it with them.

Both Allied pilots also knew that they would stand out in a crowd, even if they could beg, borrow, or steal some clothing. Unless they could travel discreetly. The first course of action was to disguise their RAF uniforms. Luckily, both had been able to keep their RAF-issue white wool sweaters, which they wore under their battle dress jackets. The jackets and sweaters were removed, and replaced in reverse order, to give the outward appearance of a pair of merchant sailors. Since Stevens spoke fluent German, it would be his job to speak for the both of them, and the two pilots invented the cover story of being aboard a freighter in the North Sea that had been strafed by murderous *terrorfliegers* of the dreaded RAF. This would account for the scrapes and cuts on Lewis's face.

Next, they started to plan their dash for freedom in earnest. Escape had earlier been a nebulous idea. Now the two men had to give it thought and definition. Where would they go? Which was the shortest route, and which the destination that would help them make a 'home run'?[21] How would they travel? Would they hide during the day and travel at night? Would they risk passenger trains? If so, how would they obtain money and civilian clothing?

There were three generally accepted routes for escaping: via Sweden, via Spain, and via Switzerland. All three countries were neutral and had agreed to return any combatants to their country of origin. The two escapees were not far from the North Sea port of Hamburg. And despite its heavy defences and military patrols, that general direction might allow them to find a ship heading for Sweden. 'Mike' Lewis thought this the safest route; Stevens favoured going overland to Switzerland. After all, he reasoned, since they were close to Hamburg, the Germans would probably look for them in that area.

Stevens had already begun a plot, and he shared some details with Lewis. They would make their way to nearby Hanover by foot or by freight train, and Stevens would attempt to contact certain 'pre-war acquaintances' who would supply food, money and civilian clothing. Then they would buy tickets on secondary trains heading to small and medium-sized towns on routes heading towards the Swiss border. Stevens persuaded Lewis that the Germans would expect them to be heading north; Spain was too far, and so Switzerland won by default. Besides, Stevens said, Swiss territory jutted into south-west Germany about one hundred miles south of Stuttgart, at Schaffhausen, and the border crossing there was long and mostly over land. Sewn inside the lining of each of their uniforms was a silk escape map that showed in some detail a spot east of Schaffhausen where the Rhine River, the border between Germany and Switzerland, was shallow enough to wade across in safety. Besides, they agreed, the Alps would indeed be pretty in the autumn.

Lewis decided to test their plan and formulated some questions. Might not Stevens's 'pre-war acquaintances' turn them in? How did Stevens know that the pair could trust them? And what would the airmen do if police or civilian officials accosted them? Lewis was acutely aware of the danger that faced them. It was entirely possible that they could be recaptured, handed over to the *Gestapo*, and simply be made to 'disappear'. The thought of this made it imperative to assure himself that any plan had to be carefully weighed, and all possible outcomes considered, prior to giving his assent.

Stevens knew that his plan was good but wasn't sure whether to tell Lewis the entire truth. He spent the next few hours thinking and finally came to a decision. If he was wrong, it could cost him his life.

As the night wore on, the two escapees shivered together and followed the train tracks south-west, on the lookout for any sign of human or train. As dawn approached on 7 October, they decided that it was just too dangerous to walk in broad daylight, especially in their air force uniforms. They headed for a nearby wooded area and prepared a hiding place where they might sleep.

Spying a small railway shed in the distance, they decided that it would be a better place to spend the daylight hours. They resolved to try and jump a freight train heading towards Hanover as soon as the sun went down.

The shed, though locked, was easy to break into. The fugitives cleared some room among the pieces of equipment inside and sat down to await the friendly darkness. Finally, as they hid, Stevens told Lewis his whole story.[22]

Stevens admitted that he was not really a British subject called Peter Stevens, but a German Jew who had been born and grew up in Hanover. He did not volunteer his real name, knowing that this valuable information could hurt his family if it fell into the wrong hands. And the 'pre-war acquaintances' were his relatives. The news shocked Lewis, but he realised that, while he wanted to know more, he didn't *need* to know any more. And the military taught people not to ask about things that didn't concern them. Lewis quickly grasped just how dangerous Stevens's admission was, and his respect for his new friend grew exponentially. Lewis knew that if the Germans ever discovered the truth, they would almost certainly torture and kill Stevens.

The mood between the two comrades changed almost imperceptibly. Lewis, the pre-war pilot and decorated veteran of two full tours of duty, now fully appreciated the less combat-experienced Stevens. The very serious Lewis now listened to Stevens even more carefully and thought harder before responding.

Dusk came at about 7 p.m., and Lewis and Stevens resumed their journey, but this time on the Hamburg–Hanover road. At about 11 p.m., they arrived at Celle (about twenty miles north-east of Hanover) and headed surreptitiously for the railway freight yard. Within an hour, they heard a train approaching. Scrambling for cover, they waited to see if it carried freight or passengers. Soon they spied a slow-moving steam locomotive pulling some twenty freight wagons. Lewis and Stevens nodded at each other and, after the locomotive had passed, ran for a freight car with a side door slightly ajar. They jumped on board and hid inside. The train soon stopped, however, so the fugitives decided to head back to the yard at Celle and wait for another train.

It was at this point that the pair's hunger got the best of them. Spying over a fence bordering the rail yard, the escapees saw a vegetable patch! They scrambled over the fence and started digging. They found mostly potatoes, which they had no way to cook – so they feasted on raw spuds. After eating their fill, they returned to the train yard.

Fortunately, another fairly slow-moving freight train soon came by, and the pair hopped on and hid in a railcar. Over several hours, the train started and stopped many times, waiting to switch tracks or shunting onto lay-bys in deference to passenger trains. Eventually, in early dawn, the number of tracks multiplied – they were approaching a city centre, but was it Hanover? The pair realised that a major railway yard would likely be crawling with armed guards, and so Lewis and Stevens decided to leave the train and find their bearings.

Unfortunately, the train showed no sign of slowing, and Stevens didn't want to head north. Despite the speed, perhaps 25 mph, Stevens jumped first. Lewis thought that he'd seen Stevens's legs knocked out from under him and was very worried about the possible consequence. What if his legs had become trapped between the rails and the massive steel wheels? Lewis took a big chance and jumped out into the void. Fortunately, when he came to rest he saw Stevens standing nearby, dusting himself off.

Although they had earlier decided to lie low during daylight hours, Stevens told Lewis about the relative in Hanover that he wanted to visit first – his mother. It being wartime, Lewis knew that such a visit would be dangerous for all three of them, but at the same time, he didn't want to be the one to deny Stevens the opportunity to see his own mother. They were quite hungry, having eaten nothing but the raw potatoes since leaving the prison camp some two days earlier. They had taken water from streams along the journey, but two stomachs were cramping up noticeably from hunger. Off they went.

Remaining under cover until about 10 a.m., Stevens instructed Lewis to walk alongside him and not say a word if they were stopped by anyone. Lewis fell in beside Stevens and heeded his instruction. Stevens quickly confirmed that they were on the outskirts of Hanover, so he could navigate them to his family home. Fortunately it was a short walk, since Stevens's neighbourhood was near the centre of the city – some two miles from where they had disembarked. Being nervous, and not wanting to appear as loiterers, they walked briskly and purposefully. Lewis thought that this expedition had turned into quite the adventure. He had been adamant up till then about having his rightful say in all decisions. After all, he was as much at risk as Stevens. But at this point in their journey, Stevens was in the driver's seat and he was along for the ride. Lewis began to understand what it felt like to be a bomber-crew member other than the pilot – complete lack of control. He did not enjoy the sensation.

Arriving on the tree-lined Rumannstrasse, Stevens pointed partway down the street to a fine four-storey building in what was clearly an affluent neighbourhood. As he had explained to Lewis, Stevens knew that the next part might be dangerous. It was approaching 11 a.m., so it was dangerous to move about openly. But Stevens had no idea whether he might find any family members at the old address. The pair exchanged brief words, and Lewis disappeared around the side to hide at the back corner of the building.

Stevens tried to appear calm as he strode up the seven stone steps to the main door. There was a board listing surnames, and he searched for his own. He knew the second-floor flat number without looking at the board, but the name beside it was not his. Scanning the other names, he saw a familiar one. Friends of his mother's, they had lived there longer than his family. Deciding to take a chance, Stevens entered the imposing but unlocked main door.

Crossing the marble-floored lobby to the main staircase, Stevens took the stairs two at a time. He glanced furtively towards the familiar door but felt no affinity for what lay behind it. After all, behind it was where his father had died and abandoned him to the unloving woman he knew as his mother.

Forcing himself to concentrate on the mission at hand, Stevens focused on the neighbours' name and slid silently over to their door. Approaching the door, he knocked quietly but purposely.

Since the neighbourhood had been completely integrated between Christians and Jews when Stevens had last lived in the flat, it would not be wise to attract the attention of anyone else in the building. Stevens whispered in German through the narrow crack as the door opened just slightly. He spent less than a minute at the door, and then rushed back down the staircase and out the main entrance. He found Lewis, and quietly explained what he'd been told by the neighbour. His mother, it was thought, had moved to another large building just a few streets away. It only took them ten minutes to walk there.

While Lewis again waited out of sight by the side of the block of flats, Stevens went up to the main door and knocked. An older woman opened it and spoke quietly with Stevens for only a minute or so.

The elderly lady disappeared, and the door closed silently. Stevens beckoned to Lewis to follow him back down to the street. Once in the open, they walked swiftly eastwards the two hundred yards or so to the dark and isolated Eilenriede Park. Stevens had fond memories of playing there as a young boy.

As soon as Stevens was sure that they were alone in the dense parkland forest, he told Lewis the sad news: his mother was dead. The neighbour, shocked to see little Georg Hein all grown up and standing at the door, had known that Georg had fled to England. What could he possibly have been doing here in the middle of the war? Perhaps it was that nervous realisation that made her say as much as she did, but the impact of Hein's presence equalled Stevens's dismay at learning of his mother's suicide in July 1939. Clearly, the thought raced through his mind, she had guessed at the horrors that were coming and had decided that she wanted no part of them. She had performed her motherly duty to the best of her ability, and her three children were safe in England. Virtually penniless, and knowing that her life was worth nothing to the Nazis, she took the brave way out. A friendly Jewish doctor had no doubt supplied the sleeping pills.

Although Stevens had felt no real affection for his mother, the revelation transformed his outward demeanour somewhat. Nevertheless, he didn't stop thinking. He shut out thoughts of his mother and told Lewis that the neighbour had revealed that his few remaining Hein relatives lived at a certain address in 'the Jewish ghetto'. A very serious discussion ensued about the advisability of two escaped prisoners of war walking into what had to be an area of some Nazi supervision in broad daylight. In the end, the pair agreed to take a chance, and walk by the neighbourhood to see the lay of the land.

Since Stevens had left Hanover as a young teenager some eight years earlier, he had had to ask the neighbour for specific directions. He also had to trust that the neighbour would not immediately call the *Gestapo* and send it to the same address. Staying on smaller residential streets rather than thoroughfares, Stevens and Lewis walked the three miles or so westwards to the old Jewish part of town. It occurred to Stevens that he was close by the An Der Strangriede Jewish Cemetery, where his father and all four of his grandparents[23] lay – and probably now his mother.

Approaching the address Stevens had been given, he again suggested to Lewis that he wait in the shadows just around the corner, in case it was a trap. Lewis watched silently as Stevens knocked quietly on the door; it was by now just after noon.

The residents were undoubtedly not expecting visitors, and the knock at the door was not welcome. After all, the only people who came knocking these days were the Nazis. With great trepidation, somebody opened the door a hair. Whispers were exchanged briefly, and Stevens motioned to Lewis that everything was safe. The door opened further, and the two fugitives slipped softly across the threshold.

Lewis recollects a warm welcome, but everyone spoke in German, so he understood nothing. The identity of their visitor shocked the residents, but after some hurried explanations by Stevens they seemed to come to grips with it. Soon they offered hot food to the two airmen, who devoured it.

Much more talk ensued (in German, of course), and the sad faces told Lewis that they had turned to the subject of Henni's death. After a few minutes, Stevens explained to Lewis that they could stay only a couple of hours and then would have to move again. After all, he explained, they didn't want to endanger their hosts, or themselves, any more than necessary. After the meal, several people brought out civilian suits; the two escapees tried on various pieces of apparel and settled on whatever fit best. The men were careful to wear articles of their air force uniforms underneath civilian clothing lest arresting officers take them for spies, suitable for torture and summary execution. The uniforms ensured them the protection of the Geneva Convention. Well, for Lewis, anyway.

Finally, the relatives offered the airmen what little money they could. They realised, it seemed to Lewis, that they could not fight the Nazis in any physical way and might be sent to the concentration camps at any time. By helping Stevens and Lewis, however, they could help the war effort in some small way.

Lewis never asked, and Stevens never volunteered, the names of the Hanoverians who helped them. They were probably from the family of one of Henni's sisters: Aunt Toni Seckel (and her husband, Stern Flatow) or Aunt Rosa (Seckel) Wertheimer. Rosa's husband had escaped to England, but she stayed behind. No records have been found, but it is thought that Toni and all of her family died in Sachsenhausen concentration camp near Berlin, and Rosa in the camp at Theresienstadt, in the Czech Republic.

Leaving the house at about 4 p.m., the two escapees planned to catch a train south towards Switzerland. The gift money would pay for their whole journey. Fellow prisoners of war had warned them to avoid the mainline trains, which attracted the attention of *Gestapo* members, who would probably stop them to check their non-existent identity papers.

According to German law, as a Jew, Stevens would have had to wear a yellow patch of material, about three inches across, bearing an embroidered six-pointed star that said *Jude*. He took a small amount of silent delight in breaking that onerous law.

The airmen reached the main Hanover station just as the evening commuter rush was beginning. In their civilian clothes, they could fit in much easier now. Lewis shadowed Stevens from a distance as he checked the large train schedule on the station wall and then ambled over to the ticket window. Stevens bought a pair of second-class tickets on a train that would stop frequently on its way south to Frankfurt am Main. The journey of some two hundred miles would normally take till about 10 p.m.

Lewis had learned quickly not to make a sound in public. Any hint of English would arouse suspicion. Stevens motioned to him to follow, and they were soon on a platform waiting for a slow train headed south. The people still in the station appeared to Lewis perfectly normal, not like mortal enemies, ready to kill him on the spot.

Clearly the war had disrupted the passenger-train schedule. The European systems had been punctual up to 1939 but were no longer. Trains were now almost always late even in Germany, and disruptions were rampant, as the *Englische Terrorfliegers* visited the German rail system from above almost every night.

Germany was rationing gasoline for all non-essential uses, so trains were now usually full to overflowing. Nonetheless the escapees could at least hope that this slow train, although departing at rush hour, would not attract commuters hurrying home. Eventually their train arrived, only twenty minutes late. They quickly found an empty second-class compartment and hoped desperately for solitude and sleep.

Before the train could depart, however, two German soldiers knocked at the door and asked about the empty seats. As Stevens and Lewis froze, the two infantrymen entered and sat down. The airmen glared at one another but were unable to speak. Stevens made a harmless comment to put at ease the soldiers, who volunteered that they were going to Frankfurt on a three-day pass for a bit of rest and recreation. The prospect of unlimited beer and some female attention clearly excited them. After a bit more small talk, Stevens stretched, curled up in his seat, and appeared to go to sleep. Lewis, not wanting to attract attention or invite conversation, tried to do the same.

The Canadian and the erstwhile Englishman could not believe what had happened to them. Of all the people to choose those seats, why were they German soldiers? After all, despite being on leave, they still had weapons. And if they so chose, they could easily raise the alarm.

As they rolled south through central Germany, the compartment seemed to house two relaxed, uniformed soldiers and two relaxed German civilians. The two real Germans never asked their neighbours why they were not in uniform. Perhaps Stevens's friendly demeanour had indeed put them at ease.

The mail-train journey, which would have taken about six hours in peacetime, now took almost eight. There were many long stops while military trains received direct routeings. But this train did indeed attract less attention from the authorities. Not once did anyone ask the escapees for their identity papers.

When the train pulled into the main station in Frankfurt late that night, the German soldiers simply rose and gathered their belongings, waved goodbye, and left. Lewis and Stevens could not believe their luck! Suddenly a huge weight lifted from their shoulders. They almost danced as they climbed down to the platform. This was their second visit to Frankfurt in just under a month; this time, however, they were free men!

It being almost midnight, there were few diners in the station cafeteria, and so the two pilots decided to stop for a bite before planning onward travel. They ordered an inexpensive but filling meal and sat down to consume it. Over dinner, they discussed what to do and where to go for the night. Frankfurt was a major centre with connections from every direction, so Stevens reasoned that they could probably spend the night in the station itself. The timetable showed a train leaving for Karlsruhe at 4.30 a.m. Lewis accepted the logic, and they agreed to stay.

At least twenty other travellers were bedding down on the waiting-room benches. Lewis and Stevens could steal a half-hour's sleep at a time, taking turns to keep guard. At about two o'clock on the morning of 9 October, however, both men woke to see a pair of German railway policemen demanding to see their tickets. Stevens immediately explained that their train had arrived quite late and they hadn't yet had a chance to buy tickets for the next leg of their journey. Not an unreasonable excuse, on the face of it. But the policemen then demanded to see identity cards.

Realising that they could not satisfy the officials, Stevens guessed that the jig was up. On the spot, he decided it would be better for them to identify themselves in a public place rather than in a *Gestapo* prison, whence they might simply disappear. They both threw their hands in the air and proclaimed, 'We are British air force officers who have escaped from a German prisoner-of-war camp. We demand to be treated according to the Geneva Convention.' The police arrested them and took them to the railway police office inside the massive station.

Lewis and Stevens had been free and on the loose in the Third *Reich* for two days and six hours.[24]

Notes

1. The Dutch boy was Bob Roele, whom I interviewed in 2001.
2. Gerrie Zwanenburg, MBE, in a letter to me, 15 November 1989. Zwanenburg is an expert on Second World War crashes of Allied aircraft on Dutch soil.
3. Short for '*Durchgangslager*' – entrance or transit camp. '*Luft*' (short form of *Luftwaffe*) is German for air, as in air force.
4. I reached Alan Payne's widow by telephone in August 2004, and she told me that he had survived the war and had become a teacher but had also reached a senior rank (group captain) in the British Air Training Corps (Air Cadets). He died of cancer on 8 May 2004.
5. Short form of *Kriegsgefangener*, or prisoner of war. *Kriegie* became a common term of endearment among the prisoners, who used it often to refer to their fellow prisoners or themselves.
6. A tour of duty in RAF Bomber Command was typically about thirty operations. When the United States entered the war after 7 December 1941, and began bombing operations

from England, it deemed that twenty-five missions was sufficient to complete an American's tour of duty.

7. William J. Wheeler, ed., *Flying under Fire* (Calgary: Fifth House Ltd, 2001), 12.
8. Sydney Smith, *Wings Day: the story of the man who led the RAF's epic battle in German captivity* (London: William Collins Sons & Co Ltd., 1968), 43.
9. Smith, *Wings Day*, 62–3.
10. Ibid., 65.
11. www.pegasus-one.org/pow/roger_bushell.htm
12. Charles Rollings, *Wire and Worse: RAF Prisoners of War in Laufen, Biberach , Lübeck and Warburg 1940–42* (Hersham, Surrey: Ian Allen Publishing, 2004), 84.
13. Ibid., 95–6.
14. www.bbc.co.uk/ww2peopleswar/stories/66/a1904366.shtml
15. Paul Brickhill, *Reach for the Sky* (London, Collins, 1954).
16. Rollings, *Wire and Worse*, 119.
17. Ibid., 150–1.
18. Ibid., 159.
19. Ibid. Roger Bushell later escaped from the same train and was at large in Czechoslovakia for seven months before his recapture.
20. National Archives, document AIR 2 / 9125 – Postwar Debrief of Peter Stevens by MI9.
21. A term borrowed from baseball for a successful escape, meaning a return to England.
22. Lewis described their escape to me during interviews and via e-mail between 1986 and 2007.
23. Selly Hein and his wife, Johanna Herzheim, and Siegmund Seckel and his wife, Rieke Moses.
24. National Archives, document AIR 2 / 9125, Postwar Debrief of Peter Stevens by MI9.

CHAPTER TWELVE

'Orderlies' and a Latrine Tunnel: Warburg and Schubin (October 1941–April 1943)

Meanwhile, back in England, the authorities finally realised what had become of Georg Franz Hein. On 7 October 1941, a sergeant (signature illegible) wrote to the chief inspector (presumably of the Metropolitan Police of London):

> In February, 1941, information came to hand that Hein was serving in the Royal Air Force, but despite exhaustive enquiries, he was not located.
>
> On 7th October 1941, information was received from Flight-Lieutenant Hixson of the A.P.M.'s office, London, to the effect that Hein is now a prisoner of war in Germany. He joined the Royal Air Force under the name Peter Stevens on 4th September 1939, and was taken prisoner whilst engaged in a raid on Berlin on the night of 7th—8th September 1941. At that time he was a Pilot Officer.
>
> It was stated that both the photograph and handwriting of Hein have been identified by his Commanding Officer as being those of Peter Stevens; further, that Stevens left directions that in the event of anything happening to him, notification should be sent to Messrs. Lake & Son, Solicitors, 61, Carey Street, London, W.C.1. and Mr. Erich Hein, c/o, Woburn House, Bloomsbury, W.C.2.
>
> Records show that Messrs. Lake & Son acted for Hein when he was last in custody, whilst Erich Hein, Registration Certificate No. 526508, is known to be his brother.[1]

The report suggested forwarding a copy of the same to the Aliens Department of the Home Office, with a request that it instruct the police what to do about the outstanding restriction order on Georg Hein.

Hand-written notes in the Home Office file for Georg Hein/Peter Stevens read 'an interesting story' (18 October 1941) and 'it is to be hoped that the Germans will not penetrate his disguise under the name Peter Stevens' (20 October 1941).[2]

Luckily, the railway police officer who arrested Lewis and Stevens in the train station at Frankfurt did not hand the airmen over to the *Gestapo*. After the Brits stripped off their outer civilian suits and showed their uniforms underneath, they were taken to the military prison, where officials questioned them briefly. The *Luftwaffe* had published details of their escape two-and-a-half days earlier, so the military already 'expected' them. A cursory and reasonably civil interrogation followed, and armed guards transferred the two pilots to their original destination – *Oflag* VI B at Warburg. The date was 12 October 1941.[3]

After arrival formalities, guards escorted the men into the general camp compound and left them to find their own beds.[4] Of course, their Lübeck friends congratulated the new 'escapers' and quizzed them endlessly on what had happened.

Eschewing their instant celebrity, Stevens and Lewis headed off to report to the Senior British Officer. He assigned them to huts and rooms, and ordered them to return for debriefing after they had settled in. After recapture, an Allied escaper underwent a quick interrogation from his own camp intelligence officer. The latter would then pass on in writing any useful information to the 'X' Organisation, such as details about train timetables, number and disposition of German soldiers at key points for escapers, and locations of and damage to any military installations.

For the next few days, it seemed to Lewis and Stevens as though every man in the camp wanted to speak with them. Many officers hoped to escape and were eager to benefit from the experiences of those who had seen life outside the wire. Many officers who had no desire to escape sought to show solidarity with those who did and so offered their congratulations and a pat on the back. Everyone realised that simply being out of German custody for a day or two constituted success. It forced the Germans to expend valuable time and personnel tracking down the escapers, redirecting assets that could otherwise help elsewhere in fighting the war.

Oflag VI B (Warburg) was about twenty-five miles north-west of Kassel, in central Germany, about sixty miles south of Hanover and eighty east of Düsseldorf. The camp was quite large: the long axis was over five hundred metres, and the short about three hundred. The ground was quite sloped; hence the 'Lower Gate' at one end and the 'Upper Gate' at the other. Twenty long barracks huts in several rows covered the camp's western half, two large sports fields the centre, and nine larger huts at a forty-five-degree angle were on the other side. The camp held approximately three thousand Allied officers and was rumoured to be the assembly point for a possible large exchange of prisoners between Germany and Britain, probably before Christmas.[5]

The barracks in German prisoner-of-war camps generally consisted of 'rooms' of six to eight (or possibly more) men. The rooms at Warburg were about seven metres by four metres, and each held from twelve to sixteen officers.[6] There were perhaps real walls inside, but the men also arranged their double-tiered bunk beds into makeshift walls to give the semblance of smaller and more personal 'rooms'. Each officer usually had a small cupboard or closet to store personal possessions (clothes, books, toiletries, and so on). A table and chairs usually occupied the centre of each room and served as the focal point for all social activity.

Most men, however, would have gone crazy if they did nothing other than talk all day indoors with the same seven men, and so everyone took advantage of the available outside activities. These would include walking 'the Circuit', the path around the inside of the camp's warning wire. The majority of prisoners were airmen and had flown many rectangular 'circuits' around their airfields at home, practicing take-offs and landings. Other activities included educational courses, musical training and practice, theatrical events, and sports such as soccer or rugby.

Warburg was not a good prisoner-of-war camp. Rats, mice, and fleas infested the huts, which had no toilets; guards locked the men in between sunset and sunrise. The infirmary held eighty-four beds, and all of these were usually filled, most often because of bronchitis and diphtheria. The rations were quite meagre: one daily serving of hot vegetable soup, plus one serving of bread, margarine, and jam. If not for the frequent Red Cross food parcels, the men would have been in dire straits.

The camp had lots of space for physical activity, including a good-sized football pitch and three netball courts. There was also a library with over four thousand books. Unlike at Lübeck, relations with the senior German officers were 'friendly'. During the eleven months that Warburg was open, the Germans built a second kitchen and improved the heating of the huts. As the flow of Red Cross parcels increased over the winter of 1941–2, however, the Germans cut back on the rations they supplied.[7]

Stevens quickly settled down. Everyday life centred around organised activities, which addressed personal cleanliness and feeding, but also occupied officers' minds and kept them from dwelling on the negative aspects of life. The Germans insisted on twice-daily *Appells*. This often became a game for the *Kriegies*, to see how they could falsify the count and frustrate the Germans. In more than one instance, they went a little too far, and the Germans reacted badly. A prisoner caught playing games might receive a rifle butt in the head. As well, the Germans would often search the huts while everyone was standing outside.

The never-ending shortage of food dominated minds and discussion. With Christmas not that far away, some prisoners began hoarding, hoping for at least some sort of Christmas pudding. It allowed the downtrodden psyche some respite from despair and loneliness.

On 2 November 1941 (the first anniversary of his commissioning as an RAF officer), news came of Stevens's promotion to flying officer. The only tangible result was a small increase in pay going to his bank in England.

Throughout November, the camp was alive with escape buzz. It seemed that most prisoners were active in planning some sort of scheme. Over the wire, under the wire, through the wire – everyone had an idea. The 'X' Organisation had been working overtime reviewing proposals and schemes. One grabbed their attention. And since Peter Stevens could speak perfect, accent-less German, he was to play a major role.

On 1 December, two armed German guards and an *Unteroffizier* (corporal) marched a group of French orderlies out of the camp's main gate. The party was about fifty yards outside when the gate guard called for it to return. The gate guard had realised that the *Unteroffizier*'s pass was missing the signature of the day's duty officer. The *Unteroffizier* admitted that the signature was missing and marched the group back into camp.

Unknown to the gate guard, all thirteen members of the party had been Allied prisoners in the charge of Peter Stevens. One of the guards was 'Prince' Palmer, another inveterate escaper. Camp tailors Dominic Bruce and Peter Tunstall had altered Allied uniform overcoats and dyed them to look like German ones. As well, the men had carved two fake German rifles from solid blocks of wood. The gate guard had not realised anything.[8]

A later account of the day's activities read:

Two officers, Flight-Lieuts. Stevens and Palmer, were dressed, not altogether convincingly, as a German N.C.O. and private soldier. Their kit was ingeniously if not very carefully contrived, and was far indeed from an exact replica of German uniform. Stevens, a really excellent German speaker, made up for this by his individual dash and resource.[9]

On 18 May 1946, the *News of the World* proclaimed 'The Boldest Escape Bid of the War':

None of the many prison camp escapes attempted by our men in Germany paralleled for daring, audacity and coolness that made by Flight-Lieut. Peter Stevens.[10]

Realising the group's good fortune, 'X' decided to use the method again, after a cooling-off period. On 8 December, *Unteroffizier* Stevens marched another work party of French orderlies to the main gate. This time, however, the gate guard was immediately suspicious and told Stevens that he did not recognise him or either of the two 'guards'. He started questioning Stevens aggressively and demanded to see the three men's military paybooks. Stevens, thinking quickly, replied that they had left the documents in the guardroom and said that they would retrieve them and return. Stevens marched the party back into the compound, but as it passed through the interior gate the German guard decided to stop it and obtain help to sort things out. He raised the alarm, and the prisoners scattered. The German guard, unaware that Stevens was a fake, yelled at him to help corral the fleeing men.[11] Unfortunately the Germans arrested Lieutenant C.H. Filmer of the Royal Navy's Fleet Air Arm and RAF Squadron Leader 'Bush' Kennedy, who spent time in the cooler.[12]

Just a day earlier, and halfway around the planet, the war had changed. On Sunday 7 December – 'a date that will live in infamy' in Franklin Roosevelt's gripping phrase – Japan attacked Pearl Harbor and other military bases in Hawaii. The United States declared war on Japan the next day. On 27 September 1940, Germany, Japan, and Italy had signed the Tripartite Pact, pledging military support to each other.[13] Pearl Harbor represented the excuse for which Roosevelt had been searching, and the US Congress approved a declaration of war against all three powers.

The jungle radio at Warburg was quite efficient, and by late on 7 December everyone in camp knew about the attack. Charles Rollings wrote: 'The local Goons (i.e. Germans) were exultant.' When the German guards gloated to their prisoners about the great success of the attack, the response surprised them: this would bring the Americans into the war, which would eventually mean the end for Germany.[14]

Christmas 1941 came and went, but escape remained foremost in the prisoners' minds. During the first eight months of 1942, Peter Stevens was helping to plan or construct three tunnels at *Oflag* VI B, but the Germans discovered all three before their completion.[15]

Stevens also became active in 'X'. His escape attempts had attracted notice, as had his fluency in German. 'X' recruited him to help in the forging of false identity documents and in scrounging. He would remain active in both throughout his remainder of his captivity.

A fellow prisoner at Warburg was Gilbert ('Tim') Walenn, a talented English artist. Tim was a natural as a forger and later headed that department within 'X'. Stevens and Walenn had been roommates at Lübeck and had worked closely together.[16] Stevens was one of very few men whom 'X' authorised to trade with the Germans. While chocolates or cigarettes could obtain most everyday items from German guards, strategically important goods such as a camera and film or radio parts were much more difficult to acquire, and needed the benefit of great tact.

'X' deputised Stevens and relied on him to obtain whatever any of its divisions needed. The most common method that prisoners used was to start off bargaining for something seemingly small and innocuous, such as tools for woodworking or sewing. Such items seemed essential for furniture and clothing and had no obvious strategic value. And so Stevens would arrange to be alone with a 'tame' guard and, in a deep but calm and soothing German voice, ask for a 'favour'. Of course, any helpful guard would receive in return a significant 'gift', for which he would sign a 'receipt' so that Stevens could show his superiors that he had not consumed the goods himself. As soon as he signed the receipt, he was vulnerable to blackmail. In this way, Stevens could bribe certain guards to provide increasingly crucial goods. A few anti-Nazi guards did not require bribes and co-operated willingly.

So Stevens acquired goods such as camp-gate passes and official German worker-identity cards for Walenn and his forgers to copy. He also became by default Walenn's 'expert' on all things German. The two men would often collaborate on the wording of letters of introduction or other 'unofficial' identification documents. Walenn's department earned the nickname 'Thomas Cook' or 'Dean and Dawson' after two well-known English travel agencies; that way an inadvertent mention of either would not alert a passing goon.

Sadly, Walenn would later become famous as one of the unfortunate '50'. 'The Great Escape', in March 1944, should have been his crowning glory. He and his brilliant artists prepared 200 sets of false documents for the mass breakout from the North Compound of *Stalag Luft* III in Poland.

Walenn, along with seventy-five other Allied officers, escaped from a 300-foot tunnel that they had dug thirty feet deep under the yellow sands of *Stalag Luft* III. As a key participant, Tim had an early spot in the line-up for the tunnel; the earlier one escaped, the more time one had to move far from the camp, perhaps catching an early train rather than a later one. Of the seventy-six prisoners who escaped before discovery of the tunnel, three made it back to England and the Germans recaptured seventy-three.

When Hitler learned of the mass breakout, he went berserk and ordered the execution of all those recaptured. This was clearly against the Geneva Convention, as the escaping officers were only doing their sworn duty. Hitler's advisers were able to mitigate his ire somewhat, and he spared twenty-three men. The *Gestapo* chose Tim Walenn as one of the fifty to die. Their cold-blooded murder stunned and shocked the Allies.

The film *The Great Escape* (1963) starred Steve McQueen (as the American 'Cooler King' escape artist called Hilts), James Garner (as the Scrounger), Sir Richard Attenborough (as Roger Bartlett, 'Big X'), Charles Bronson (as the 'Tunnel King') and Donald Pleasance (as the forger). For people who had studied the events, Pleasance's character appeared, apart from the blindness that the film added, to be Tim Walenn.

As 1941 gave way to 1942, camp life focused on food and escape. There was never enough food, so escape served as a diversion from constant hunger. Not every officer participated in the effort, and that was acceptable. Despite the officer's duty to escape, every prisoner had already risked his life to arrive at that place. Most of the hard-core escapers realised that not everyone had the nerve for the task.

Some abstainers helped in one way or another: they might take dirt from the tunnel digging and disperse it as inconspicuously as possible – a dangerous business in winter, when piles of dry dirt on clean snow would readily attract attention. Others would help out as forgers, as tailors (converting Allied uniforms into German military or civilian clothing), or as 'stooges' (keeping track of, and reporting, movements of German guards and ferrets in and out of the camp). 'Ferret' was the nickname given by Allied prisoners to German guards who specialised in searching for tunnels. Because their duties required that they climb in, around and under the prisoners' huts, they wore dark blue jumpsuits over their uniforms.

Other non-participants in escape activities occupied their time reading, teaching or attending courses, playing in the camp orchestra, or taking part in theatrical productions. The Germans were usually happy to provide equipment, because a prisoner playing music or sports was at least not digging a tunnel at the same time.

After the war, however, stories showed how these diversions could disguise tunnelling activities. Orchestra practice could cover the heavy hammering of breaking through concrete and tile. While the Drama Society was rehearsing, escapers could hide the dirt from a tunnel under the sloping theatre floor (as happened in North Compound of *Stalag Luft* III). Art classes often served as mass document-forging clinics.

In 1942, German High Command decided that the camp at Warburg had outlived its usefulness. During the summer, the Germans were still advancing deeper into Russia on the Eastern Front and felt that it would be wise politically to move as many prisoners as possible out of Germany proper. The highest levels of government thought that locating prisoners of war in Poland would boost the morale of German civilians. It would free the homeland of the fear of Allied escapes, place more distance between prisoners and Britain, and render useless any escape plans and tunnels already under way. Charles Rollings wrote that *Oflag* VI B spawned no fewer than 110 tunnel starts![17] Peter Stevens had taken part in three.[18]

On 19 August 1942, there was the ill-fated Canadian assault on the French port of Dieppe. This attack, which lacked sufficient naval and air support, was almost certainly a feint, as British commanders sought to assess German coastal defences. Of the 5,000 or so soldiers who hit the beach, just over 2,000 returned to England. The Germans took almost 2,000 prisoners and killed 807 men.[19] When this news reached Warburg, it must have hurt morale.

Sometime during the second half of 1942, 'Mike' Lewis, after months of reflection, decided that the story of Peter Stevens could not remain a secret for just the two of them. Besides, Lewis thought, if the Germans should somehow learn the truth, the Geneva Convention could not help Stevens, nor could the British. He went to Stevens and persuaded him to inform the Senior British Officer. At least that way, Lewis rationalised, if the Germans found out, the British might somehow be able to protect Stevens. And so Peter Stevens duly spoke with 'Wings' Day, who met the story with typical aplomb, although the man's courage amazed him. Day himself first told the world (in a 1968 biography of him) the true story of Peter Stevens.[20]

At the end of August 1942, the Senior British Officer at Warburg learned that the camp was closing and that all the prisoners would transfer elsewhere. Warburg had been originally intended only for army men, and the Germans saw that mixing prisoners from different branches of the armed forces created discord and extra work for them. They therefore decided to send all the air force officers to be with colleagues, to *Oflag* XXI B at Schubin, in central Poland. And so, in late August and early September 1942, Peter Stevens and most of the airmen at Warburg entrained for Poland. Stevens arrived at Schubin on 5 September.[21]

Surprisingly, the new camp was a former girls' school, about two miles outside of town. It consisted of a large white school building, several outbuildings, a chapel, a stable, and a good amount of space, boasting a sports field and two large vegetable gardens. The ground sloped noticeably from one end of camp to the other, but the sports field at least was now level.[22]

Feldwebel Hermann Glemnitz, the *Luftwaffe*'s senior non-commissioned officer at Warburg and Sagan and the bane of all escapers, accompanied the next transfer of prisoners to Schubin on 9 September. That group included 'Wings' Day and about a hundred of the best RAF escapers.

Harry Melville Arbuthnot Day was an odd bird. Born in northern Borneo in 1898, he attended private schools in England. A great-uncle was naval Captain George Day, who won the Victoria Cross[23] during the Crimean War. His great-great-great grandfather was Royal Navy Captain George Miller Bligh, a hero of the Napoleonic wars. Day himself had already served with distinction during the First World War. As an eighteen-year-old second lieutenant serving with the Royal Marines on board HMS *Britannia* when it was torpedoed in 1916, he went below in the burning vessel, at great personal risk, to carry several wounded crewmen to safety. He received the Albert Medal for bravery.[24]

Between the wars, Day took up flying and became a pilot. He transferred to the RAF in 1929 and was already an 'old man' by September 1939. The Germans shot down his Blenheim bomber during a photoreconnaissance mission on 13 October 1939, and he was to become one of the most avid, and greatest, escapers of the war.

Feldwebel Glemnitz thought it madness to put such a large group of experienced escape artists together in one camp. He attempted to warn the *Wehrmacht* guards at Schubin, but they ignored his advice. As he left for *Stalag Luft* III at Sagan (further south-west in Poland), he actually reminded the Allied officers that it was their duty to escape! In response, several yelled out in German, '*Befehl ist Befehl!*' (An order is an order!)[25]

Glemnitz was one of the few German camp guards who was completely incorruptible. A veteran of the Great War, he 'knew the score'. While he served patriotically, he was no Nazi. But he was dangerous. He knew many, if not most, of the escapers' tricks and tried to stay one step ahead of them. Despite the nickname 'Dimwits' from the *Kriegies*, he earned the prisoners' grudging respect.[26] He would later be guest of honour at the Ex-Air Force POW Reunion in Toronto in 1970 and actually spent several days as a guest in the home of Peter Stevens. One wonders what they discussed over a drink late on those evenings…

Incidents occurred in the early days at Schubin. RAF Flight Lieutenant R.H. Edwards decided that he had had enough of prison life. On 26 September 1942, he walked calmly towards the barbed wire. Surprisingly, he didn't stop. As he reached the fence, he began climbing. A German guard stationed outside the wire told him to climb down, but Edwards ignored the order. Rather than calling for help with a clearly deranged man, the guard simply shot Edwards, who died soon afterwards. On 12 November, RAF Flying Officer P.A. Lovegrove fell out of a third-storey window and landed on his head. He also died.[27]

In November 1942, Peter Stevens learned about another promotion. On the anniversary of his elevation to flying officer (2 November 1941), he became a flight lieutenant (equivalent of a captain in the army).

The new inmates of Schubin soon figured out the lay of the land. Some started tunnels, one of them destined for infamy. Eddy Asselin, an entrepreneurial Canadian officer from Montreal, realised that the closest building to the wire was the latrine (*Abort* in German). He brilliantly realised that the beehive of activity could easily cover the comings and goings of many men working on a tunnel.

Analysing the set-up of the building and its underground cesspit, Asselin soon discovered an ingenious possibility. The structure had a concrete foundation and consisted of two sections, one with urinals and the other with stalls. Descending through the first stall near the entrance, one could cut a hole in the foundation, just above the cesspit. That hole led to the area under the urinals, which were built over solid earth. The men excavated a room there, where most of the administration work could take place under cover. The location for this tunnel offered a built-in disposal site for excavated earth. Most of the soil could, and did, go straight into the cesspit, whence the camp's 'honey wagon' took it away regularly.

William ('Tex') Ash, an American Spitfire pilot in the Royal Canadian Air Force, directed tunnel construction with Asselin. In early 1940, terribly disappointed that his own country was unwilling to fight Fascism, Ash had left Texas for Canada to become a pilot. He had crash-landed his badly damaged fighter in France in March 1942 and was on the run for almost three months with members of the French Resistance, before his capture in Paris.[28]

Edmund Tobin Asselin became famous during his incarceration for finding ways to enrich his life. Often his labours brought him cigarettes and chocolate bars. Eddy liked to play cards and to bet on the outcomes of various situations. 'Tex' Ash wrote:

Eddy was a survivor, a philosopher, a helper of others but also someone with a finely developed sense of when to push and when to step back in the cause of self-preservation. Maybe that's why he made such a great poker player. Having decided on his strategy for the rest of the war, he yawned, stretched and joined in a game of cards with the motley group of pimps, deserters and refugees with whom we shared our cell. Very soon, as always, Eddy Asselin was winning.

Once he got back to Schubin camp, Eddy did as he had said, both there and later in *Stalag Luft* III, where he ran a vast and never-ending poker game, racking up huge amounts of money in back pay from those less sharp of mind.[29]

Ash later observed:

It seemed sad to me that some people spent their time cutting deals with guards while fleecing other prisoners rather than trying to escape or just getting on with life as a prisoner, but they were always in the minority. Others thought they were an admirable example of entrepreneurial spirit. Similarly there were a handful of sharks who specialized in long-running poker schools where the more foolish players ended up owing literally years of back pay. Luckily the majority of prisoners, if not anxious to get themselves shot while escaping, were more interested in helping other escapees than in being reduced to the miserable state of preying on each other. My old escape buddy Eddy Asselin and I never did manage to see eye to eye on that one, yet we stayed friends.[30]

Despite what anyone thought of him, Asselin had resourcefulness and initiative. One story has it that he disappeared immediately after the war. His family complained to the Royal Canadian Air Force that he had never returned to Canada, and it launched a search. It later found him living the high life in Paris and sent him home to Montreal forthwith.

He went on to a career in politics. He served on Montreal city council and from 1963 to 1966 was a Member of Parliament. As a mature student, he attended law school and later became a municipal court judge. He died in 1999, leaving six children and his fourth wife.

Excavation to begin the tunnel at Schubin was unpleasant. Men cut the seat of the stall strategically and replaced it with a hinged trapdoor that looked like and was a functional toilet seat. To cut through the concrete and brick foundation, workers took turns hanging upside down over the cesspit, drilling and digging until noxious fumes or blood rushing to their head overcame them.[31]

Others participating included 'Prince' Palmer (of the Warburg gate walkout attempts), 'Duke' Marshall, and Tommy Calnan. Palmer and Marshall helped with shoring (using 'liberated' bed boards), ventilation, traps, and lighting. Calnan, a Spitfire reconnaissance pilot who had been shot down and badly burned, was responsible for tunnel security.[32]

Another ten or so officers joined the venture, and they began by digging straight down to a depth of seventeen feet – deep enough, they hoped, to avoid triggering the Germans' buried seismometers. In early February 1943, a rumour spread like wildfire that the prisoners would be leaving for another location, probably in March.[33]

During construction in winter 1942–3, other preparations for the escape were under way. The camp tailors were making sets of civilian clothing, often dying uniforms and making them look like suits. As well, each escaper was to receive a set of forged identity documents. Thirty-three officers would go out the tunnel, and all would need this escape material.

In many cases, would-be escapers made up their own stories (or 'legends') and had their false documents custom-designed to fit. As the best German speaker, Peter ('Steve') Stevens often advised colleagues about the viability and wording of most documents. Soon, Stevens was so active that the escape group asked him to join it, which he did readily. It was general policy to invite on board any *Kriegie* who was helping in a big way. 'Big X' would occasionally name someone to the scheme arbitrarily, because he felt that person had an excellent chance on an escape. Sometimes the fellows who had done the hard work underground resented these interlopers. After Stevens joined, Tommy Calnan wrote:

> Steve, the German expert, was another ['Big X' appointee]. Without him, none of the documents we were using would have been even slightly plausible. All of us who were travelling 'legitimate' with forged documents were delighted to have him with us.[34]

The men made the entrance chamber for the underground tunnel sizeable – about ten feet wide by fifteen feet long by six feet high. In it, Cyril ('Sid') Swain and his carpenters made the tunnel-shoring system from liberated bedboards and other 'found' materials. [35]

During the course of tunnel construction, Peter Stevens happily took part in such Christmas festivities as there were, but noted how they differed from those of the religion of his birth. Mostly, he and his fellow prisoners just tried to put on a brave face in front of the Germans, for it was by no means clear that the Allies would win the war.

In early February 1943, Soviet forces finally turned the tide on the Eastern Front. They defeated the German war machine at Stalingrad, a decisive victory for a people desperately in need of hope. Soviet citizens noticed that the victory occurred at the city named after their feared leader, Josef Stalin. For the Germans, it proved the straw that broke the camel's back. Hitler's army, like Napoleon's, had over-extended itself and, with few minor exceptions, would not win a major land battle again.

At the time of the February 1943 rumour that hit Schubin about another move (probably in early March), the only tunnel anywhere near ready was Asselin's.

METROPOLITAN POLICE.

CRIMINAL INVESTIGATION DEPARTMENT

New Scotland Yard,

7th. day of October, 194 1

SUBJECT

Aliens

(1).

To Chief Inspector.

Reference to Papers.

79/H/1717.

    With further reference to the attached correspondence respecting Georg Franz HEIN -German- H.O. reference H.549/2 wanted for failing to report to Police, vide Police Gazette Supplement 'C' of 15th. November, 1939, Case No.3 ; and against whom a Restriction Order under Article 11 of the Aliens Order, 1920, was made on 8th. September, 1939, :-

    In February, 1941, information came to hand that Hein was serving in the Royal Air Force, but despite exhaustive enquiries, he was not located.

    On 7th. October, 1941, information was received from Flight-Lieutenant Hixson of the A.P.M.'s. Office, London, to the effect that Hein is now a prisoner of war in German He joined the Royal Air Force under the name of Peter STEV on 4th. September, 1939, and was taken prisoner whilst eng in a raid on Berlin on the night of 7th.-8th. September,19 At that time he was a Pilot Officer.

    It was stated that both the photograph and handwriti of Hein have been identified by his Commanding Officer as being those of Peter Stevens; further, that Stevens left directions that in the event of anything happening to him, notification should be sent to Messrs. Lake & Son, Solicito 61, Carey Street, London, W.C.1. and Mr. Erich Hein, c/o, Woburn House, Bloomsbury, W.C.2.

    Records show that Messrs. Lake & Son acted for Hein when he was last in custody, whilst Erich Hein, Registration Certificate No. 526508, is known to be his brother.

    I suggest that a copy of this report be forwarded to Aliens Department, Home Office, with a request that we be notified of the position in regard to the Restriction Order, the copy of which is still attached to this correspondence.

Sergeant.

Ch. Insp

7/ 10 · 41

Metropolitan Police Report of Oct 7/41 detailing their discovery of the fate of fugitive alien Georg Hein. (*National Archives File HO 405/20069, photo by author*)

Telephone Clerkenwell 7952

My Reference L.S/P.M/4616

Your Reference

PROVOST MARSHAL'S DEPARTMENT,
ROYAL AIR FORCE,
30/34 MOORGATE,
LONDON, E.C.2.

31st May, 1946.

RECEIVED
30 AUG 1946
No.

PERSONAL

Dear Marshall,

S/Ldr. P. Stevens (88219)

I am enclosing the "Naturalization Form S" completed by the abovementioned officer. The application is supported by letters which were obtained by the late W/Cdr. W.R. John from persons including a number of Senior R.A.F. Officers, who knew this officer before the war, during his internment as a prisoner-of-war in Germany, and after the war. You will observe that all of these persons write about him in terms of the highest praise.

2. The case is absolutely unique. He is actually a German Jew Georg Hein, who enlisted in the R.A.F. as an aircraft hand at the beginning of the war. He volunteered for aircrew, and was trained as a pilot. He did twenty-two operational flights over Germany, and the Commanding Officer of his station has stated that he acted with conspicuous gallantry and went quite low before dropping his bombs. He was shot down on the 7th September, 1941, and was made a prisoner-of-war in Germany.

3. He is now personal assistant, interpreter and pilot to Air Vice-Marshal A.P. Davidson, C.B.E., whose letter about him is attached. You will see that the Air Vice-Marshal states that Stevens saved his life as recently as last Christmas.

/4.

S/Ldr. C. Marshall,
Directorate of Foreign Liaison,
8/9 Buckingham Gate,
LONDON,
S.W.1.

HOME OFFICE
ALIENS DEPT.
2 - SEP 1946
FILE NUMBER
H 5471

(b) Nature of occupation :
i.) Temple Press — Advertisement Representative.
Intelligence Officer (S.O.1)

A report by the Provost Marshal of the RAF detailing the application by Georg Franz Hein for naturalization in the UK as Peter Stevens, giving full details of his case. (*National Archives File HO 405/20069, photo by author*)

4.   One thing in his favour is, that he voluntarily told the Air Vice-Marshal and also a Senior Intelligence Officer the whole of his story before being asked to do so. His conduct while in the R.A.F. has been exemplary, and there is no doubt that he is an exceptionally brave man, whose instincts are to help this country.

5.   You will find also attached, a letter from the Head Master of the Latymer Upper School, Hammersmith who adopted him with a full knowledge of the Home Office. Though I understand that this was not an official legal adoption. One difficulty is, that when he was a very young man, he got into trouble with the police about some money and a vacuum cleaner, but in view of his exceptional service to the state, I strongly recommend that his application for naturalisation should go through.

6.   I am sure you will pass all the recommendations to the appropriate quarter and expedite as far as possible the naturalisation of the officer.

Group Captain
FOR Provost Marshal

From; W/Cdr.E.T.Smith. R.A.F.

Empire Central Flying School,
R.A.F. Hullavington.
13 th.February, 1946.

Ref IS/IM/4616

Dear John,

Thank you for your letter dated 4 th.February.

I have known A/S/Ldr.P.Stevens since October 1941, when I first met him as a fellow Prisoner of War, at Oflag 6B, Warburg, Germany. Until May 1945 I was in daily personal contact with him.

His conduct was always of the highest order. He took an active part in most camp activities, was well liked, and his keenness to assist and participate in all escaping activities was most noticeable.

In my opinion, every assistance should be given him to put forward his case for naturalisation.

Yours sincerely,

W/Cdr, W.R. John O.B.E. P.M.1.
Air Ministry.

Naturalization reference letter of Feb 13/46 from Wing Commander T.E. Smith ["his keenness to assist and participate in all escaping activities was most noticeable"]. (*National Archives File HO 405/20069, photo by author*)

From:- G/Capt R.C.M. Collard, D.S.O., D.F.C.

R.A.F. Station,
GRAVELEY,
Huntingdonshire.

14th March 1946.

<u>SECRET AND PERSONAL.</u>

GY/RCMC/DO.

Dear John,

I have only just received your letter IS/PM/4616 dated
2nd February 1946, regarding Acting Squadron Leader P. Stevens.
I have been moving about and the letter seems to have gone
temporarily astray.

I knew Stevens at Stalag Lufte III during a period of
some 18 months and knew him to be a German by birth.   He
worked extremely hard as a "contact man" in various activities
against the Hun, particularly in connection with escaping and
propaganda.   I would say, but this must be regarded as
simply my own personal opinion, that he is a fit and proper
person to hold a British Passport.   I must emphasise that
I know nothing of his history and background.

Yours sincerely,

R.C.M. Collard.

Wing Commander W.R. John, O.B.E.,
Air Ministry (P.M.1.),
30/34, Moorgate,
<u>LONDON, E.C.2.</u>

PROVOST MARSHAL
RECEIVED
1 5 MAR 1946
AIR MINISTRY

Naturalization reference letter of Mar 14/46 from Group Captain R.C.M. Collard ["he worked extremely hard as a 'contact man' in various activities against the Hun, particularly in connection with escaping and propaganda."]. (*National Archives File HO 405/20069, photo by author*)

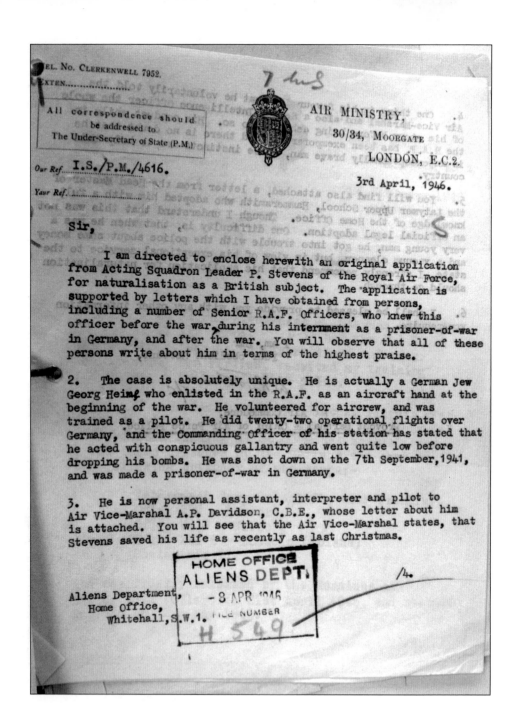

All correspondence should
be addressed to
The Under-Secretary of State (P.M.)

AIR MINISTRY,
30/34, MOORGATE
LONDON, E.C.2.

Our Ref. **I.S./P.M./4616.**

Your Ref. ....

3rd April, 1946.

Sir,

    I am directed to enclose herewith an original application from Acting Squadron Leader P. Stevens of the Royal Air Force, for naturalisation as a British subject. The application is supported by letters which I have obtained from persons, including a number of Senior R.A.F. Officers, who knew this officer before the war, during his internment as a prisoner-of-war in Germany, and after the war. You will observe that all of these persons write about him in terms of the highest praise.

2.   The case is absolutely unique. He is actually a German Jew Georg Heim who enlisted in the R.A.F. as an aircraft hand at the beginning of the war. He volunteered for aircrew, and was trained as a pilot. He did twenty-two operational flights over Germany, and the Commanding Officer of his station has stated that he acted with conspicuous gallantry and went quite low before dropping his bombs. He was shot down on the 7th September,1941, and was made a prisoner-of-war in Germany.

3.   He is now personal assistant, interpreter and pilot to Air Vice-Marshal A.P. Davidson, C.B.E., whose letter about him is attached. You will see that the Air Vice-Marshal states, that Stevens saved his life as recently as last Christmas.

Aliens Department,
    Home Office,
        Whitehall, S.W.1.

HOME OFFICE
ALIENS DEPT.
- 8 APR 1946
FILE NUMBER
H 549

/4.

Letter from Wing Commander W.R. John of the Provost Marshal's office, Air Ministry, to the Aliens Department, Home Office, detailing the application for naturalization by S/Ldr Stevens. W/C John wrote "The case is absolutely unique. He is actually a German Jew Georg Hein who enlisted in the R.A.F. ... at the beginning of the war...

4.   One thing in his favour is, that he voluntarily told the Air Vice-Marshal and also a Senior Intelligence Officer the whole of his story before being asked to do so. His conduct while in the R.A.F. has been exemporarily, and there is no doubt that he is an exceptionally brave man, whose instincts are to help this country.

5.   You will find also attached, a letter from the Head Master of the Latymer Upper School, Hammersmith who adopted him with a full knowledge of the Home Office. Though I understand that this was not an official legal adoption. One difficulty is, that when he was a very young man, he got into trouble with the police about some money and a vacuum cleaner, but in view of his exceptional service to the state, I strongly recommend that his application for naturalisation should go through.

6.   I shall be pleased to provide you with any other information you require.

I am, Sir
Your obedient Servant,

W.R. John   w/c

For Air Commodore,
Provost Marshal & Chief of Air Force Police.

... He did twenty-two operational flights over Germany, and the Commanding Officer of his station has stated that he acted with conspicuous gallantry and went quite low before dropping his bombs... the Air Vice-Marshall states that Stevens saved his life as recently as last Christmas...there is no doubt that he is an exceptionally brave man." (*National Archives File HO 405/20069, photo by author*)

48 Lowndes Square,
London S.W.I

20th. February 1946.

D ear W/Cdr. John,

Your Ref IS/PM/4616, 15th. Feb.

In reply to your letter of the above reference. My knowledge of A/S/Ldr Stevens covers only that time during which I was Senior British Officer of the East Compound of Stalag Luft i.e. from 4th. Sept 1943 to Jan. 1945. During all this time A/S/Ldr Stevens was in my Compound.

If enthusiasm for the British Cause during the war is a sufficient qualification for naturalisation, then S/Ldr Stevens is supremely suitable. His risk of falling foul with the Germans was greater than the other prisoners and the consequences to him had his true identity been discovered must have been unpleasantly fatal. In spite of this S/Ldr Stevens was above a very good average in dangerous activities such as E-scape, Intelligence and underground wireless work. At times I had to assert my authority as S.B.O. to stop him imperilling his saf-ety unduly.

He was popular among the other prisoners and always willing to help to the best of his ability He kept himself f-it, and, if a little highly strung at times, there was excuse enough f-or it. I found him unusually unselfish.

I cannot give an opinion if the above makes him suitable to become a British subject; I hope it does.

Yours sincerely,

[signature]

I have destroyed your letter to me.

Naturalization reference letter of Feb 20/46 from Group Captain A.H. Willetts, who wrote that he was the Senior British Officer in East Compound, Stalag Luft 3, and that Stevens' "risk of falling foul with the Germans was greater than the other prisoners and the consequences to him had his true identity been discovered must have been unpleasantly fatal. In spite of this S/Ldr Stevens was above a very good average in dangerous activities such as Escape, Intelligence and underground wireless work. At times I had to assert my authority as S.B.O. to stop him imperilling his safety unduly." (*National Archives File HO 405/20069, photo by author*)

It was already 150 feet long and reached some thirty feet beyond the outer wire. Asselin and the other men in charge decided that the tunnel could hold thirty-three men and so allocated departure numbers. The lowest (or earliest) numbers promised the most time outside before the Germans discovered the tunnel and thereby the best chance of success. Spots one and two went to Asselin and 'Tex' Ash. Peter Stevens was to be twenty-one,[36] and 'Wings' Day thirty-three.[37] The tunnel was ready on 3 March, and the breakout was to take place two days later, on a relatively moon-free night.[38]

In the early evening of 5 March, the lucky thirty-three received a schedule for arrival at the latrine:

Numbers 5–9	17:30 hours
Numbers 10–14	17:40 hours
Numbers 15–19	18:30 hours
Numbers 20–24	18:20 hours [sic]
Numbers 25–29	18:30 hours [sic]
Numbers 30–33	18:40 hours [sic]

The large gap between numbers fourteen and fifteen would allow the first fourteen men to reach the far end of the tunnel before the next large group arrived. 'Prince' Palmer and 'Duke' Marshall were numbers three and four, and Tommy Calnan, fourteen.[39]

'Dean and Dawson,' the *Kriegie* 'travel agency', prepared superbly for the event. Two or three primary forgers drew up a mass of false German identification papers, leaving names and dates blank for completion just before the escape. They worked an average of three to four hours each day. They produced *Ausweis* identity cards for German, Polish, and foreign workers and police passes and travel permits to accompany them. As each traveller needed at least three or four documents, this escape required more than a hundred customised items – a very tall order indeed.

Two subsidiary groups of 'Dean and Dawson' also came into being – the letterhead draftsmen and the photographic people. The first group produced falsified letters of introduction from specific (real) companies, introducing their carriers to all and sundry as bona-fide commercial travellers. Obviously, these documents were in German or another language (depending on the escaper's legend), had to be letter-perfect in grammar and tone, and had to match the social station of the false identity. Here Peter Stevens's fluency in German proved invaluable. The forgers personalised each letter with the company's name and address and possibly embossed the corporate trademark or listed the names of directors on the letterhead. These items were works of art. In many cases, the forgers applied false, official-looking stamps carved from rubber boot heels to documents to add credibility.

The second auxiliary section produced new or altered photographs for identity documents. Somehow a young Polish woman working in the camp would smuggle in a camera, and escapers took photos in great secrecy. She would then smuggle out the camera and film and the next day return with the printed snapshots. In a few cases, the forgers altered pictures of relatives by darkening hair, changing neckwear, or adding a cigarette. This type of work was extremely difficult and hence very rare. The prisoners bribed a friendly guard to allow them access to a typewriter in the *Kommandantur* (German headquarters in the camp, usually off-limits to prisoners). When that access was unavailable, the escapers would draw and paint typewritten letters by hand!

The official postwar 'Schubin Camp History' that MI9 gave to senior officers and participants comments:

> One officer travelling first class reached Innsbruck and only had his papers discovered on his eighth check. Two officers reach Koln (Cologne) and were caught on the seventh check. One officer reach [sic] Hanover after 6 checks. Two officers reached their destination Warsaw, where they remained for 6 months. Two other officers reached their immediate destination Copenhagen, but were later shot when crossing to Sweden in a canoe.[40]

So the false papers, despite rudimentary methods and equipment, were actually quite good. As long as the escaper could use a language other than English, the documents could hold up to at least mild scrutiny.

But as they entered the tunnel, the would-be escapers did not know exactly how good their fake documents actually were. Climbing down through the toilet-seat trapdoor, they must have been nervous. They had to climb down into a partially full cesspit, oozing and stinking, and be certain of their grip so as not to slip and fall in. Then they had to shift themselves and whatever luggage they were carrying over to the entry in the concrete sidewall and into the tunnel's entrance chamber. Thirty-three men had to go through this process, all within about ninety minutes, while German guards were patrolling within the compound. The duty pilot and the other members of his team had to be especially alert. If any goon threatened to go anywhere near the *Abort* (latrine), the team would temporarily close the tunnel and suspend above ground operations.

Once inside the entrance chamber, each man would wait until he heard his number and then crawl into a two-foot-square opening and work his way up the tunnel until he hit the previous man's feet. And, of course, he had to drag or push his belongings with him. For most escapers, this was the most difficult part of the operation. During digging, lamps filled with clarified margarine lit the tunnel; it wasn't very bright, it was smoky, and the space was confining. Eventually the lamps would dim as the fresh air and oxygen diminished.

But on the night of the escape, the tunnel was eerily dark. Anyone with even a hint of claustrophobia would have a tough time. Sometimes an escaper who had never been inside a tunnel would panic and have to back all the way out, but that didn't happen here.

The sun set at about 5.20 p.m., and the day's final *Appell* was at 5.00 p.m. A rugby match between England and Australia helped to cover the groups of two or three prisoners making their way to the latrine before curfew. As the last man, 'Wings' Day went through the trap and the entrance was closed; the long wait began. A man-operated bellows pump made from a duffel bag sent fresh air all along the tunnel to the escapers-in-waiting, using empty tins of Klim (powdered milk from Red Cross parcels) as a conduit. The waiting was not easy, with nervous men stretched along the entire tunnel dressed in heavy overcoats and winter clothing and with a declining oxygen supply; rumours circulated later that some men had passed out. Certainly, complete darkness outside would have been two to three hours away.

Robert Kee later recalled:

Once there was the dreaded sound of boots running overhead. My heart beat so loudly that I couldn't tell which was boots and which was heart. Sammy [his escape mate, Tommy Calnan] took my ankle.

'We've had it,' he said.

But ten minutes passed and nothing happened. Then Warburton said:

'It must've been the patrolling goon trying to keep warm.'[41]

Finally, Eddy Asselin judged the time to be right and began digging at the top of the exit shaft. Using a trowel, he began breaking out through the final layer of sod into the clear night air. As he did so, the tunnel began to fill with fresh air, alerting those inside. As Asselin eased his head through the small opening, he looked around and saw that his tunnel had come out exactly where he predicted, inside a ditch just outside the wire. But a guard was patrolling just inside the camp.

After the danger passed, Asselin scrambled out and made for the safety of the trees. Gradually, one by one, the officers emerged into the night, watching out for the goon on sentry duty. Luckily, all of the camp floodlights aimed into the compound, leaving the exterior in shadow. Progress was agonisingly slow, partly because communication in the tunnel was so bad. As Robert Kee reached the exit, the man in front of him struggled desperately to climb out through the narrow vertical shaft. Kee endured dirt kicked in his face from above, but then came silence and complete darkness. Kee assumed that the fellow had become stuck, but the man had left and was already free. Several minutes later, Kee finally realised that he was looking not at the behind of the man in front, but at the dark night sky.[42]

Peter Stevens escaped from the tunnel late at about 10.30 p.m.,[43] once again a free man. It was eighteen days after his twenty-fourth birthday.

Feeling the cold fresh air on his face after several hours in the tunnel, Stevens hurried to move away from *Oflag* XXI B. Most of the escapers did not have the linguistic skills to pass a document challenge by the German police or *Gestapo* and had chosen to go 'hard arse' (on foot) across country.

'Wings' Day emerged from the tunnel just before midnight.[44] Early the next morning Squadron Leader Don Gericke, a South African, realising that the Germans had not yet discovered the tunnel or the escape, gathered together a few things and crawled out of the tunnel. He was at least a hundred yards away before the alarm finally went up.[45]

Like several of the officers who spoke German, Stevens could take the train. He headed straight for the Bromberg station, some twenty-one kilometres to the north-east, and caught up with Sgt Brock of the RAF. They walked together quickly but quietly until they reached the town's outskirts and then separated. Stevens was wearing a double-breasted civilian suit crafted from the uniform of a British naval officer. He also carried an RAF officer's greatcoat, similarly altered to appear less military.

Stevens entered the railway station at 4.30 a.m. on 6 March and promptly bought a ticket to Berlin.[46] Waiting on the platform, he of course encountered many of his colleagues. Tommy Calnan was dressed as a munitions worker and relied on a very formal letter of introduction from the Krupp armaments firm that befitted a man of his obvious importance! He later recalled:

> If the identity cards I had manufactured for Robert (Kee) and myself were of doubtful value – they were palpable forgeries if viewed in a good light – the Krupp letter was a masterpiece. The heading was embossed in rich black print of impressive dimensions. It was all Indian ink and careful brushwork and the embossing had been achieved by delicately pressing out each single letter in the title with an exactly formed wooden block, cut with a penknife. The final result was imposing.
>
> The address, telephone number and cable address were genuine, obtained from newspaper advertisements. The text of the letter, in brush-forged typescript, required all and sundry to support and assist the bearers, who were named, in their work, vital to the German war effort. It also explained the rather vague itinerary which Robert and I might be following, using the broad phrase 'at our factories or associates with the territory of the Third Reich'.
>
> The letter terminated with a formal 'Heil Hitler' and was apparently signed by the equivalent of the Director General.
>
> The German text had been drafted by Steve who had been educated more in German schools than in English. He was completely bilingual.[47]

'Tex' Ash wrote in his memoirs:

> Near by, but pretending not to know him, would be German-born Flying Officer Stevens. He was a brave man. His advantage was that he spoke

native German. His disadvantage was he was Jewish as well as a German fighting for the British. If he was captured and either of these interesting facts came out, he knew he would be both tortured and executed.[48]

On the way to Berlin, Stevens passed safely through two identity checks. Arriving in the capital at about 2 p.m. on 6 March, Stevens found that the train to Cologne, his next destination en route south to Switzerland, would not leave until 10 p.m. He spent most of the time walking around the city, with memories of the 1936 Olympics and his Aunt Sophie (Hein) Beer flooding his consciousness. He could not have known of her death in that city on 13 November 1940.

At 9.30 p.m., Peter Stevens returned to the Hauptbahnhof and boarded the train for Cologne, which travelled by way of Hanover. Calnan wrote:

On Hanover station we met Steve, who greeted us warmly. As he had been largely responsible for drafting the miraculous Krupp letter, he was most interested to hear of our adventures. He looked like a thoroughly respectable business man and, as he was completely bi-lingual in German, he was full of confidence. Although he was a little ashamed of being seen in the company of two tramps [Calnan and Robert Kee], he insisted on buying us beer and another Stammtisch [plate of typical German food]. We spent a happy hour in his company and then left the station. He stayed behind in the warmth of the second-class waiting room, discounting the possibility of a police check. I believe he was arrested there.[49]

Stevens's own account claims:

When the train was approaching Hanover I was asked for my identity card by a Gestapo official. I produced my identity papers and he informed me that they were forgeries. I was arrested and taken off the train at Hanover.[50]

It seems odd that either one should be wrong. Perhaps Calnan meant to write 'Berlin' instead of 'Hanover', since it seems impossible that he could have imagined the whole meeting. Perhaps Stevens was just confused when MI9 was debriefing him after the war. He was by then suffering from extreme malnutrition and was probably a bit out of sorts psychologically.

Either way, Peter Stevens's second successful escape ended after only twenty-seven hours of freedom. In fact, it was partly this fact that nearly saw him shot as a spy. The *Gestapo* officers interrogating him at their Hanover prison patently refused to believe that he was an escaped RAF officer. They had learned of the mass escape from Schubin but could not believe that Stevens had travelled 350 miles that quickly. It took him several hours of explanation, including details of trains and times, to convince them.[51] They held him for three days, and he was finally sent back to Schubin on 9 March 1943. Back at *Oflag* XXI B, after waiting five days in the cooler, he received a sentence of fourteen days of solitary confinement there.[52]

Time in the cooler was not always hard. Certainly the meals were pathetic and the surroundings Spartan, but after eighteen months of captivity Stevens was used to lack of food. But at least one had privacy there – something sorely lacking in the camps.

The accounting came later, and it wasn't good: the Germans recaptured thirty-two of the thirty-four escapers. Royal Navy Lieutenant Commander Jimmy Buckley (head of 'X') and young Danish soldier Jorge Thalbitzer (serving under the identity Flying Officer Thompson) had stolen a small boat and attempted to cross the Baltic. Thalbitzer's body washed up on shore about a week later, and Buckley's never reappeared. An ocean-going vessel had probably inadvertently run over their craft. Nonetheless, this was the largest escape of the war to that time, and the highest levels of the Third *Reich* took note of it.[53]

According to a later report, the Germans detailed some 300,000 troops to search for the thirty-four escapers.[54] Certainly a massive response, and exactly what 'X' had hoped for.

Notes

1. National Archives, file HO405 / 20069, Home Office file on Alien Registration of Georg Hein.
2. Ibid.
3. National Archives, document AIR 2 / 9125, Postwar Debrief of Peter Stevens by MI9.
4. In ibid., Stevens says that the two men received no punishment for this escape. In *Wire and Worse*, Charles Rollings notes their remand to the 'cooler,' or solitary-confinement punishment cells, on their arrival at Warburg (p. 165).
5. Rollings, *Wire and Worse*, 163–6.
6. National Archives, document WO 208 / 3290, History of *Oflag* VI B Dossel/Warburg.
7. Ibid.
8. Rollings, *Wire and Worse*, 190.
9. T.C.F. Prittie and W. Earle Edwards, *Escape to Freedom* (London; Hutchinson & Co., 1953), 128–9.
10. *News of the World*, 18 May 1946, 1.
11. Clutton-Brock, *Footprints on the Sands of Time*, 59.
12. National Archives, document AIR 2 / 9125, Postwar Debrief of Peter Stevens by MI9.
13. /www.ibiblio.org/pha/policy/pre-war/361125a.html
14. Rollings, *Wire and Worse*, 191.
15. National Archives, document AIR 2 / 9125, Postwar Debrief of Peter Stevens by MI9.
16. Rollings, *Wire and Worse*, 149.
17. Rollings, *Wire and Worse*, 177.
18. National Archives, document AIR 2 / 9125, Postwar Debrief of Peter Stevens by MI9.
19. www.civilization.ca/cwm/chrono/1931disaster_e.html
20. Smith, *Wings Day*, 121.

21. National Archives, document AIR 2 / 9125, Postwar Debrief of Peter Stevens by MI9.
22. Clutton-Brock, *Footprints on the Sands of Time*, 86.
23. Britain's highest military award for valour.
24. Smith, *Wings Day*, 26–7.
25. Clutton-Brock, *Footprints on the Sands of Time*, 86.
26. Smith, *Wings Day*, 95.
27. Clutton-Brock, *Footprints on the Sands of Time*, 87.
28. William Ash with Brendan Foley, *Under the Wire: The Wartime Memoir of a Spitfire Pilot, Legendary Escape Artist and 'Cooler King'* (London: Bantam Press, 2005), 95.
29. Ibid., 172–3.
30. Ibid., 192.
31. Jonathan F. Vance, *A Gallant Company: The Men of 'The Great Escape'* (New York: ibooks, inc., 2000), 64.
32. Ibid., 64.
33. Clutton-Brock, *Footprints on the Sands of Time*, 88.
34. T.D. Calnan, *Free As a Running Fox* (New York: Dial Press, 1970), 203.
35. Vance, *A Gallant Company*, 66.
36. National Archives, document AIR 2 / 9125, Postwar Debrief of Peter Stevens by MI9.
37. Clutton-Brock, *Footprints on the Sands of Time*. 87–8.
38. Ash, *Under the Wire*, 163.
39. Calnan, *Free As a Running Fox*, 204.
40. National Archives, document AIR 40 / 274, Postwar history of escape activities at *Oflag* XXI B Schubin. Peter Stevens reached Hanover.
41. Robert Kee, *A Crowd Is Not Company* (London: Sphere Books Ltd, 1989), 125. The book appeared in 1947 as a novel, primarily because that's what the market demanded. As a result, Kee had changed the names of the major players.
42. Ibid., 127.
43. National Archives, document AIR 2 / 9125, Postwar Debrief of Peter Stevens by MI9.
44. Ash, *Under the Wire*, 165–9.
45. Smith, *Wings Day*, 122.
46. National Archives, document AIR 2 / 9125, Postwar Debrief of Peter Stevens by MI9.
47. Calnan, *Free As a Running Fox*, 202.
48. Ash, *Under the Wire*, 169.
49. Calnan, *Free As a Running Fox*, 221.
50. National Archives, document AIR 2 / 9125, Postwar Debrief of Peter Stevens by MI9.
51. It seems highly unlikely that Stevens used his German to make the *Gestapo* understand that he was not a spy.
52. National Archives, document AIR 2 / 9125, Postwar Debrief of Peter Stevens by MI9.
53. Clutton-Brock, *Footprints on the Sands of Time*, 88.
54. James, *Moonless Night*, 74.

CHAPTER THIRTEEN

A Wooden Horse and the Great Escape: *Stalag Luft* III (April 1943–March 1944)

lmost immediately after Stevens returned to the main camp at Schubin in March 1943, the prisoners learned of the planned move to *Stalag Luft* III. On 21 April 1943, all RAF officers boarded a train for the infamous prisoner-of-war camp at Sagan, some two hundred kilometres to the south-west.

The Germans had designed *Stalag Luft* III to make escape impossible. Several features had affected selection of the site, in the middle of a heavy pine forest. The subsoil consisted mainly of yellowish sand, difficult to tunnel through and lacking holding power. Any attempts seemed likely to endure endless cave-ins. And disposal of such brightly coloured material would be very difficult. Of course, the Germans took the usual precautions during construction. They buried seismometers and microphones throughout the camp to detect furtive digging.

The camp lay about 160 kilometres south-east of Berlin. It was about a kilometre south of the train station at Sagan, itself on the town's southern edge. The ground between the camp and the station was a pine forest that gave ample opportunity for cover. At the southern edge of the station, closest to the forest, German fortifications included two armed blockhouses and at least one underground bomb shelter. A concrete tunnel leading from the south side of the station and passing underneath the various east–west tracks ended inside the station's passenger ticket hall.

The prisoners at *Stalag Luft* III were well aware of the camp's 'escape-proof' reputation, especially after the *Kommandant*, Col Friedrich-Wilhelm von Lindeiner-Wildau, mentioned it in his welcoming speech. The colonel, in his early sixties, was a full-time professional soldier and, like Hermann Glemnitz, respected the Allied officers and understood that it was their sworn duty to attempt escape. He had joined the German army in 1908 and had won two Iron Crosses in the Great War, sustaining wounds three times. Leaving the army in

1919, he launched a flourishing career in international business. He married a Dutch baroness and lived in Holland for most of the period from 1919 to 1932. After his recall to Germany in 1932, both he and the baroness fervently opposed the Nazis. Thanks to his previous military experience, however, he was expected to serve. To avoid conflict, he joined the *Luftwaffe* and was appointed to *Feldmarschall* Hermann Göring's personal staff in 1937. Realising his own aversion to Nazi policies, he unsuccessfully applied three times for retirement. Finally, he took what he hoped would be a relatively stress-free posting at *Stalag Luft* III when it opened in spring 1942.[1]

Half of the Schubin escapers, including Peter Stevens, went to the original part of *Stalag Luft* III, the East Compound. The other half, including 'Wings' Day, Tim Walenn, 'Jimmy' James and Army Major John Dodge ('the Dodger') went to the newest part, North Compound.[2] Waiting for them there was their old nemesis, *Feldwebel* Hermann Glemnitz. John Dodge was a nephew (by marriage) of Winston Churchill. Immediately before war's end, the Germans released Dodge and sent him back to England (via Switzerland), hoping that he would use his influence with Churchill to bring peace.

Settling into East Compound, Stevens found himself a room and bunk in Hut 69, at the furthest south-east point in the compound, closest to the outside wire. His old escape-mate 'Mike' Lewis was in Hut 63. Lewis had been part of the original purge to *Stalag Luft* III from Warburg but later had gone to Schubin.

Stalag Luft III was to become the largest German prisoner-of-war camp, holding about 10,000 men by January 1945. It went up in stages, with East Compound being the oldest part. Immediately to the west was Centre Compound (housing primarily non-commissioned officers), and to its west a large area for camp administration. Further west lay a small bit of forest, then North Compound, and finally West Compound, along the camp's western boundary. South Compound, immediately south of North Compound, became home to the growing contingent of downed American fliers.

Soon schemes were reaching the 'X' Committee at a furious pace. On 3 June 1943, Peter Stevens implemented his fifth escape attempt in less than twenty-one months of captivity. He heard that RAF Warrant Officer C.B. Flockhart had tried the scheme two weeks earlier and felt that he could make it work too.

At the north end of the camp was the generally off-limits *Vorlager*, which administered both East and Centre Compounds. Its buildings included the hospital, the Red Cross parcel storeroom, the clothing depot, the coal-storage shed, and the bathhouse. Stevens's plan was to hide in the bathhouse overnight, then surreptitiously work his way into a shower party of German guards. He would eventually be able to leave the camp without hindrance.

Following Flockhart's example, Stevens took his usual weekly turn in the prisoners' shower party. As he was dressing afterwards, a German *Feldwebel* became suspicious of him, probably because of his extra pack of clothing (a fake German uniform). Stevens had planned on concealing himself within the roof area but found that the *Feldwebel* kept him in sight. Stevens found a way to pass off to his fellow prisoners most of his escape clothing, except for the jacket. While they were marching back to the East Compound, the guard stopped Stevens and had him searched. Of course, the incriminating uniform tunic surfaced, and interrogation followed. Stevens remained silent, and the Germans never discovered his plan. He waited three days in the cooler for notification of a seven-day sentence – a total of ten more days in solitary confinement.

Oliver Clutton-Brock later described this attempt somewhat differently. He wrote that, on 10 June, two fake German guards led a group of twenty-six officers out of East Compound towards the showers outside the camp. The shower gang disappeared into the pine forest in uniform, then reappeared out the other side disguised as civilians. Discovery of the plot came in less than an hour, and only four prisoners actually escaped the Sagan area.[3]

The next month brought very good news. As usual, the camp radio was presenting the nightly BBC news, and on 10 July 1943, it announced that the Allies had landed in Sicily. Two weeks later it reported the overthrow of Mussolini! The Germans had lost 300,000 men at Stalingrad several months earlier and another 70,000 at the Battle of Kursk from 5 to 16 July. Rumours were rife among the prisoners that they would all be home for Christmas.[4]

Back in East Compound, plans were under way for one of the most audacious escapes of the war, with behind-the-scenes help from Peter Stevens. Eric Williams and Michael Codner had come up with an ingenious plan: using plywood left over from Red Cross packing cases, they constructed a gymnastics vaulting horse. Assuming that the device would help the prisoners keep in good shape, the Germans said nothing. Before digging began, the prisoners deliberately knocked the horse over in full view of the guards to prove that the apparatus was harmless.[5]

In reality, the device was a modern Trojan horse. Completely hollow inside, it could carry two men and some sandbags. The prisoners placed it over the same spot each morning and afternoon, with one or two men inside. They dug a trap and re-covered it with a wooden trapdoor, under a good depth of earth. Camouflage rendered the trap essentially invisible when the horse was not there. Vaulting produced noise and vibration that masked the tunnelling from the Germans' underground sensors. As well, the exercise ground was closer to the outside wire than any of the barracks huts. The spot was only five yards from the warning wire. This gave Williams and Codner an automatic head start!

Digging began, and the German guards initially followed the vaulting intently; after a while, the activity became routine, and they lost interest completely. The tunnel made slow but steady progress, and bags filled with sand would accompany the digger back to the cookhouse at each lunch and suppertime. The men would dispose of the sand wherever possible, but after three months of tunnelling they had completely filled in the space under the floor of the 'barber shop'.[6] The cookhouse roof might have been sagging a bit as well! While digging was physically demanding, so was vaulting, especially on slim rations.

Oliver Philpot was a member of the above-ground crew that helped plan the escape. He was one of East Compound's leading organisers and hated being a prisoner of the Germans. He had been the pilot of a Bristol Beaufort torpedo-bomber and had crash-landed in the North Sea off the coast of Norway in December 1941. Philpot had been at Schubin with Stevens and the others and had witnessed at first hand the success of the *Abort Dienst* [latrine tunnel].

Williams and Codner, after months of taking turns digging one at a time, revised their plan slightly in September or October 1943. Having two men in the tunnel at the same time would hasten progress, as would adding a third man. The good weather would soon turn to the typical cold and wet Polish autumn. If they were unable to break out before then, vaulting and digging would have to stop and the escape delayed until the following spring.

In order to avoid that possibility, the pair invited Philpot to join them. He took a bit of persuading, because he wasn't at all sure that the plan would succeed. Finally, he accepted the offer.

As time passed, and the tunnel grew longer, Philpot and the others also sought altered civilian clothing and false identity documents. Philpot was quite picky and devised an extensive false legend for himself. His plan entailed making his way to a Baltic seaport and stowing away aboard a freighter heading for neutral Sweden. On arrival there, he would declare himself to the British embassy in Stockholm, which would immediately return him to London. He would travel as a Norwegian businessman, a supporter of Vidkun Quisling, the collaborationist leader.

Philpot had learned well the importance of travelling by train and having the best possible false identity documents. The further and faster he moved away from the camp, the less chance the enemy had to catch him. The better his documents, the more likely he was to pass through random identity checks.[7]

I tracked Stevens down. He was an expert on nearly everything German, especially documents. I whispered to him my plan; said I had got some papers under way, what next, please?

'You'll need an Arbeitskarte – a work card.' He peered down the passageway of the hut, then out of the window, and in an instant was down through a homemade hatch in the room's floor boards. He reappeared, a trifle sandy, carrying a large book, like a dictionary. This was a priceless camp possession, smuggled in. This was what the doctor had ordered – *Der Auslander Arbeiter in Deutschland – The Foreign Worker In Germany*. The Reich had gone to town on the fullest possible description of the formalities and papers necessary for the foreign worker to operate in Greater Germany. Stevens, leaning over the book with his big head and black hair, turned over the pages thoughtfully. He came to a written description which applied to an adjoining sketch of an Arbeitskarte.[8]

Stevens explained the other documents and papers that he would need, and Philpot asked for the *pièce de résistance*:

'A letter, Steve. I want to carry a letter written in German introducing me to all and sundry. It must be issued by the Margarine Sales Union, who are looking after me – although they don't know it – and it must make out that I am a fairly respectable person – a business man – who is visiting all parts of Germany and is examining Union depots, offices, factories, and sales units – anywhere in Germany.'

'That should be all right … Yes, I'll do that for you … you let me have an English draft.'

'Thanks very much. Now, I want to stress one point. This chap must not only be a salesman, or a factory man, he must just be a general business man. Let the exact type of business be settled by me when I am questioned – but I must have an interest in *all* sides of the business. Also, I shouldn't be too high in status, my clothes won't stand it, but I must, nevertheless, be managerial – a sort of person it is clearly worth a Company spending some railway fares on.'

'Seems to require a nice balance, but I think I've got it … By the way, shouldn't we put a statement in this "To whom it may concern" letter, to the effect that the Union has got permission – official permission – from the German authorities to send you on this tour?'

'That sounds fine … couldn't do any harm at all … Now, I'll do my draft, then over to you for the thing in German – I daren't tackle that … I couldn't get it letter-perfect, or hope to.'[9]

Philpot did not expect Stevens to do all of the forging. For that, he went to 'Dean and Dawson'. He took Stevens's list and presented it for completion.

His old friend Tommy Calnan helped Philpot with the typing of introduction letters. Philpot was making use of his pre-war business with a genuine organisation (the Margarine Sales Union).

Fortunately, the weather remained warm and dry throughout the autumn of 1943. The threesome completed the tunnel and made their daring breakout on 29 October.

Philpot's Margarine Sales Union letter and other false documents served him well. He took a train to the port of Danzig (now Gdànsk) in less than twenty-four hours and stowed away on a ship bound for Sweden. He arrived on neutral territory late on the night of 3 November, just five days after his escape.

Williams and Codner had travelled by train to the port of Stettin (Szczeczin), where they sought transport to Sweden. They settled for a ship to Denmark and waited there for three days before sailing for Sweden, where they arrived on 11 November. On 13 November, all three escapers were reunited at the British embassy. Because of bad weather, it was late December before they reached the United Kingdom.[10] News of their success bolstered morale at *Stalag Luft* III tremendously.

The aftermath of the escape consisted of a memo to Group Captain Willetts, the Senior British Officer, from von Lindeiner. It instituted new security measures, which included:

1. Three daily Appells, to take place at 8.30 am, 1.00 pm, and 4.30 pm. [This was an increase from the previous schedule of one in the morning and one in the late afternoon.]
2. Permission for movement between the barracks huts during the period from darkness until 9.00 pm was cancelled. All prisoners were to be confined to their own barracks from dusk until dawn.
3. Window shutters were to be closed at dusk. [There were several later reports of German guards actually shooting at windows that they claimed were unshuttered.]
4. The ground in East Compound was to be levelled, in order to prevent the construction of tunnels and the dispersal of sand therefrom.[11]

Peter Stevens helped in another escape attempt involving a tunnel.[12] No further details are available, but the official postwar history of East Compound notes that Stevens was active in 'X' in Forgery and Contacts. The study lists Stevens as head of Contacts from April 1943. He personally obtained dyes, passes, radio parts, and clothing.[13]

In the meantime, North Compound was also abuzz with plans for 'The Great Escape', in which Peter Stevens did not participate. Squadron Leader Roger Bushell, the South African who had jumped off the same train as Peter Stevens and 'Mike' Lewis in late 1941, was 'Big X', head of the Escape Committee. He was in the advance contingent from East Compound that had helped to prepare North Compound before its opening. In this way, he and several colleagues had already searched out the best possible escape opportunities before the compound opened.[14]

One early incident at North Compound could have come right out of the Hollywood movie *The Great Escape*. Squadron Leader Ian Cross, sensing an opportunity, crawled under a fire engine that had entered North Compound to flood certain tunnels that the authorities had discovered. When it had finished its work, Glemnitz directed the driver towards the main gate over the bumpiest area with the most tree stumps sticking out of the ground. At the gate, Glemnitz hopped out of the truck's cab and announced loudly, '*Herr* Cross, I hope you enjoyed the ride. You must get down from under. The rest of the journey to the cooler must be done on foot.'[15]

Paul Brickhill, author of the book *The Great Escape*, wrote:

Glemnitz was the archenemy. We didn't exactly like him, but we certainly respected him. He was a droll fellow in a sardonic way, with a leathery face you could crack rocks on. He didn't wear overalls like the other ferrets, but was always in uniform complete with peaked cap and the dignity of rank. A good soldier, Glemnitz, efficient and incorruptible, too good for our liking. Griese, his second in charge, was the other dangerous ferret, a lean *Unteroffizier* (corporal), with a long thin neck and known, naturally, as 'Rubberneck'. He was smart but he didn't have Glemnitz's sense of humour.[16]

The 'duty pilot' logged in and out of the compound each of the 'goons', so that the prisoners could be certain that there weren't any German guards hiding inside the camp, waiting to catch them out. Both sides knew about the procedure, which sometimes produced humourous results. One day, as Glemnitz entered the compound, he went over to the duty pilot and told him: 'Sign me in.' He then asked who else was in the compound and learned that he was the only one. Looking at his watch, he asked to see the list. Knowing that several of his men had compound duty until five o'clock that day, Glemnitz was furious and left to find out why they had left early. In due course, he sent two of his own guards to the German cooler and assigned 'Rubberneck' two weeks' extra duty and placed him under house arrest![17]

Not all the guards at *Stalag Luft* III strongly opposed the Allies, and one or two even assisted the prisoners in their escape quest. A senior officer, *Hauptmann* (Captain) Hans Pieber, was an Austrian who vehemently opposed Hitler. He aided the prisoners in many ways, supplying them with many innocuous-seeming items to help. In perhaps his most outrageous act, he carried in his briefcase from the East Compound to the North the camp's radio receiver and booklets with flying instructions for the Messerschmitt Bf 109 fighter and the Dornier Do X aircraft.[18]

Planning for the escape began after the North Compound opened in March 1943. Bushell hoped to make it the largest escape to date, involving 250 men. This would require unprecedented organisation.

He deputised each department head in 'X' to assemble a group to prepare the vast amounts of escape materials necessary. The plan would require clothing, maps, travel and identity documents, food, compasses (made by melting and reshaping vinyl gramophone records into small round compass bodies and using magnetised razor blades as pointers), and tunnelling equipment (wire for electric lights and boards for shoring tunnel walls and to make rails and carts to haul sand away from the tunnel face). As well, the project would need to dispose of vast quantities of sand, and obtain intelligence (train timetables and so on). Then there was the issue of who would dig the tunnels.

The original plan called for three separate tunnels, 'Tom,' 'Dick,' and 'Harry'. The combined effort was more than three times the amount necessary to dig one tunnel, but Bushell felt it likely that the Germans would discover at least one before completion. The tunnels, and many other aspects of the escape, were given inocouous names to deceive any German eavesdroppers.

The Germans truly believed that *Stalag Luft* III was escape-proof. Twin barbed-wire fences, each nine feet tall, surrounded it. In between stood more barbed wire, rolled up in concertina fashion. About eight feet inside the inner fence was a single strand of barbed wire about eighteen inches above the ground – the warning wire. The guards would shoot anyone who crossed this barrier at any time. Raised guard towers surrounded the outer fence at a distance of between 100 and 150 yards. The tower guards had rifles, semi-automatic weapons, and machine-guns. Each tower had large searchlights to cover the compounds at night. Guards locked the prisoners into their barracks between dusk and dawn, and each hut stood on brick 'stilts', about two feet off the ground. This allowed ferrets easy access under the huts to ensure that prisoners were not building tunnels. The camp rested on light yellow sand, immediately under the thin topsoil. Tunnelling would soon make that sand visible.

If the huts were above ground, how to dig tunnels? One could cut a trapdoor in the floor and begin digging from the ground two feet below, but regular inspections by ferrets under the huts made such a scheme vulnerable.

The officers of North Compound had to be much smarter than that. Work on the tunnels began on 11 April 1943, and the traps were works of art. Men chiselled out the opening to 'Harry' through clay tiles under the barracks stove. They made removable wooden handles to allow the stove to be moved at any time, whether it was lit or not, so that it was always possible to open the tunnel.

The escapers cut the trap for 'Tom' through the concrete floor in a hut passageway. It was very fine work, requiring incredible attention to detail to render cracks in the grout invisible and to avoid breaking any tiles. As well, it required heavy hammering to break the mortar, and a diversion was necessary.

'Dick' was just as ingenious and involved a false floor drain in Hut 122's lavatory. Men constructed a false bottom so that it would hold water, and the tunnel began in the new hollow waste column that carried the vertical drainpipe leading downwards that removed wastewater. Polish airmen with pre-war experience in this type of work built all the traps. These items had to be absolutely perfect, as the goons could spot anything that wasn't quite right. The traps were indeed ingeniously designed and flawlessly constructed.

Tunnelling itself was the bailiwick of a tall Canadian Spitfire pilot, Wally Floody. Although most sources describe him as a mining engineer, Floody had actually been a labourer in the gold mines of northern Ontario. He finished high school and then immediately went to work to help support his family. Late in the Depression he dug for precious metals. The money was good (up to $4.75 per day), and he could play on the company sports teams. In his few years mining, he learned a great deal.[19]

Both 'Tom' and 'Dick' headed westerly from neighbouring huts (123 and 122, respectively). 'Harry' headed northwards from Hut 104, and the shortest distance lay under both the cooler and a guard tower.[20]

Dispersing sand from the tunnels was a large team of 'penguins'. Their duties involved carrying two large bags of dirt inside their trouser legs, which they suspended from their necks by a piece of rope. They would waddle around (the dirt could weigh twenty pounds or more) with hands in pockets, holding the bag-release mechanisms, until they found a good spot to dump their load.

During construction, Glemnitz and his team often found evidence of tunnelling, as the escapers had to leave some sand out in the open. And Glemnitz seemed to know where to find it. At one point, triangulating his finds *vis-à-vis* possible tunnel locations, he sent six or seven ferrets into North Compound at 2 a.m., hoping to catch men tunnelling. Since a similar situation in *Stalag Luft* I at Barth had resulted in disaster for the prisoners, nobody in North Compound worked underground at night.[21]

On several occasions, Glemnitz and the goons spotted sand-dispersal activities. At first, not realising that each tunnel was thirty feet below the surface, they tried driving heavily laden wagons around the compound. They hoped that the sheer weight would collapse any shallow burrows.

In order to decrease suspicion and to give the best possible chance to one tunnel, 'X' decided to stop digging on 'Dick' and 'Harry.' But what to do with all the yellow sand coming from 'Tom'? The heads of 'X' held a strategy session. Peter 'Hornblower' Fanshawe, a Fleet Air Arm (Royal Navy) pilot, suggested storing the sand from 'Tom' inside 'Dick'.[22]

Effort then concentrated on 'Tom', with substantial advances occurring (between eight and ten feet per day), until the Germans started clearing the land outside the western fences to add another compound. 'Tom' was already well over 200 long, and its utility now in serious doubt.[23]

The addition of the new West Compound would mean doubling the length of 'Tom', so a strategy review was necessary. The men decided to halt work on 'Tom' and make 'Harry' number one.

At that point, 'Tom' was 260 feet long and reached about 140 feet outside the wire. It was still about forty feet short of the newly extended western treeline, but Roger Bushell decided that it was long enough. After all, it was beyond the area that the searchlights covered. Better to use it now, rather than to wait for the Germans to discover it.

But Glemnitz's goons were unrelenting. During routine searches, they had discovered under prisoners' bunks Red Cross parcel boxes filled with yellow sand. And then one of them spied a few officers carrying similar boxes out of Hut 123. That was enough for Glemnitz, and on 8 September 1943, he called a snap search of Hut 123. Bushell had recently ordered re-cementing shut 'Tom', in case of exactly such action, but a goon was poking around with a long, thin metal probe that stuck in the wet cement. At some 260 feet in length, 'Tom' was no longer a secret![24]

The tunnel was such a miraculous work of engineering that the Germans did not know how to dismantle it. In the past, they would simply carry in hoses, turn on the water, and cause the flooded tunnel to collapse on itself. In the case of 'Tom', however, with 100 per cent wooden shoring, that would not work. The authorities brought in a demolition expert, and for two days he set underground charges the entire length of the tunnel; after evacuation of the area, the fireworks started. Sure enough, a rumble followed, but the well-built shoring caused the force of detonation to return back up through the tunnel. It literally blew the roof off Hut 123![25]

That looked like the end of escape attempts. Detection of 'Tom' lulled the Germans into a false sense of security – the goons walked around the camp for weeks with silly smiles. Glemnitz had explored the entire length of 'Tom' and, seeing the huge number of boards shoring up its walls, pronounced that the *Kriegies* had clearly exhausted the camp's supply. But Roger Bushell now redoubled the escape efforts. Before the Germans could do an inventory of bedboards, 'Big X' ordered the largest-ever appropriation; some two thousand boards went into storage down 'Dick' and in other safe spots.[26]

The new South Compound was finally ready for occupation in September 1943.[27] The Germans moved to that section all the camp's officers who were Americans, regardless of force (US Army Air Force, Royal Air Force, or Royal Canadian Air Force). A few Americans had played critical roles in helping 'X' in North Compound, including 'Bub' Clark, but were now out of the circuit. There were to be no Americans in 'The Great Escape'.

Having lost 'Tom', Bushell decreed in January 1944 that North Compound would now direct all its efforts to 'Harry'. Work proceeded at a good pace, but the distance into the forest would be almost 400 feet! The project would require removal, transport, and hiding of 130 *tons* of sand. The escapers built a time-saving trolley which – instead of men on hands and knees – would carry sand from the tunnel face back to the work area below the entrance shaft. They connected a rope to the trolley on each side; that way, a digger could pull the empty wagon back to the tunnel face and a man at the tunnel entrance could pull it full of sandbags back from the digging area. The conspirators even hid sand under the seats in the North Compound theatre, which prisoners had built with a sloping floor and empty space below. The entrance to the secret space lay under seat number thirteen![28]

The tunnel advanced about three feet per day. By its completion in late March 1944, 'X' grasped the enormity of the three construction projects. Prisoners had dug a total of 645 feet of tunnel, two feet square. They had installed 1,000 feet of electrical wire, used over 4,000 bedboards to shore up the works, and fitted together 1,400 Klim tins to provide fresh air throughout.[29]

'Harry' was so long, in fact, that it had needed two hollowed-out 'turnaround' spots, where the trolley and rails had ended. The rope runs had become too long, and so the escapers broke them into one-third lengths to facilitate movement of sand. The men gave these 'halfway houses' names: the one closest to the entrance was 'Piccadilly Circus', and that nearest the exit was 'Leicester Square'.

In early March, Glemnitz was again worried that something was afoot. But what to do? His plan was almost as ingenious as any of his opposition's. A new compound, called Belaria, had just opened in a former German army training camp a few miles away from the main part of *Stalag Luft* III. Glemnitz determined that he would transfer to it the most ardent escapers, his 'usual suspects'. These twenty officers included some of the leaders of 'X': Wally Floody, George Harsh, 'Hornblower' Fanshawe, and fighter-pilot ace Bob Stanford-Tuck.[30] Roger Bushell, knowing that he was under constant surveillance, had (as a diversionary tactic) become very active in the camp theatre. He fooled even Glemnitz, who told *Kommandant* von Lindeiner that Bushell had seemingly given up his dreams of escape![31] The Belaria purge was a blow to 'X' but came too late to have any serious effect.

At a meeting of 'X' in early March 1944, Bushell pushed for speedy completion of 'Harry'. Sure that the Germans were on the verge of discovering it, he noted that 'Rubberneck' was about to go away on two weeks' leave and would return mid-month. During his absence, tunnelling would accelerate.[32]

Completion came in mid-March 1944. Concurrent work on clothing, papers, and other escape materials had produced the required 250 sets. Bushell and the others were increasingly nervous about discovery and decided to break out as soon as possible. Weather was a factor, as was the phase of the moon. The leaders wanted a moonless night for the escape, just as for bombing missions: the less ambient light the better.

The most important factor, however, was the goons' increasing attention to Hut 104. Glemnitz and his able team had noticed the excessive traffic in and out of 104 and had searched it several times. Around 14 March, 'Rubberneck' (just returned from leave) and his ferrets evacuated the hut and scoured it for some four hours.[33] Bushell realised that, despite the harsh winter weather, they would have to move on the moonless night of 24 March. To wait one more month almost guaranteed discovery.

And so, on the evening of 24 March, some two hundred Allied prisoners of North Compound, *Stalag Luft* III, congregated as close as possible to Hut 104. Each carried his personal escape kit and as many supplies as he had been able to accumulate.

The organisation of the escape was military in its precision. Each officer had a number for the tunnel and a time to arrive. The first men went down the tunnel at 9 p.m. and waited there while those at the head of the line broke out the last few feet of vertical shaft. The Germans would come by at 10 p.m. as usual, to lock up the huts from the outside, so all the escapers had to be inside Hut 104 prior to that. Obviously, space was at a premium and the heat became intense; occasionally nerves snapped.

One of the officers controlling operations above ground, David Torrens, suddenly spotted a German *Gefreiter* (lance corporal) at the far end of the hut. Making a mad dash to cut him off, he realised when directly in front of the man that it was actually Flying Officer Pavel Tobolski, a Polish officer who would escape with 'Wings' Day![34]

Below ground, there was difficulty with opening the far end of the tunnel. Also, a minor cave-in occurred near 'Leicester Square'. Henry Birkland, a Canadian, cleared the cave-in, and operations resumed. As the first person's head emerged cautiously from the tunnel exit, a sinking feeling came over him. The exit was about ten feet short of the woods! The shaft opening was in plain view of the guards and only fifteen feet from a manned guard tower. Plenty of snow still covered the ground, enough to highlight the silhouette of any man in dark clothing.

Quick thinking ensued, and the escapers devised a system using a rope. As each man scrambled out of the tunnel to the woods, he would wait a moment and tug a couple of times on the rope to signal the next in line when the way was clear.[35] Movement through the tunnel became regular, and every few minutes another man would make a break for the woods.

In the midst of all this hectic activity, the camp searchlights (and consequently the electric lights inside the tunnel) went out and the air-raid sirens sounded. 24 March just happened to be the night of the RAF's final heavy bombing attack on Berlin, some 160 kilometres to the north-west.[36] The escapers delayed exits, but the hiatus (and 'lights out') ended relatively quickly. Nonetheless, it must have heightened anxiety among those in the tunnel, especially for first-timers.

It was as man number seventy-seven poked his head out of the ground that a German guard unexpectedly walking on the forest side of the road spotted the motion. All hell broke loose, and the guard fired his rifle, screaming 'Halt!' at the man lying motionless on the snow. The escaper in the forest tugging on the rope came running out of the woods yelling over and over, *'Nicht schiessen!'* (Don't shoot!). Two other escapers, hiding close by, immediately put their hands up and came forward, while two others made a break for it through the woods. Those still in the tunnel reversed course and scrambled back into Hut 104.

On learning of what had happened, Hitler flew into a rage, the likes of which no one had seen before. He ordered that all the escapers recaptured be executed. It took a bit of time, but his senior advisers persuaded him that this would be cold-blooded murder and that the British and Americans might reciprocate against German soldiers they held prisoner. Hitler relented slightly and told the *Gestapo* to murder fifty.

And so, a massive effort by the Germans gradually rounded up the escapers, while a deadly lottery was under way at *Gestapo* headquarters. General Artur Nebe laid out photos and biographies of each conspirator on a table and decided who was to live and who was to die. He chose many inveterate escapers for execution, including Roger Bushell. Enmity between 'Big X' and the *Gestapo* stemmed from an earlier incident when it had recaptured Bushell, who had then spent time as its guest. The selection of the fifty was complex, sometimes factoring in age and family status. A married prisoner was more likely to live, and eastern Europeans more likely to die. Remarkably, the *Gestapo* spared 'Wings' Day.

In the end, Nebe passed a list of fifty names down through the *Gestapo* chain of command. During the first week after the breakout, as authorities rounded up the escapers they conveyed the prisoners, mostly in small groups, to vacant fields and shot them in cold blood. They cremated the remains and eventually returned them to *Stalag Luft* III.

In the meantime, Colonel von Lindeiner had become the scapegoat; authorities arrested him and held him for court martial. His successor, Colonel Braune, summoned the Senior British Officer, Group Captain Massey, in early April 1944. Unlike von Lindeiner, Braune did not speak English, and he asked Massey to bring a translator; the latter chose Squadron Leader 'Wank' Murray.

Instead of the usual handshake, Braune stood and bowed slightly. While the Britons sat down, the *Kommandant* remained standing, and he delivered a prepared speech. In German, he reported that he had instructions from a 'higher authority' to communicate to the prisoners the news that German soldiers had shot forty-one Allied prisoners while they attempted to escape during or after recapture.

Murray at first could not understand and asked the colonel to repeat the number. 'Forty-one' came the reply. Murray repeated the number to Massey, who immediately asked how many had only suffered wounds. Braune replied only that he was under instruction to deliver the message as it was and was unable to answer any questions. Pressing for more information and the names of the dead, Massey received the same reply. His superiors, Braune repeated, had directed that this was the only information he was to give. He added only that the *Luftwaffe* was not responsible for these dreadful and terrible events.[37]

Many camp guards met the prisoners' resulting outrage with obvious sadness and shock. Worrying how the thousands in the camp would react, the *Kommandant* put all his men on alert. Eventually, the Germans posted a list of the dead, and an alert prisoner pointed out that the number was actually forty-seven! The butcher's bill included Henry Birkland, Roger Bushell, Al Hake (the Australian making compasses), Tom Kirby-Green (head of Security), Wally Valenta (head of Intelligence), Tim Walenn, and many other popular men.

A few days later, another short list, with just three names, appeared beside the earlier enumeration. The three were Danny Krol (a Polish officer who had escaped from Schubin with Peter Stevens), Pavel Tobolski (who had scared Torrens so badly the night of the breakout and was 'Wings' Day's escape partner), and 'Cookie' Long.

In the end, the totals came to seventy-six escaped, seventy-three recaptured, three 'home runs', and fifty murdered.

Fifteen of the twenty-three recaptured officers returned to *Stalag Luft* III, but 'Wings' Day, Jimmy James, Sydney Dowse, and Major John Dodge ('the Dodger') were sent to Sachsenhausen Concentration Camp, just north of Berlin. There they had housing with the *Prominenten*, or VIP famous political and military prisoners, just outside the camp's main part, which was for political, criminal, and Jewish prisoners. James and Dowse, using a simple table knife with a serrated edge, dug another tunnel about one hundred feet long and, with Day, Dodge, and Jack Churchill, escaped *once again*!

After the Germans again recaptured these five men, they moved them all around Germany and Italy ahead of advancing Allied troops, who eventually liberated all but Dodge in northern Italy in May 1945. (The Germans had sent Dodge to Switzerland in February 1945 to try to persuade the Allies to accept a peace treaty.)[38]

Of the three 'Great Escapers' who were not recaptured, Dutchman Bram (Bob) Vanderstok made his way overland through France and across the Pyrenees into Spain, and Norwegians Peter Bergsland ('Rocky' Rockland) and Jens Muller reached Sweden via Stettin (Szczeczin).[39]

In due course, the Germans returned the cremated remains of the fifty murdered escapers to *Stalag Luft* III and handed them over to the Senior British Officer. After consultation, the *Kommandant* permitted a full military funeral and also allowed the prisoners to build a stone monument that listed the names.[40]

The Geneva Convention provided protection for escaping military prisoners. But Colonel von Lindeiner's recent warnings that 'Escape is no longer a sport' had come to fruition. As a result of the *Gestapo*'s criminal behaviour and the reversing tides of war (with Germany slowly pulling back on the Eastern and Italian fronts), the *Kriegies* in *Stalag Luft* III ceased all escape attempts.

Notes

1. Arthur A. Durand, *Stalag Luft III: The Secret Story* (Baton Rouge, La.: Louisiana State University Press, 1988), 125–6.
2. Smith, *Wings Day*, 126.
3. Clutton-Brock, *Footprints on the Sands of Time*, 72. Stevens's postwar debrief lists the date of the escape as being 3 June.
4. Dupuy and Dupuy, *The Harper Encyclopedia of Military History from 3500 B.C. to the Present*, 1,202–3.
5. Tim Carroll, *The Great Escapers: The Full Story of the Second World War's Most Remarkable Mass Escape* (Edinburgh: Mainstream Publishing Company Ltd, 2004), 115–16.
6. Eric Williams, *The Wooden Horse* (London: Reprint Society Ltd, 1950), 96.
7. Oliver Philpot, *Stolen Journey* (London: Hodder and Stoughton Ltd, 1950), 186–7.
8. Ibid., 198.
9. Ibid., 199.
10. Clutton-Brock, *Footprints on the Sands of Time*, 74.

11. National Archives, document AIR 40 / 266, Translation of 30 October 1943 memo from Colonel von Lindeiner to Group Captain Willetts, SBO of East Compound. The memo incorrectly spells Willetts's name as 'Kellett'.
12. National Archives, document AIR 2 / 9125, Postwar Debrief of Peter Stevens by MI9.
13. National Archives, document WO 208 / 3283.
14. Smith, *Wings Day*, 126.
15. Ibid., 127.
16. Paul Brickhill, *The Great Escape* (London: Cassell, 2000), 32.
17. Ibid., 102.
18. Smith, *Wings Day*, 129.
19. Barbara Hehner, *The Tunnel King: The True Story of Wally Floody and the Great Escape* (Toronto: HarperCollins Publishers Ltd, 2004), 4–5.
20. Brickhill, *The Great Escape*, 28.
21. Ibid., 98–9.
22. Ibid., 100–1.
23. Ibid., 103–4.
24. Ibid., 105–8.
25. Anton Gill, *The Great Escape: The Full Dramatic Story with Contributions from Survivors and Their Families* (London: Headline Book Publishing, 2002), 144.
26. Brickhill, *The Great Escape*, 110.
27. Durand, *Stalag Luft III: The Secret Story*, 118.
28. James, *Moonless Night*, 91.
29. Ibid., 202.
30. Hehner, *The Tunnel King*, 88–9.
31. Carroll, *The Great Escapers*, 122.
32. Ken Rees with Karen Arrandale, *Lie in the Dark and Listen: The Remarkable Exploits of a WWII Bomber Pilot and Great Escaper* (London: Grub Street, 2004), 171.
33. James, *Moonless Night*, 95.
34. Ibid., 99.
35. Brickhill, *The Great Escape*, 175–6.
36. Clutton-Brock, *Footprints on the Sands of Time*, 75.
37. Brickhill, *The Great Escape*, 224–7.
38. James, *Moonless Night*, 158.
39. Ibid., 105–6.
40. This monument is on the north-west edge of what remains of *Stalag Luft* III, just south of Zagan, Poland. A Great Escape Museum is about two hundred yards from the monument. I visited both in September 2005.

CHAPTER FOURTEEN

End of the Road: *Stalag Luft* III and Luckenwalde (March 1944–May 1945)

It was not long before some very welcome good news arrived at *Stalag Luft* III, near Sagan. The wireless receiver for East Compound was hidden in Block 69, Room 14 – Peter Steven's room.[1] As usual in the evening, the prisoners were listening to the BBC news on their illicit short-wave radio, when the announcement came of the landings in Normandy on 6 June 1944. Even the most ardent escapers now realised that to continue in the face of Nazi desperation was insanity. The Senior British Officer issued a directive to refrain from all escape activities.

Ceasing escape planning was not easy for these prisoners of war, but they grasped the logic. They began to channel their focus into other diversions, such as educational and arts programs.

Life in the camp had become increasingly difficult. Boredom and lack of purpose strained relations among prisoners. Bickering and petty infighting resulted in more arguments than normal, and incessant chatter exhausted many quieter types.

Peter Stevens eventually took the common way out – 'sick report'. On 8 November 1944, Stevens complained to the camp doctor that his nerves were bothering him. He feigned some sort of tic and received a few days in the camp hospital, where he could obtain a decent night's sleep – certainly the sound of snoring was much less! Unfamiliar faces and new topics of discussion provided some relief and helped to alleviate the ennui.

By mid-1944, food was becoming a major issue at *Stalag Luft* III. Prisoners of war of the Third *Reich* had never received much food, but Red Cross parcels made life at least sustainable. As a result of battle losses and the Allies' disruption of transportation and logistics across western Europe, these supplies became more erratic. The prisoners were no longer receiving enough for survival, and the long, slow process of starvation was beginning.

During the last three months of 1944, malnutrition began to take its toll on prisoners' health. Factors that slowed food parcels also affected medical supplies. Peter Stevens – a typical case – had lost perhaps ten pounds between his capture in September 1941 and D-Day – 6 June 1944. Between the latter and the New Year, he lost about ten more pounds.

During that same second half of 1944, hope began to take root among the *Kriegies*. The daily reporting of the news that had arrived the previous evening via short-wave radio preoccupied most officers. And the news was mostly good. While Allied ground troops had taken about a month to obtain a good footing in France, by August and September they were advancing across France and into Belgium and Holland. And day and night bombing raids by the *Kriegies'* colleagues back in England were wreaking havoc on the Third *Reich*. Soviet forces were applying heavy pressure from the east, and by late 1944 it seemed clear that Germany was losing the war.

That realisation affected the attitude of most guards at *Stalag Luft* III. Those who had been friendly were now asking their prisoner contacts to vouch for them at war's end. Those who had avoided, even taunted, Allied officers now became more sociable. Despite High Command's false reports to the populace about Germany's continuing to win the war, most guards tended to ask for (and believe) the truth from their captives.

The Allies' only major setback took place in December 1944 and January 1945. The Battle of the Bulge consisted of a brilliant and valiant counterattack by German tanks and troops in Belgium and Luxemburg. Achieving complete surprise on 16 December 1944, the large German force attempted to split the Allies' ground troops and overrun their supply lines. Bad winter weather added to the surprise, and the German offensive penetrated deep into Belgium, reaching within twenty-five miles of the coast and cutting off a large portion of Allied forces. For several weeks, the outcome was in grave doubt.

US General Dwight Eisenhower, Supreme Commander of all Allied Forces in Europe, committed his reserves to the battle, and by 26 December the Allied recovery had begun. After a fierce battle for Bastogne, the Allies repulsed the Germans in early January 1945, and their counterattack rolled across German lines, forcing the Panzer tanks into retreat.[2]

Halfway across Europe, the Soviet army was squeezing the Germans on the Eastern Front. On 15 September 1944, the Soviets had advanced to within twenty miles of Warsaw, whence they watched German suppression of the Warsaw Uprising and destruction of the capital. By 15 December, they had taken Budapest and Belgrade.[3]

Christmas 1945 provided good feeling and levity in East Compound at *Stalag Luft* III. The prisoners prepared the usual Yuletide Festive Dinner, with personalised menus. One side lists the (perhaps fanciful) menu:

MENU
Soup
Sausage Roll
Turkey
Roast Potatoes, Cabbage and Carrots
Xmas Pudding
Mince Pies
Biscuits
Cheese
Fruit and Nuts
Sweets – Coffee

The top left corner sports a drawing of a luscious fruit pie; the top right, a large piece of fruit, drizzled in a sweet sauce; the bottom left, a freshly plucked turkey; and the bottom right, a large slice of double layer cake with thick icing. In the middle, on each side of the food listing, sits a pair of army boots, perhaps for making the soup!

The reverse side contains a caricature of a prisoner, with the legend 'Happy Xmas' at the top. Peter Stevens's likeness, for example, is striking and revealing. A heavy day's growth of beard is evident, as is the *Kriegie*'s ever-present cigarette stuck in the mouth. A prominent chin and a large red nose suggest a forceful personality. Stevens is wearing a wide pinstriped suit, with a blue-and-white-striped shirt and a multi-coloured tie with polka dots. A white carnation serves as *boutonnière*, and a dark fedora finishes the outfit.

Overall, the study presents a serious man of good upbringing, but perhaps with a naughty streak. It almost puts one in mind of a gangster. At the bottom left appear the words, 'Sagan, Room 14, Block 69'. This simple document seems an ideal and evocative memento of life as a prisoner of war.

Another undated caricature, probably by the same highly talented amateur artist (Tom Slack) depicts Peter Stevens as a young boy in short pants and sports shirt, carrying a wide-brimmed straw hat with a red band and pulling a string attached to a toy dog mounted on a wheeled platform. Stevens is standing inside a barbed-wire fence and again has heavy five-o'clock shadow. He is frowning and again displays the forceful jaw and long red nose, along with close-cropped, curly hair. It seems likely that the artist was pointing out character flaws (childish persistence?), yet the subject kept it among his treasured mementoes all his life.

Tom Slack's memoirs noted that: 'Steve Stevens spoke German fluently and was the unofficial camp interpreter. Steve had the German eating out of his hands and little did they know that his parents were German Jews.'[4]

As Allied forces began to close in on Germany, the guards at *Stalag Luft* III became increasingly anxious. Regular rumours were in circulation, and ten thousand prisoners began to wonder about their fate. As 1945 dawned, it was possible to hear Soviet artillery pounding German positions, albeit tens of miles away.

For a brief time, prisoners of war in many camps worried that German High Command might order their mass murder, and senior officers secretly drew up plans on how to respond. Certainly prisoners vastly outnumbered guards and should have been able to overrun them, if it proved necessary.

There were other concerns. The Eastern European officers in camp made it clear that they hoped for liberation by American and British forces rather than by the Soviet army. They knew that the Communists would not be kind to them and their newly 'liberated' territories.

Perhaps not surprising, the guards agreed wholeheartedly with these sentiments. The Germans knew how badly their own advancing brethren had treated civilians and the military as the *blitzkrieg* had rolled eastward in 1941, and they assumed that Soviet troops would now ignore the Geneva Convention. Many threatened to desert in the face of the oncoming Soviet hordes.

The food situation hit rock bottom in January 1945. But careful hoarding during good times had created a surplus of Red Cross food parcels in storage. Anticipating difficult times ahead, the Germans ordered their distribution. The *Kommandant* and his staff began meeting with the senior Allied officers to discuss the camp's future.

In the second half of January, rumours again abounded, but this time about evacuation of *Stalag Luft* III. It was the middle of a cold and snowy winter, and a long journey would be difficult. Since the Third *Reich* was disintegrating, motorised transport seemed doubtful; hence a march across country became likely. This concept set off a firestorm of activity among the prisoners. They began making equipment to carry, or better yet drag, their supplies with them. Packsacks and sledges were under construction all over the camp.

Since the Germans would clearly not take their prisoners eastwards, it seemed obvious that they would cross the River Oder (or another) and head westward into Germany. On the morning of 27 January 1945, Peter Stevens and the rest of the men in East Compound learned that they would march at eleven o'clock that evening. This was it! While the war was almost over, the prisoners' fate seemed very uncertain. Fifty-three prisoners too ill to travel were left behind at *Stalag Luft* III.

Tom Slack wrote that 'Steve, in his capacity as camp interpreter, was able to visit the German Administrative block outside the camp where he managed to steal the German record cards of the two of us to provide a unique memento of our stay at Sagan.'[5]

After a great deal of preparation and several false starts, the men finally departed about 6 a.m. on 28 January. Each man received one Red Cross parcel, but that was all. Of course, each prisoner was free to carry anything and everything else that he could. All of them wore every stitch of clothing they owned and took whatever food they possessed, but some carried non-essential belongings. These items soon fell by the roadside, leaving a trail of litter behind the long column of slow-moving prisoners. On that first day, the prisoners slogged seventeen kilometres (about ten miles) southwards through the fierce wind and the crusty snow, stopping at Halbau at about 4 p.m.[6]

Very quickly most guards stopped being jailers and became participants in a mass migration. While they carried guns, most fraternised with the men they had come to know and respect. There were, however, occasional incidents of barbarity and ill treatment. At each stop, townspeople reminded the guards that the prisoners were *Luftgangsters* and child murderers'.[7]

Most of the prisoners lacked proper cold-weather clothing or gear. As many had been prisoners for at least a year, they were always short of clothing. They took whatever they could obtain from Red Cross shipments, but no one was ready for mid-winter outdoor duty lasting a week or more. Most prisoners had no more than two sets of clothing, alternating them daily to keep some semblance of cleanliness. They wore a mish-mash of what they could find in the clothing stores, plus whatever had arrived from home. If a prisoner even *had* boots, they were almost certainly in bad repair. Many men began the trek with shoes wrapped in scarves or towels or whatever insulation they could find. As the march wore on, and temperatures fluctuated between freezing (0°C) and about –30°C (with the windchill factor), these outer coverings thawed, became soaked, and froze. Frostbite soon became a major issue.

At Halbau, the group spread out in the town square, waiting for a billet for the night. The civilian population, mostly German, seemed relatively friendly and supplied hot water and, in some cases, *ersatz* coffee. The men split into two groups; one went to a church, the other to a school. Conditions were harsh at best (concrete and stone floors to sleep on, with no mattresses). The temperature during the day had been –10°C, and it went down to –18°C that night and neither building was heated.

On Monday 29 January, the officers from East Compound stayed in Halbau while the groups from North Compound and Belaria marched ahead. The departing groups left at 1 a.m. and covered eleven kilometres (seven miles) to Leippa, where they arrived at 4 p.m. For the second day, there was no food, and the billet was in a school.

Leaving Leippa at 4 p.m. on 30 January, the prisoners headed for Muskau in Germany, just across the Neisse River[8] – some thirty-one kilometres (twenty miles) away. Again no food and deplorable weather. High winds and snowfall combined with an afternoon thaw to make the marching extremely difficult. Those prisoners who had brought or bartered with civilians for sledges had a very hard time dragging their goods. And lack of sanitation had begun to cause dysentery. Jim Hunter described 30 January: 'A very hard day – hardest yet.'

After resting at Muskau on 1 February, the party had to leave three men behind because of illness. The group from East Compound split into two, and 568 men joined up with the men from North Compound, who ended up in Tarmstedt, about thirty miles west of Hamburg.

Peter Stevens remained with the original East Compound/Belaria group – some two thousand prisoners – and continued on the freezing march westwards. On 2 February, that group of East Compounders marched eighteen kilometres (eleven miles) straight west to Graustein. Along the way, they realised that the civilians were increasingly nervous. The residents offered to trade household goods for coffee, chocolate, or cigarettes, easily transportable and useful as currency in time of war. Sensing the approach of invading Soviet troops, they were as afraid as the camp guards. Some chose to stay, but many packed whatever they could carry and joined the march westwards.

On 3 February there was a short day of marching – only ten kilometres (six miles) to Spremberg, the site of a German railhead.⁹ The *Kriegies* had been on the march a full week, with no heat and precious little food.

There the Germans separated groups of prisoners and shipped them onward by train. They sent 4,000 Americans from South and Centre Compounds to *Stalag* VII A at Moosberg; 2,500 Americans from North and West Compounds to *Stalag* XIII D at Langwasser-Nürnberg; 2,000 RAF and Allied officers from Belaria and 1,000 prisoners from East Compound to *Stalag* III A at Luckenwalde (thirty kilometres south of Berlin); and 1,500 RAF and Allied officers from North Compound plus 1,000 from East Compound to Marlag und Milag Nord (Tarmstedt).¹⁰

Once again, train conditions were deplorable: unheated cattle cars ('40 *hommes ou 8 chevaux*') with no comforts, fresh water, or sanitary facilities. Peter Stevens and the RAF prisoners from East Compound arrived at Luckenwalde station at about 5 p.m. on 4 February after a day on the freezing cold train.

During the brief but horrific journey from Sagan to *Stalag* III A at Luckenwalde, at least fifteen officers, including Wing Commander Bob Stanford-Tuck, escaped.

After the prisoners stood in the rain for two hours at Luckenwalde, guards marched them into *Stalag* III A, but many found this effort quite difficult physically. The arrivals received delousing before entering the barracks, and processing them took all night. It was 6 a.m. on 5 February when they finally found their new bunks. The huts had dirt floors, leaking roofs, and rats. Three-tiered beds took up almost all the living space.¹¹

The daily food ration was pitiful: one-fifth of a loaf of bread, half a litre of soup (such as it was), six potatoes, and an ounce of margarine. Some six hundred Norwegian prisoners already in the camp donated some of their Red Cross parcels, and each officer from *Stalag Luft* III obtained one-fifth of a parcel¹² – less than a subsistence diet. The men were starving. Finally, after two weeks, a plea to the International Red Cross brought each man one full food parcel.

For the next two months, activity was minimal. Everyone, including the Germans, knew that it was simply a matter of time, and the main subject of discussion was who would liberate the camp, the western Allies or the Soviets. Peter Stevens feared that it would be the Soviet forces. During his captivity, he had heard many stories of their brutality, and he did not want to test their validity. His own personal secret worsened his anxiety. The Soviets did not like people who kept secrets, and they had their ways to deal with such people. The simplest was a bullet to the back of the head. Even worse was exile to the Siberian gulag, whence people rarely returned. Amazingly, the gulag inspired Stevens's greatest wartime fear. He had survived countless near-death experiences, yet liberation by Soviet forces scared him most!

As mid-April approached, the men could hear Soviet heavy artillery coming from the east. Allied aircraft were often visible. The news on 12 April reported the sudden death of American President Franklin Delano Roosevelt, and this only added to the general anxiety in camp. Sadly, on 13 April, guards shot two airmen trying to escape. One of the two, a Canadian officer named Crosswell, died from his injuries.[13]

On 21 April, about noon, the guards quietly disappeared. The prisoners felt shock and disbelief. Realising their danger, the Senior British Officer immediately confined all prisoners to camp – it was much safer to be inside the wire than out!

At 6 a.m. on 22 April, the first Soviet troops arrived at *Stalag* III A Luckenwalde. By 10 a.m., Soviet tanks and armoured cars entered the camp, to very minor German resistance from the surrounding woods. This fearsome Soviet force acted quite sociably, with its members cheering and waving to the prisoners. It did not stay long, breaking down the fence on the far side of the camp as it exited, intent on advancing into Berlin.

Some 9,000 Soviet prisoners at Luckenwalde left in short order, but almost 18,000 Allied prisoners remained. As order gradually broke down, many simply disappeared, wanting to make a break westwards and hoping to encounter advancing American or British troops.[14]

Peter Stevens had, in the period from leaving *Stalag Luft* III on 28 January until his final liberation, lost another twenty pounds, for a total of forty pounds during his captivity. He now weighed less than 140 pounds.

On 5 May 1945, an advance party of American troops reached Luckenwalde. It promised a later arrival of a convoy of trucks, but Peter Stevens was not about to wait and, in any case, it never came. Waving to an American officer commanding an armoured car and putting on his thickest British accent, he casually asked for a lift back to England. The American, clearly amused, waved Stevens aboard.[15]

'For you, mate, the war is over!' was all he said.

And this time it really was.

Notes

1. Tom Slack, *Happy is the Day – A Spitfire Pilot's Story* (Penzance, England: United Writers Publications Ltd, 1987), 100.
2. Dupuy and Dupuy, *The Harper Encyclopedia of Military History from 3500 B.C. to the Present*, 1217–18.

3. Ibid., 1,219.

4. Slack, *Happy is the Day*, 106.

5. Ibid., 110–12.

6. National Archives, document TS 26 / 348, United Nations War Crimes Commission report concerning the evacuation of *Stalag Luft* III.

7. Clutton-Brock, *Footprints on the Sands of Time*, 133.

8. W.J. 'Jim' Hunter, *From Coastal Command to Captivity: The Memoir of a Second World War Airman* (Barnsley, Yorkshire: Leo Cooper, 2003), 110.

9. National Archives, United Nations War Crimes Commission report.

10. Clutton-Brock, *Footprints on the Sands of Time*, 83.

11. Ibid., 136.

12. Ibid., 136.

13. Ibid., 137.

14. Ibid., 137–8.

15. National Archives, document AIR 2 / 9125, Postwar Debrief of Peter Stevens by MI9.

Part Five: Epilogue

CHAPTER FIFTEEN

Patterns of a Lifetime: Hanover, London, Montreal, Ottawa, Toronto

Flight Lieutenant Stevens was in no hurry to return and see his siblings. Nonetheless, when he finally reached England by plane in May 1945, it felt good to be back on British soil. People greeted him as a conquering hero. The best things were the food and the beer. He had lost some forty pounds and now sought to return to a decent fighting weight as quickly as possible. While the rest of the country remained on strict food rationing, he as a soldier with special medical needs was exempt. Like most returning prisoners of war, he devoured all the eggs and meat (and, of course, beer!) that he could comfortably hold, and more. Within a month, he had put on almost ten pounds and had begun to look and feel almost human again. He would never again however, take a good meal for granted. And for the rest of his life, there were certain vegetables (turnip, for example) that had become staples in POW camps, that he refused to eat.

Eventually, after a few weeks back, he tracked down his sister, Trude, who was now living in Manchester. She had done reasonably well during the war and worked as a nursing assistant in a children's ward at a local hospital. To make her name easier for her colleagues and to obscure her German nationality, she had changed the pronunciation of her name from Trude (pronounced 'Trood') to 'Trudy'. Stevens introduced himself to the head nursing sister, who immediately went to find the young woman. 'Your brother is here to see you,' she told Trude. 'My brother?' she replied, 'That's not possible, he's in Canada.'

Authorities had early in the war arrested Erich, who (oddly) had refused to take out British citizenship. They had sent him to Canada and interned him on Prince Edward Island for the duration. Trude had received sporadic postcards from him but was not expecting him back soon. It never even occurred to her that her visitor might be Georg.

She had had not a word from him since the war started, and she considered him dead. It was quite a shock to meet the uniformed Flight Lieutenant Peter Stevens, and she broke down. They spent a few hours together, during which he told her about their mother's death. Trude had been too realistic to hope that their family had escaped the Holocaust. In fact, they had lost some fifteen relatives, mostly cousins, aunts, and uncles. Peter soon returned to London and his RAF duties. Trude was to hear from him only occasionally over the next twenty years.

On his return to England from Canada later that year, Erich went back to his work as an optician. By now suffering the pronounced symptoms of schizophrenia, he had to share digs with his sister. His general health was not the best, and he led a very sheltered life with little physical activity. Trudy took good care of him until his death, of a heart attack, on 1 December 1960.

On 18 September 1945, the air vice marshal commanding No. 5 Group of RAF's Bomber Command recommended an award for Peter Stevens. It took him more than two pages to document his heroics, and it concluded:

> Throughout his captivity Flight Lieutenant Stevens' [sic] demonstrated an outstanding devotion to duty and his determination to cause the enemy the maximum annoyance on every possible occasion never waned. Although on several occasions he had been severely punished for attempted escapes, his tenacity and courage never failed. I strongly recommend that Flight Lieutenant Stevens be awarded the Military Cross, for his fine contribution to the War effort.[1]

Bomber Command Headquarters approved the recommendation, and the commander-in-chief, Air Marshal Sir Norman Bottomley, forwarded it to the Air Ministry on 3 October 1945. On 31 January 1946, the War Office replied to the Ministry that:

> ... the names of F/Lt B.A. James and F/Lt P. Stevens will be submitted to The King in the near future for awards of the Military Cross.[2]

On 17 May 1946, the *London Gazette* noted: 'The King has been graciously pleased to approve the following award: *Military Cross* Flight Lieutenant Peter Stevens (88219), Royal Air Force Reserve, No 144 Squadron.' The *News Chronicle*, in a front-page story on 18 May 1946, called one of his escape attempts – dressing up as a German guard and attempting to march out of Warburg with a group of prisoners – 'The War's Coolest Escape Bid'.

It turned out that, after his liberation debriefing and that of his fellow prisoners of war, someone senior had decided that he had deserved a 'gong' (i.e. medal). It was perhaps 'Wings' Day, by then a household name. While the official story mentioned the basics of several escapes and attempts, it left out the telling subtext. A German-Jewish refugee had survived for almost four years as a prisoner of war right under German noses and had several times attempted escape, succeeding twice.

Because he was still on active service, Stevens received the award in Berlin, missing the opportunity to go to Buckingham Palace for the usual ceremony. Nonetheless, there was a big party at the Mess that night. Now he was truly a war hero; people could look at the understated white-and-purple ribbon on his chest. Now, white-and-purple ribbon was relatively common in the RAF, but usually with very thin bands of colour at a 45-degree angle (Distinguished Flying Cross to officers or Distinguished Flying Medal to non-commissioned officers). Stevens's ribbon stripes were broad and vertical. The Military Cross is for *ground* action in any branch of the armed forces and is extremely rare in the RAF. And so his honour became a natural focus for discussion with friends and colleagues for the rest of his life.

Throughout the process, no reference appeared to the fact that Peter Stevens was actually a German Jew, and deserved (or was actually given) special consideration in light of that fact. It is unclear whether this information was even known to the officer who made the initial recommendation.

Because of his fluency in German and his lack of civilian trade skills, Stevens applied for and received an RAF position as aide-de-camp to Air Vice Marshal Davidson, working in Berlin with the occupation forces. He received promotion to the rank of squadron leader and was authorised the use of an RAF aircraft at any time, for any reason – generally a twin-engined Avro Anson, originally a navigation trainer but now used for carrying VIPs.

Because some of his work as personal assistant to an air vice marshal was secret, Stevens decided in February 1946 to apply for naturalisation as a British subject. His pre-war criminal record might have doomed his application. However, he enlisted in advance the aid of Air Vice Marshal Davidson, as well as several other senior RAF officers with whom he had been a prisoner of war. Several of them wrote glowing recommendations, which are on file at the National Archives.[3]

The Air Ministry's letter, which included the application for naturalisation, went to the Home Office and reads in part:

> The application is supported by letters which I have obtained from persons, including a number of Senior R.A.F. Officers, who knew this officer before the war, during his internment as a prisoner-of-war in Germany, and after the war. You will observe that all of these persons write about him in terms of the highest praise.
>
> The case is absolutely unique. He is actually a German Jew Georg Hein, who enlisted in the R.A.F. as an aircraft hand at the beginning of the war. He volunteered for aircrew, and was trained as a pilot. He did twenty-two operational flights over Germany, and the Commanding Officer of his station has stated that he acted with conspicuous gallantry and went quite low before dropping his bombs.[4]

The letter mentioned another incident. During his time in Berlin in late 1946, Stevens and Air Vice Marshal Davidson were passengers in an Anson, and the pilot suddenly went berserk. It being a local trip, there was no co-pilot. Stevens and another passenger disabled the pilot, and Stevens took command of the aircraft, taking the flight to an uneventful end. When the plane landed, Davidson credited Stevens with saving his life. For his calm but decisive action under extreme pressure, Davidson gave him a pair of engraved solid-gold cuff links.

Davidson wrote in his supporting letter for Stevens:

His skill and determination under the most trying circumstances undoubtedly saved my life and those of four other passengers in my aircraft.[5]

The application for naturalisation succeeded, and on 18 October 1946, Georg Franz Hein became a British citizen: Squadron Leader Peter Stevens, MC.

During his two years with the RAF in Berlin, Stevens wove himself neatly into the fabric of the remnants of German high society. As a devoted opera fan, he took to hobnobbing with several of the more famous local singers, including Frida Leider and Gunther Treptoe. As part of their crowd, he also came to know many highly placed industrialists, connections that would later come in quite handy.

While food was scarce in England, it was even more so in Germany. Therefore, having at his disposal the Anson, plus a reasonable amount of cash from his German friends, he regularly went on scavenger hunts to Zurich and Copenhagen. Often he returned with an aircraft full of fresh meat and dairy products, for which his friends were immensely grateful. Later, several of them credited Peter with their survival through 1946 and 1947.

Germany was undergoing a lot of change, not all of it for the good. The Soviet Union, as Churchill predicted, was becoming extremely aggressive and less and less the 'friendly ally'. The exodus of German citizens from the Eastern sector to the Western sector was growing from a trickle to a flow and upsetting the Soviets. They began to take extreme measures, and leaving the Soviet Sector of Germany soon became very difficult for German citizens.

In 1947, Stevens was only twenty-eight years old, but had had several lifetimes' worth of excitement. When British Intelligence (MI6) approached him covertly about working for it in Germany, he jumped at the chance and resigned his commission in the RAF. Ian Fleming's books had not yet appeared, and nobody had yet heard of James Bond, but here was a chance for Stevens to be a genuine secret agent! His cover was as an employee of the Control Commission for Germany and Austria, but the real job entailed running agents in eastern Germany and the Soviet Control Zone. It was clear that the rebuilding of German industry and society would rely on German industrialists, and so one of the primary goals was expediting their resettlement from East Germany into the British Sector.

An MI6 colleague of Stevens's, Rodger Morro, wrote about the kind of activities that they undertook in his thinly veiled autobiography, *Spy Tapestry*.[6] Suffice to say that they had plenty of adventure and lots of sex. In the mid-1970s Stevens and Morro would meet again by sheer chance on a street corner in Toronto. Morro was living in Taiwan managing a rubber company, but was visiting Toronto on a business trip. Stevens recognised him immediately and invited him home to dinner with the family. Morro loved to tell the story of how Stevens had waltzed into the office in Cologne one day and demanded $5,000 in US cash – an incredible sum in 1950. He received it, and no accounting was necessary. Where and to whom it went was nobody's business. Morro also pointed out that Stevens had bought (or more likely commandeered) for his private use the largest American car in Germany. Apparently, Stevens didn't know the meaning of 'inconspicuous'!

Stevens never spoke of his time with British Intelligence, but he did maintain correspondence with another old colleague from those days, one George Bowen. Bowen had grown up in Belgium, the son of a banker, and had been a Royal Marine commando during the war. He too had gravitated to Intelligence work during the Cold War. In the 1960s and 1970s, he served as a translator at SHAPE (Supreme Headquarters Allied Powers Europe) near Paris. The two lost touch after meeting on a Stevens family trip to Europe in 1967.

According to Rodger Morro, in 1952, after five years in Intelligence, Stevens realised that he did not have the right background (i.e., English private schooling) to advance. He decided to make a clean break and start afresh somewhere new. After looking around and speaking to acquaintances (being a 'spook', he had few true friends), he decided to try either Canada or Australia. Remembering his escape partner 'Mike' Lewis, he wrote him a note care of the Royal Canadian Air Force, asking about the prospects. The letter eventually caught up with Lewis on a posting in the wilds of northern Labrador. Lewis replied that, being 'somewhat off the beaten track', he could not help personally, but he did add that there was plenty of opportunity in Canada. Stevens went ahead and emigrated to Montreal in mid-1952.

Arriving with just a few suitcases and his British government retirement allowance of a few hundred dollars, he set about finding a job. As a decorated veteran, he found one quickly. The Canadian subsidiary of England's Bristol Aeroplane Company hired him as personnel manager. He also joined 401 Squadron of the Royal Canadian Air Force Reserves, based at St Hubert, Quebec. He reverted to junior rank (pilot officer) and flew high-performance, single-engine Harvard trainers on weekends. The camaraderie of the Officers' Mess was what really attracted him, and exchanging war stories with the other pilots (many of whom had also flown in combat) gave him much pleasure. The squadron was also just beginning its transition to jets (de Havilland Vampires), which Stevens found very tempting. He had yet to try his hand with jets, and like most pilots, he found them incredibly exciting.

On one occasion at RCAF St Hubert, he took a passenger up for a few quick circuits in a Harvard. The man was a long-suffering squadron mechanic, who had never before flown. All went well until, at about 300 feet above the ground, the engine sputtered and died. This was no serious problem for Stevens, who completed a safe emergency landing. The mechanic, however, had an unfortunate accident in his trousers! The incident resulted in a special RCAF warning to all air bases about not filling the tanks of a piston-engined aircraft with jet fuel.

At Bristol Aeroplane, the dashing war hero with the deep voice and seeming Oxford accent cut a swath through the secretarial pool and went straight to the top. He began calling on a very attractive twenty-nine-year-old French-Canadian woman, the executive secretary to the general manager. Her name was Claire Lalonde, and she had excellent education, spoke well, and had travelled. She and a girlfriend had taken a three-month leave of absence in 1951 and had toured through much of Europe first class (inexpensive in those days).

Lalonde's father owned a plumbing-supply business and she had attended a private school run by nuns. She had several suitors but immediately fell for the war hero. She had always liked men in uniform. Her older brother, Lucien, had been the commanding officer of a Canadian army unit, the *Régiment de Maisonneuve*, and had served with distinction during the liberation of France and Holland and received the Distinguished Service Order (DSO). Stevens told Claire Lalonde little of his past, telling her that he was an Anglican and an only child. They married in a Catholic chapel on her thirtieth birthday, 27 June 1953.

The next year, on 10 October, their first son arrived. They named him Peter Frederick (in honour of Fred Wilkinson, the English headmaster who had adopted Georg Hein in 1936, allowing him to stay in Britain). On 15 January 1957, came another son, Marc Hugh (the author). Our parents baptised both of us and our mother raised us as Catholics.

At Bristol Aeroplane the post-war boom work slowly wound down, and it became clear in 1957 that the factory had too many workers. It was Dad's job to announce the layoff of some two hundred employees. He took this task to heart and promised to find every single man a new job elsewhere. He lived up to his pledge, but it took a toll: at thirty-eight, he suffered a heart attack. Luckily, being so young (though a very heavy smoker), he recovered well. Nonetheless, from then on he eschewed any form of physical exercise. He left it to Mother and his boys to shovel snow from the driveway in winter and to push the lawn mower in summer.

In December 1958, Dad accepted a new job as Director of Labour Relations at the Canadian Construction Association in Ottawa. He continued to present himself as a (non-practising) member of the Anglican faith. He attended services once or twice a year, especially on Battle of Britain Memorial Day (15 September).

In early December 1960, bad news arrived from England. Dad's only brother, Erich, had had a massive heart attack and died. Of course, Peter Stevens now had to 'come clean' with Mother about his family past, but he continued to hide his Jewish roots. He told her that Germany's political situation in the early 1930s had distressed his mother, who had sent all three children to England. The story was not completely ridiculous, and so his trusting spouse accepted it.

In 1961 came another complication: a visit from Trude. She had made a post-war life for herself as a civil servant in London, England, and lived quite frugally. This income, along with an insignificant inheritance from Erich and later small reparations from the West German government (in 1962 or 1963), allowed her to travel. Henni (their mother) had nieces and nephews who had resettled in the United States, and Trude now visited them every five or ten years. She was much closer to them, in fact, than to her own brother.

In any case, Trude announced to Peter in 1961 that she was going to visit her American cousins and would like to stop in Ottawa to meet her nephews, if possible. As she was still a practising Jew, this offered a challenge. How to hide the family religion from his wife? We boys were too young to notice or care, but Mother was still very Catholic, and such news might upset her.

Trude's flight landed in Montreal, a two-and-a-half hour drive from Ottawa. Mother was genuinely looking forward to spending the time in the car getting to know Trude, but Dad wouldn't allow it. He determined that he would drive to Montreal alone to pick up his sister. On the drive back to Ottawa, he insisted that Trude not let slip his secret to Mother. Trude, though somewhat offended, acceded to the demand. The visit went very well, with Trude treating Peter and me to a trip to the circus.

Upon Trude's return to London, relations deteriorated between brother and sister, and there was the inevitable fight over money *vis-à-vis* the reparations. Dad (wrongly) claimed to have been cheated and cut off all communication with his closest living blood relative from the Old World. From then on, he never spoke or exchanged letters with anyone in his family.

In late 1966, the Stevens family moved again, this time to Toronto. We settled down to a relatively mundane suburban life, and soon all religious adherences ceased.

Dad and Mother's marriage was always difficult, mainly because Dad refused to act like part of the family. He had been on his own since the age of seven, not trusting anyone and relying for survival only upon his own wits. This pattern followed him throughout his life. When he married, he had no idea how to relate to a wife. He lied to Mother continuously, often for no apparent reason. Not that he was a terrible husband or provider, not at all. But unwilling and unable to communicate with an intimate confidante, he made a poor mate. Probably for the same reasons, he made no long-lasting friendships during his lifetime.

The Stevenses took only one vacation together, in 1967. Dad decided that we boys needed to see the world and arranged a grand tour of Europe. First came London, where he showed Mother and us 'his town'. He arranged for Peter and me to meet our 'grandfather', Fred Wilkinson. A big highlight of our stay in

London was a meeting that Dad had prearranged with his personal hero, 'Wings' Day. Although Day was sixty-nine years old and somewhat tired, he was very friendly to us and made us feel welcome in his small apartment. He had a humble smile and an easygoing manner, but what was keenly evident at that meeting was the high regard in which Day was held by my father. Dad was very proud to be able to introduce his family to someone he considered a true war hero.

Later on that same trip came Paris, Zurich, Berlin, Bonn, Salzberg, and Copenhagen. At almost every stop, Dad's postwar acquaintances feted us in grand style. To a man, the Germans credited him with saving their lives, by saving them from the Communists or by supplying them with food from his personal RAF aircraft. It was a fabulous learning experience for Peter and me, and left us both with a bad case of Dad's wanderlust. Both before and after 1967, we took all our vacations without Dad, he being too busy (!) to join us.

By 1968, when Peter and I were thirteen and eleven, respectively, Mother decided that she had had enough. She hadn't married Dad only to remain single, and that was what it felt like. There was no sharing, no emotion, no sense of partnership. Dad lived with her as though she was his housekeeper. Without a job or any income, she couldn't support us sons, yet she was slowly suffocating, and so she made a very difficult choice. She packed up her things, hopped in her car, and left. She didn't do it out of any malice, or without deep misgivings (especially her feeling of deserting us), but she couldn't continue with the status quo.

She drove back to Montreal and stayed with her sister. Our desperate pleas to Dad had little result. Unfortunately for Mother, the cure seemed worse than the disease. She couldn't stand the guilt of abandoning Peter and me and returned home after only two weeks away. Perhaps the situation between them improved a little bit, but not a great deal. Mother had known that she was the glue that kept the family together, and she could not bring herself to be responsible for its destruction.

The next year, Mother decided that she wasn't going to deny herself any longer. She determined that we needed a dog (and she, companionship), so she made the announcement one night at dinner. Dad, in outrage, replied: 'It's either me or a dog, make your choice.' Well, Mother had already decided, and the next week she picked up a lovely two-month-old miniature poodle. Within six months, Niko was spending early evenings cradled inside Dad's curled-up legs in front of the television. Make no mistake, he was Mother's dog, but Niko didn't mind spending time with Dad either.

In 1970, the RCAF Ex-Air Force POW Association organised a reunion to mark the twenty-fifth anniversary of liberation. It was a week-long celebration in Toronto, culminating with a gala dinner at the Royal York Hotel. As a special treat, one of the association's senior members, Don Morrison (who also just happened to be a vice-president at Air Canada), arranged the donation of airfare from Germany for a special honouree – *Feldwebel* Hermann Glemnitz. As Glemnitz and Dad had had something of a close working relationship at *Stalag*

Luft III, Dad volunteered to billet him at home. A nicer, kinder old gentlemen you couldn't find, and Mother, Peter, and I spent several enjoyable days with him, hosting him on the grand tour. To see him and the former prisoners of war enjoying their time together, you would never have known that they had ever been enemies. Dad had always been reluctant to discuss the war with us, so it was very good to see that camaraderie.

To occupy himself in his spare time, Dad had found himself a hobby: politics. Since his day job entailed lobbying the provincial government on behalf of the construction industry, he knew several cabinet ministers well, both socially and professionally. He became active in the Progressive Conservative Party's local constituency association, rising to president.

Humour played a large part in our household. With us boys now teenagers, Dad could use his quick wit to get a rise out of us, and he enjoyed this immensely. One of his favourite television programs was *Hogan's Heroes*, the madcap adventures of American, British, and French prisoners of war who secretly ran '*Stalag* 13' under the noses of their German captors. It was good to hear his belly laughs whenever Sgt Schultz (one of the camp guards) would profess to everyone within hearing, 'I see nothing, I know nothing!'

Later in the 1970s, with Dad's health beginning to fail (thanks in large part to his smoking three packs of cigarettes a day), he and Mother agreed essentially to disagree. After fighting continuously for a good ten years (mainly over Dad's inability to act as a real husband), they actually began to tolerate one another. Dad asked Mother to join him on long vacation trips to the Canadian Rockies and twice to Hawaii.

In April 1979, at age sixty, Dad learned that he had acute lymphoma. He started on chemotherapy and insisted on complete secrecy on our parts. In mid-July, he suffered another heart attack and drove himself to the hospital, which discharged him after three days. A few days later, on 16 July, he was due for another round of chemotherapy. That night, just after dinner, he told us that he wasn't feeling well and asked if someone could drive him to the hospital. On arrival at the Emergency Department, Dad suffered a massive heart attack and died.

He had wanted us to donate his body to medical science, and this we did. Consequently, there was no burial, but acquaintances from his political connections and the Royal Canadian Legion organised a large and heart-warming memorial service. There were tributes, speeches, and letters of condolence – for example, from the prime minister of Canada, other politicians, office colleagues, and war heroes. I think that he would have been pleased.

Notes

1. National Archives, file AIR 2 / 9125.
2. Ibid.
3. The National Archives sealed file HO 405 / 20069 until the year 2051. My Freedom of Information Act application led it to open the file in December 2006. It contains the

entire Home Office file relating to Georg Hein/Peter Stevens, including details of his criminal conviction in 1939, his wartime RAF service, and personal letters of reference from Davidson, Group Captains Willetts and Keily and Wing Commanders Trenchard-Smith and Collard.

4. Letter from Wing Commander A.R. John, writing on behalf of the provost marshal and chief of Air Force Police, to the Aliens Department, Home Office, Whitehall, on 3 April 1946.

5. National Archives, file HO 405/20069, handwritten letter from AVM Davidson to W/C A.R. John dated February 24, 1946.

6. Rodger Morro, *Spy Tapestry* (Sussex: The Book Guild Ltd, 2001).

CHAPTER SIXTEEN

Rediscovering My Father

During the 1980s, while researching my father's life, I met with several of his wartime RAF colleagues and with people who knew the stories of many RAF prisoners of war. It was only then that I began to learn about his Jewish heritage. It came as a shock to me to hear, 'Oh yes, your father was Jewish.' This message came first from W.J. 'Mike' Lewis, who had jumped from the train in December 1941 with my father, and later from Charles Rollings, a Briton preparing a series of books about POWs and escapes.

For some years afterwards, I still felt disbelief. And yet, looking back, and reading other wartime escape stories, I found it all there for the taking. It appears in print in Sydney Smith's 1970 biography of 'Wings' Day and in *Moonless Night* (1983) by B.A. ('Jimmy') James. Strange then that the Day story did not show up in my father's collection of escape books. Any other volume that mentioned his name he displayed prominently on the bookshelf. Neither Douglas Wark nor John Matthews (Dad's air gunners on the deadly operation of 6/7 August 1941) seemed to have any knowledge of my Dad's Jewish background. Of course, they were not officers when they served with him and so had not socialised with him. But then, his true origin and religion he shared with very few people, and certainly none in England, before the Germans shot him down and took him prisoner.

In an e-mail to me dated 8 July 2004, John Matthews wrote:

Your father and I were on the Squadron together for just over a month – a brief interlude in my 6 years' service. We had little intimate contact...
   But I could assess his skill and character as a pilot and Captain.

1. There was none better. The evasive action he took when we were attacked was like the skill of a fighter pilot. I realized this some years later when I was on a Gunnery Leaders' Course. The belly landing when we crashed was smoother than a three pointer with an under-carriage. He inspired confidence.
2. He was quite unflappable, courageous and determined. Those characteristics were evident in his escapades as a POW.

3. When he wrote to my father there was a warmth that made me wish I had known Peter better.
4. How he behaved on that Karlsruhe flight should have been recognised by the award of a D.F.C. (Distinguished Flying Cross)

What was Peter Stevens really like? Well, from the viewpoint of a son, he was a man with a brilliant mind but misplaced priorities. He almost always put himself and his work ahead of family. In his life, he had known neither love nor trust until he married at thirty-four. Even then, however, despite Mother's selfless love, he was unable to reciprocate. He always felt that his father had abandoned him (by dying when Georg/Peter was only six) and that his mother never loved him (she was unable to cope with his constant demands and sent him away to boarding school). As well, he blamed his mother for squandering the family fortune; in fact, a large portion of that wealth was undoubtedly lost in the 1929 stock market crash that led to the Great Depression. She spent much of the remainder sending him and his siblings to safety in England and lost the better part of what was left to Nazi persecution. He himself squandered the sizeable nest egg that she sent to London for the support of her children. His youth, and then his adolescence, were years of desperate uncertainty for him. He moved to a land where he didn't speak a word of the language and had to survive almost on his own.

In 1939, fearing deportation, he 'did the right thing' and enlisted in the RAF. What was his motive in volunteering to serve? Was it to fight the Nazis? Was it to defend his family and his people? Was it to avoid another upheaval or imprisonment? Was it for the excitement? We will never know for sure, but it was probably a combination of all four factors.

How did he survive for almost four years as a prisoner of war? Why did he admit his Jewish heritage first to 'Mike' Lewis, and then to the Senior British Officer in the camps? Why, after the war, did he involve himself with the British Secret Service? Why did he emigrate, and why to Canada?

His life provided more questions than answers. All of this uncertainty is more than any one man can bear, and it is therefore no surprise that Peter Stevens was incapable of love, for he had seen too little of it. He never once told my brother and me that he loved us and never used the word 'love' in our presence, even though he did enjoy our company. He was not a bad father, but he did not take an active role in our upbringing or spend much time playing or interacting with us. He did not help us with our homework, nor did he play sports or games with us the way our mother did. He let Mother shoulder most of the burden of their life together, without offering any semblance of love or gratitude in return.

There were only two times that I can remember seeing him cry: watching on television the funeral of Sir Winston Churchill in 1965, and wandering the Allied Forces Cemetery in Berlin in 1967, looking for the grave of his lost crewman, Sgt Ivor Fraser. How does one describe or understand a man who cried only twice in his adulthood? Why didn't Peter Stevens know how to love? Was it a case of nature versus nurture? The sad and pitiful truth here is that he experienced no nurturing. Georg Hein, after his father's death, never knew or felt love for anyone or anything. Or if he did, he was simply incapable of expressing it.

There were other Jewish refugees who fought in the British and Allied forces. Just under one hundred of them were set up as a highly secret Royal Marine organisation called 'Ten Commando';[1] another group that trained in the United States became 'The Ritchie Boys'. Their stories begin in much the same way as that of Peter Stevens, as refugees able to escape to England or the US just before the war. Each of them, however, initially kept his own identity, and the government arrested and interned most of those in Britain. Of course, while the United Kingdom considered these brave young men 'enemy aliens' and regarded them with suspicion, they themselves knew that they were the furthest thing from being agents for the Nazis.

Early on, some of the internees expressed their desire to fight for their new country, and the military secretly recruited some into this special unit (Ten Commando). Most had earlier joined the Pioneer Corps, which took on such 'important' duties as unloading coal wagons. In other words, the highly suspicious government gave them work that, while necessary, was not strategic in nature. Eventually, after vetting by MI5 and acceptance into the Royal Marines, each man had to come up with a new (British) identity and to destroy all documents showing his true name. Lengthy military training as true commandos followed, and the unit finally did acquit itself well in combat in several theatres of operation, though rarely before D-Day. These men too were heroes.

Peter Masters, an Austrian-Jewish refugee, was one of these commandos and told his story in *Striking Back*. In it, he rationalises as follows:

> We young Jews had experienced life under the Nazis, so it was natural for us to push ourselves forward whenever anything needed to be done. Although all Army Commandos were volunteers, we volunteered on top of volunteering. In our case, when straws were drawn, it was the man who drew the short straw who didn't get to go on a hazardous mission. Our more dangerous undertakings were often entirely self-motivated; nobody had to give us orders to do what we did.[2]

A renowned Jewish scholar, Professor Norman Bentwich, wrote several books about Jewish life and culture in Britain, including *I Understand the Risks: How Those Who Fled to England from Hitlerite Oppression Fought – Understanding the Risks – Against Nazism* (1950). The work details the lengths to which some European Jewish refugees went to join the fight.

During the first three years of the war, the [Royal] Air Force was closed to volunteers of enemy origin. When an Army Council Instruction was published in 1940 about transfer of suitable persons to the Air Force for fighting duties, numbers of men in the [Jewish] Pioneer Companies volunteered. Some of them formed study groups to brush up their mathematics and technical knowledge; and when they were called to a test, they did well, but only to be told in the end that they could not be accepted. From 1943, the Air Force was in principle open to volunteers, but was, in fact, restricted in admitting them.[3]

Bentwich went on: 'In England, [RAF] admission was granted to a few refugees who were naturalized or had allied nationality, Czech or Polish; but those who were legally "enemy aliens" were debarred.'[4] He concluded:

In the later period of the war the restrictions on transfer and commissions for foreigners were a little relaxed. First, those refugees from Germany who had allied or neutral nationality, Czech, Polish, Rumanian, etc., were admitted to aircrews. About a dozen were commissioned [i.e., as officers], among them two brothers Adam, Squadron-Leader Silverman, Flight-Lieutenant Lichte and Flight-Lieutenant Deventer. Then a few German and Austrian subjects were admitted, provided that they had no kith or kin in the enemy countries. The R.A.F. had its own security rule, to exclude those who had parents or near relations in Germany.[5]

Appendices in Bentwich's work show that forty Jews enlisted in the RAF, all after 1942,[6] and that six 'non-British members of H.M. Forces [all Army] were awarded the Military Cross for their actions during World War 2'.[7]

If Bentwich is correct, then the RAF should never have accepted the enemy alien Georg Hein/Peter Stevens in September 1939. It should never have allowed him to fly bombers, as he had immediate relatives in Germany. In fact, during one mission on 14 July 1941, he actually bombed his hometown of Hanover. One can only guess at the thoughts going through his mind on that operation. It is hard to believe that he didn't just grit his teeth and avoid looking at the ground. At least it wasn't he who released the bombs.

No mention of Hein/Stevens occurs in Bentwich's book – presumably because Peter Stevens never went public with his story. He legally assumed the name 'Peter Stevens' and received naturalisation as a British subject on 18 October 1946.

One might argue that Georg Hein/Peter Stevens never practised Judaism and was therefore not a Jew. This argument would not have satisfied the Germans, who almost certainly would have tortured and killed him. Being a Jew, according to Hitler, was a function of bloodlines, not of whether one attended synagogue or lit candles at Sabbath dinner. And Georg Hein's parents were Jews, so *he* was a Jew. Plain and simple.

Of the 125,000 or so Allied airmen who fought in Britain's Bomber Command during the Second World War, almost 56,000 (44 per cent) were killed. No other British wartime unit incurred higher losses.

While accepting the justifiable and earned praise that went along with the Military Cross awarded for his innumerable escape activities, Peter Stevens never felt that it was his place to make any kind of statement about being a Jew and fighting the Nazis. Was he ashamed of his true heritage? Everything he had done during the war had screamed out against the tyranny and murder of his people, yet perhaps he felt guilt that he had not been more successful in trying to stop them. Perhaps he felt a failure for not being able to at least save his mother or other members of his family. Perhaps he went through his entire life wanting to forget that greatest of inadequacies. Regardless, he did, in his own small way, fight back and take some measure of personal revenge.

Notes

1. Ian Dear, *Ten Commando 1942 –1945* (New York: St Martin's Press, 1987).
2. Peter Masters, *Striking Back: A Jewish Commando's War against the Nazis* (Novato, Calif.: Presidio Press, 1997), 190.
3. Norman Bentwich, *I Understand the Risks* (London: Victor Gollancz Limited, 1950), 122.
4. Ibid., 122.
5. Ibid., 123.
6. Ibid., 176.
7. Ibid., 181.

Postscript

In 1996, while conducting genealogical research on the family at home in Toronto, I finally located a telephone listing for a Gertrude Hein in London. I had had no contact whatsoever with my aunt since about 1963 (when I was six), and I called her immediately. Trude's first question startled me: 'Is my brother still alive?' Not having anticipated the obvious, and choking back tears, I had to reply, 'No.' My first question to her was 'Are you Jewish?' To which her response was, by then, obvious.

Further research showed me that some ten or fifteen members of the extended Hein-Seckel family died as a direct result of the Holocaust (whether in concentration camps or by suicide). We cannot know the number for sure, as there is no record of cause or location of death for some relatives.

To the day he died, Peter Stevens admitted his Jewish heritage to no one in his own family. It is somewhat ironic, then, that his eldest son, Peter Jr, married a Jewish woman in 1983 and later converted to that religion himself. Together, Peter Jr and his wife, Dr Billie Goldstein, had a daughter, Ruth, and a son, George, whom they named in honour of his grandfather. And so despite the incredible Nazi barbarity, and thanks in some small part to the wartime actions of my father, the line carries on...

Thanks, Dad.

Bibliography

Mission Debriefing Reports and Squadron Records
National Archives, Kew, London, England – Crown Copyright

Books

Air Ministry. *Bomber Command Continues – The Air Ministry Account of The Rising Offensive Against Germany, July 1941 – June 1942*. London: His Majesty's Stationery Office, 1942.

Aretha, David, ed. *The Holocaust Chronicle*. Lincolnwood, Illinois: Publications International, Ltd, 2001.

*Ash, William (with Brendan Foley). *Under The Wire*. London: Bantam Press (Transworld Publishers), 2005.

Bentwich, Norman. *I Understand The Risks*. London: Victor Gollancz Ltd, 1950.

Bentwich, Norman. *The Refugees From Germany April 1933 To December 1935*. London: George Allen & Unwin, Ltd, 1936.

Bowyer, Chaz. *The Encyclopedia Of British Military Aircraft*. London: Arms and Armour Press Limited, 1982.

Bowyer, Chaz. *Hampden Special*. Shepperton, Surrey, UK: Ian Allan Ltd, 1976.

Brickhill, Paul. *Reach For The Sky*. London: Collins, 1954.

Brickhill, Paul. *The Great Escape*. London: Cassell Military Paperbacks, 2000.

Brokaw, Tom. *The Greatest Generation*. New York: Random House, 1998.

Burgess, Alan. The Longest Tunnel – The True Story Of World War II's Great Escape. New York: Grove Weidenfeld, 1990.

*Calnan, T.D. *Free As A Running Fox*. New York: The Dial Press, 1970.

Carroll, Tim. *The Great Escapers*. Edinburgh: Mainstream Publishing Company (Edinburgh) Ltd, 2004.

*Chorley, W.R. *RAF Bomber Command Losses of the Second World War – 1941*. Leicestershire, England: Midland Counties Publications, 1993.

Congdon, Philip. *Per Ardua Ad Astra – A Handbook Of The Royal Air Force*. Shrewsbury, England: Airlife Publishing Ltd, 1987.

Crawley, Aidan. *Escape From Germany*. London: Her Majesty's Stationery Office, 1985.

*Clutton-Brock, Oliver. *Footprints On The Sands Of Time – RAF Bomber Command Prisoners Of War In Germany 1939–45*. London: Grub Street Press, 2003.

Dear, Ian. *Ten Commando – 1942–1945*. New York: St Martin's Press, 1987.

Dear, Ian. *Escape and Evasion – Prisoner of War Breakouts and the Routes to Safety in World War Two*. London: Arms and Armour Press, 1997.

Deighton, Len. *Bomber*. New York: Harper & Row, 1970.

Dupuy, R. Ernest and Dupuy, Trevor N. *The Harper Encyclopedia Of Military History: From 3500 B.C. to the Present, Fourth Edition*. New York: HarperCollins, 1993.

Durand, Arthur A. *Stalag Luft III – The Secret Story*. Baton Rouge, Louisiana: Louisiana State University Press, 1988.

Elon, Amos. *The Pity Of It All: A Portrait Of The German-Jewish Epoch 1743–1933*. New York: Picador, 2002.

Falconer, Jonathan. *Bomber Command Handbook 1939–1945*. Stroud, Gloucestershire, England: Sutton Publishing Limited, 1998.

Fisher, David E. *A Summer Bright And Beautiful – Winston Churchill, Lord Dowding, Radar, And The Impossible Triumph Of The Battle Of Britain*. Emeryville, California: Shoemaker & Hoard, 2005.

Gill, Anton. *The Great Escape – The Full Dramatic Story With Contributions From Survivors and their Families*. London: Review, Headline Book Publishing, 2002.

Halpenny, Bruce Barrymore. *Action Stations – 2. Military Airfields of Lincolnshire and the East Midlands*. Wellingborough, Northants, UK: Patrick Stephens Limited, 1981.

Hehner, Barbara. *The Tunnel King – The True Story Of Wally Floody and the Great Escape*. Toronto: HarperCollins Publishers Ltd, 2004.

Hodgson, Lynn Philip and Longfield, Alan Paul. *Camp 30 – Word Of Honour – Bowmanville*. Port Perry, Ontario: Blake Books Distribution, 2003.

Jary, Christopher. *Portrait Of A Bomber Pilot*. Bristol, England: Sydney Jary Limited, 1990.

Kee, Robert. *A Crowd is Not Company*. London: Eyre & Spottiswoode Ltd, 1947.

*James, B.A. 'Jimmy'. *Moonless Night*. London: Leo Cooper, 2001.

Levy, Harry. *The Dark Side Of The Sky – The Story Of A Young Jewish Airman In Nazi Germany*. London: Leo Cooper, 1996.

London, Louise. *Whitehall And The Jews 1933–1948 – British Immigration Policy and the Holocaust*. Cambridge, England: Cambridge University Press, 2000.

MacMillan, Margaret. *Paris 1919 – Six Months That Changed the World*. New York: Random House, 2001.

Martin, Gwyn. *Up And Under*. Aberystwyth, Wales: Gwyn Martin, 1989.

Masters, Peter. *Striking Back – A Jewish Commando's War Against The Nazis*. Novato, California: Presidio Press, 1997.

Middlebrook, Martin and Everitt, Chris. *The Bomber Command War Diaries – An Operational Reference Book 1939–1945*. Leicester, England: Midland Publishing Limited, 1996.

Morro, Rodger. *Spy Tapestry*. Lewes, Sussex, UK: The Book Guild Ltd, 2001.

*Moyle, Harry. *The Hampden File*. Tonbridge, Kent, UK: Air-Britain (Historians) Ltd, 1989.

Postlethwaite, Mark. *Hampden Squadrons In Focus*. Walton on Thames, Surrey, England: Red Kite, 2003.

*Philpot, Oliver. *Stolen Journey*. London: Hodder & Stoughton Ltd, 1950.

*Prittie, T.C.F. and Edwards, W. Earle. *Escape To Freedom*. London: Hutchinson & Co. Ltd, 1953.

Rees, Ken. *Lie in the Dark and Listen*. London: Grub Street, 2004.

Roberts, Nicholas. *Handley Page Hampden & Hereford Crash Log*. Leicestershire, England: Midland Counties Publications, 1980.

*Rollings, Charles. *Wire And Worse – RAF Prisoners Of War In Laufen, Biberach, Lübeck And Warburg 1940–42*. Hersham, Surrey, England: Ian Allen Publishing Ltd, 2004.

Sherman, A.J. *Island Refuge – Britain And Refugees From The Third Reich 1933–1939*. Ilford, England: Frank Cass & Co. Ltd, 1994.

*Slack, Tom. *Happy is the Day – A Spitfire Pilot's Story*. Penzance, England: United Writers Publications Ltd, 1987.

*Smith, Sydney. *Wings Day*. London: William Collins Sons & Co Ltd, 1968.

Stevens, Austin. *The Dispossessed – German Refugees In Britain*. London: Barrie & Jenkins Limited, 1975.

Terraine, John. *The Right Of The Line – The RAF In The European War 1939–1945*. London: Hodder & Stoughton Limited, 1985.

*Vance, Jonathan F. *A Gallant Company – The True Story Of 'The Great Escape'*. New York: ibooks, inc., 2003.

Wheeler, William J., ed. *Flying Under Fire – Canadian Fliers Recall The Second World War*. Calgary, Alberta: Fifth House Ltd, 2001.

Williams, Eric. *The Tunnel*. London: William Collins Sons & Co Ltd, 1951.

Williams, Eric. *The Wooden Horse*. London: William Collins Sons & Co Ltd, 1949.

Wilson, Patrick. *The War Behind The Wire*. Barnsley, Yorkshire, England: Pen & Sword Books Limited, 2000.

Woods, Eric. *While Others Slept – The Early Years Of Bomber Command*. Bognor Regis, England: Woodfield Publishing, 2001.

*Denotes books that mention Peter Stevens (or 'Steve', his RAF and prison camp nickname)

Websites

The Village of Marquartstein: www.marquartstein.de

Destruction of European Jewry Timeline: www.ess.uwe.ac.uk/genocide/destrtim.htm (Copyright Stuart D. Stein, University of the West of England, Bristol)

The Holocaust Chronicle: www.holocaustchronicle.org (Copyright Publications International, Ltd)

Index

Subheadings appear in approximate chronological order where appropriate.